Dante Gabriel Rossetti

Julian Treuherz, Elizabeth Prettejohn, Edwin Becker

Dante Gabriel
Rossetti

With 190 illustrations, 140 in color

Thames & Hudson

Endpapers
Based on a motif from the endpapers of *Poems* by Dante
Gabriel Rossetti, published by F.S. Ellis, 1870

Page 6
Rossetti letter heading. Before August 1863

This book has been published to accompany the exhibition *Dante Gabriel Rossetti*, the Walker, Liverpool, 16 October 2003 – 18 January 2004; Van Gogh Museum, Amsterdam, 27 February – 6 June 2004.

First published in the United Kingdom in 2003 by
Thames & Hudson Ltd,
181A High Holborn,
London WC1V 7QX

www.thamesandhudson.com

First published in hard cover in the United States of America by
Thames & Hudson Inc,
500 Fifth Avenue, New York,
New York 10110

thamesandhudsonusa.com

© 2003 Uitgeverij Waanders b.v., Zwolle / Van Gogh Museum,
Amsterdam / National Museums Liverpool

Authors
Julian Treuherz
Elizabeth Prettejohn
Edwin Becker

Catalogue texts
Julian Treuherz: 1-38, 47-59, 61-93, 156-185
Elizabeth Prettejohn: 39-46, 60, 94-155, chronology

Translation
Wendie Shaffer and Kate Williams (text by Becker)

Design
Joseph Plateau graphic designers, Amsterdam

Photographs
All photographs were supplied with the permission of the owners of
the works reproduced.

British Library Cataloguing-in-Publication Data
A catalogue record for this book is available from the British Library

ISBN 0-500-09316-4

Printed and bound in the Netherlands by Waanders Printers, Zwolle

Contents

Preface

This exhibition presents a rare opportunity to see the full range of Dante Gabriel Rossetti's work. During his lifetime Rossetti hardly ever exhibited. The year after his death saw two memorial exhibitions, but after that the public had to wait another ninety years to see a comprehensive exhibition of his work – in the 1973 Rossetti exhibition, held first at the Royal Academy, London, and then at Birmingham Art Gallery. Since then, despite a great deal of research on the artist, a new generation has grown up which has never had the opportunity to see Rossetti's art at first hand in any depth. We are confident that they will be surprised and delighted by a body of work that is more varied and original than the popular conception of Rossetti might suggest.

The Walker has long been associated with Pre-Raphaelite studies, and the Van Gogh Museum has organized a series of important exhibitions by Van Gogh's contemporaries, including notable displays of European symbolism. After the success of the Alma -Tadema exhibition, on which we collaborated, it is especially appropriate for the Walker and the Van Gogh Museum to join forces again for Rossetti, one of the founding members of the Pre-Raphaelite Brotherhood and an artist whose work was a touchstone for later Symbolist painters.

We thank the curatorial team responsible for the exhibition and catalogue, all of whom are specialists in the art of the late 19th century: Edwin Becker, Exhibitions Curator at the Van Gogh Museum, who first proposed the idea of a Rossetti exhibition; Julian Treuherz, Keeper of Art Galleries for National Museums Liverpool, who visited many public and private collections in order to make the best possible initial selection; and our Guest Curator Elizabeth Prettejohn, Professor of Modern Art at the University of Plymouth, who contributed her expertise and knowledge of late Victorian art. The works in the exhibition have been chosen first and foremost on the grounds of visual quality, and, with only a few exceptions, museums and private collectors have responded generously.

We are grateful to all the lenders, but particularly to Birmingham Museums & Art Gallery, which has lent an exceptional number of works; and to the Dean and Chapter of Llandaff Cathedral and the Representative Body of the Church in Wales, which has for the first time allowed Rossetti's altarpiece to be made accessible to a wider audience. We would like to thank the staff of National Museums Liverpool and the Van Gogh Museum, who have worked tirelessly to ensure the success of the exhibition.

We are indebted to the Yale Center for British Art, New Haven, USA, which awarded Julian Treuherz a Visiting Fellowship to enable him to undertake research on Rossetti for the exhibition.

Finally, we join with the curatorial team in dedicating this catalogue to two pioneering Rossetti scholars without whose outstanding work the present exhibition would not have been possible, Mrs Virginia Surtees and Dr Alastair Grieve.

Dr David Fleming
Director, National Museums Liverpool

John Leighton
Director, Van Gogh Museum, Amsterdam

fig. 1
William Holman Hunt
Dante Gabriel Rossetti
c. 1870
Birmingham Museums & Art Gallery

'The most startlingly original living'

ROSSETTI'S EARLY YEARS

Julian Treuherz

When Coventry Patmore visited the Oxford Union in 1857 to see the mural paintings of the legend of King Arthur by Rossetti and his friends, Patmore was bowled over. Rossetti, he wrote, 'is, among painters, what Mr. Butterfield is among architects — that is to say, about the most startlingly original living. Original artists, in every kind, are almost always mannerists — though it by no means follows that mannerists are original; and when the peculiar *mannerism* is added to the peculiar *style* — ... the result is a departure from precedent as indescribable as it is complete.'[1] In the 1890s, this judgement was endorsed by the perceptive German writer Richard Muther, who wrote that 'a new stage in the culture of modern England dates from the appearance of Rossetti. He borrowed nothing from his contemporaries and all borrowed from him.'[2] Even Roger Fry, referring to the 20th century's 'renascence of the art of expressive design', wrote in 1916 that 'Rossetti more than any other English artist since Blake may be hailed as a forerunner of the new ideas.'[3]

It is important to return to these views, because, just as the brilliant colours of the Oxford murals have faded, so Rossetti's real achievements have become obscured, and he is now associated not so much with originality or modernity as with a morbid and languorous sensuality. It is easy to see why this has happened. Much of his art is concerned with ideas about women, beauty, love and sexuality, and images of the same women are repeated obsessively in his paintings. Though Rossetti sometimes used professional models, the women he painted most often were those with whom he had close personal relationships,

his wife Elizabeth Siddal, his presumed mistress Fanny Cornforth, and Jane Morris, the wife of his friend William Morris. It is undeniable too that certain episodes in his career, notably the burial of his poems with the body of his wife and the subsequent exhumation of the manuscript, give his life a novelistic quality different from the lives of most of his contemporaries. Thus the understanding of his work has been clouded by overdependence on biographical interpretation, often depicted in exaggerated terms. Whilst the events of his life cannot be ignored when considering his art, it is important to look at and read his pictures more closely. They are far more rewarding, richer and more complex than they would be if they were simply the expression of his personal liaisons.

There are other factors too in the obscuring of his achievements. He is now principally known for his late paintings of beautiful women, which have attained wide currency through the proliferation of colour reproductions. Apart from his first two oil paintings (figs. 9, 10), prominently placed in the Tate, his early works, mostly on a small scale and often in fragile media such as watercolour, are less easily visible, yet their freshness and experimentalism gives an added dimension to the understanding of his work as a whole. Rossetti is also criticized for his lack of drawing skills. He was his own worst enemy: mercurial, bursting with ideas but impatient of discipline, he never completed a formal art education. His grasp of anatomy and perspective was imperfect, but they were less important to him than meaning and expression. He began many works that were never fully realized and exist only as tantalizingly slight sketches, unsatisfactory in themselves.

fig. 2
Self-portrait
1847
National Portrait Gallery, London
cat. I

Latterly dogged by illness and dependence on medically prescribed drugs, he released for sale paintings of uneven quality and studio replicas, thus allowing his work to be judged from inferior examples. Later still, understanding of Rossetti's achievement was clouded by the work of imitators, who watered down the emotional charge of the originals. Yet he could draw with skill and painstaking elaboration (for example, figs. 6, 21, 32). In his best work his technical inventiveness combines with richness of imagery to produce an intensity of effect rarely seen in the work of his academic contemporaries.

This first chapter introduces the work of Rossetti up to about 1860, putting forward the view that it was original, innovative and avant-garde, leading the way for other advanced painters. Originality is not currently a fashionable concept amongst art historians, who tend to place more importance on the role of context in the formation of art. This is in part a reaction to the 19th-century cult of the artist as an isolated figure working in a sacred realm apart from everyday concerns, an idea Rossetti himself expressed in watercolours such as *The first anniversary of the death of Beatrice* (fig. 15) and *Fra Pace* (fig. 3). During his lifetime, his paintings, apart from his very early work, were hardly exhibited. His work was little known at first hand to anyone outside his immediate circle, and towards the end of his life he became something of a recluse. This fostered the idea of his art as the product of personal genius, standing outside society and independent of it.

Artists do not work in a vacuum; they absorb ideas from the world around them and from the art of earlier periods, they are influenced by the need to earn a living,

by deadlines and by patrons. To say that Rossetti was original does not preclude his being influenced by the context into which he was born, nor by his fellow artists or his patrons. His Italian ancestry, his literary bias and his idiosyncratic art training all contributed to his originality, and a crucial influence on his work was his membership of the Pre-Raphaelite Brotherhood and his closeness to his fellow members William Holman Hunt and John Everett Millais. Rossetti made of these and other influences something completely his own: the way that Rossetti's mind, hand and eye worked was quite different from that of other artists. After the break-up of the Brotherhood, he went on to develop his art in a personal direction, independently of his friends and away from the realism prevalent in the Victorian art world.

Literary and artistic imagination

Rossetti's Anglo-Italian family background, atypical at a time when the British art world was somewhat insular, was the root of his originality. His father, an Italian political émigré, was Professor of Italian at King's College, London, a poet and a Dante scholar; his maternal grandfather, also Italian, had served as Count Alfieri's secretary in Paris until the French Revolution. The family was brought up to be bilingual and politically aware; the house was often full of foreign revolutionaries discussing politics. Unlike his brother William Michael, Rossetti never went to Italy. He was born and educated in London, he was a British national and, as an adult, had no particular political

fig. 3
Fra Pace
1856
private collection

affiliations, but his membership of the Anglo-Italian community gave him the attitude of an outsider, detached from conventional British society. This outlook was reinforced by the bohemian milieu in which he mixed and by the apartness of his art from the conventional academic norm.

From an early age Rossetti was encouraged by his family in writing and drawing and became adept at both. At the start of his career, he vacillated between poetry and painting, deciding on painting because it was more likely to earn him a living, though never abandoning poetry. He published poetry and prose in *The Germ*, the shortlived magazine produced by the Pre-Raphaelite Brotherhood in 1850, and produced a collected edition of his poems in 1870 (cat. 161). He often made paintings and poems designed to go together as 'double' works of art, sometimes including texts on his picture frames, sometimes within the pictures themselves; the reciprocity between word and image was a means of enlarging both.[4] Rossetti was an admirer and an early advocate of the work of William Blake, acquiring a Blake notebook in 1847, when Blake's reputation was at a low ebb.[5] Rossetti's combination of painting and poetry bridges a gap in British art between Blake and David Jones and makes him unique in Victorian art.

His literary bent had another consequence for his painting. Rossetti's imagination was fired by his voracious reading, so that by the time he began his studies in art he was already familiar with a wide range of European literature. He read old English ballads, the historical romances of Sir Walter Scott, French novels by Dumas and Hugo,

fig. 4
The Raven
c. 1848
Victoria & Albert Museum, London
cat. 4

and the Gothic fantasies of Maturin and La Motte Fouqué. He could recite passages from Browning and Patmore by heart. He translated part of the Nibelungenlied from German and made translations of Dante, Cavalcanti and other medieval Italian poets, that he eventually published (see cats. 90, 156). Much of the originality of subject matter in his painting came from literature, either his own or that of others, and he had at his disposal a range of literary reference that was rare for a painter at any time. Visually his earliest work was derivative, not unexpected in a young man trying his strength. It betrays the influence of French printmakers, including Gavarni and Delacroix's *Faust* lithographs, and of the English follower of Fuseli, Theodor von Holst.[6] But his literary tastes were advanced; his first

drawing of Edgar Allan Poe's *The Raven* (cat. 2), still in the style of the illustrator Sir John Gilbert, dates from 1846, the year after the poem was first published, and makes Rossetti one of Poe's first English admirers;[7] the subject matter of lovers separated by death inspired his own poem and his later paintings of *The Blessed Damozel* (figs. 69, 103). He was also a devotee of English romantic poetry before it was generally appreciated; when his mentor Ford Madox Brown chose his favourite poets for his painting *The Seeds and Fruits of English Poetry*, Rossetti wanted him to include Keats and Shelley instead of Burns and Pope.[8]

Rossetti's father devoted his life to his interpretation of Dante and christened his son Gabriel Charles Dante Rossetti in honour of his hero; the son developed a deep

fig. 5
The Salutation of Beatrice
1849–50
Fogg Art Museum, Harvard University Art
Museums. Bequest of Grenville L. Winthrop

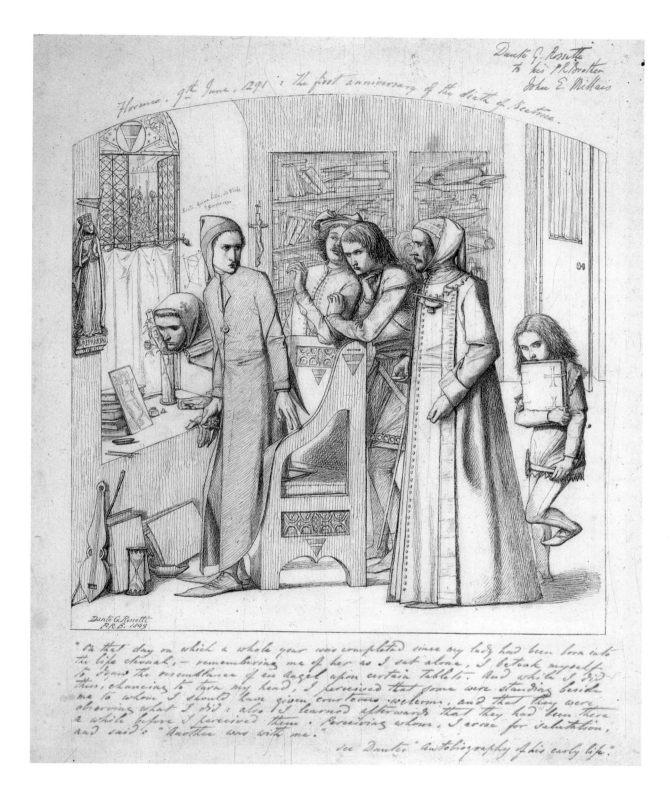

fig. 6
**The first anniversary
of the death of Beatrice**
1849
Birmingham Museums & Art Gallery.
Presented by subscribers
cat. 11

knowledge of Dante and later changed the order of his names to Dante Gabriel Rossetti, in homage to his literary inheritance. He translated the *Vita Nuova* and constantly returned to it, not only as a source of subjects, but also as a means of interpreting his own life and as a way in to an interior world of ideal love, that became one of the well-springs of his art. He was also one of the first to take up the *Morte d'Arthur* as a source for paintings, his earliest subject from Malory being *Arthur's Tomb* (fig. 25) of 1854–5; Malory too was the springboard for the creation of an imaginary interior world.

Rossetti did not receive a conventional or a complete art education. Though this was the source of his technical difficulties with his drawing, perspective and anatomy, it was one of the foundations of his originality. It freed him from the shackles of the conventional academic vehicle of a figure group, with carefully balanced light and shade, in a correctly constructed perspective setting, and it freed him from the deadening effects of the long-drawn out curriculum taught at the Academy Schools, starting with drawing from antique casts and only progressing to drawing from the life and eventually to oil painting after six years. Rossetti had no patience with such drudgery. After desultory studies at Sass's, a preparatory art school for the Academy, he was accepted at the Academy Schools first as a Probationer and then in July 1846 as a Student in the Antique School.[9] But after two years he left, briefly taking private lessons with Madox Brown, at that time his hero and mentor. He soon became impatient with the exercises Brown set him and for a time attended classes in life-drawing. But he seems to have been happier as a member

fig. 7
John Everett Millais
Isabella
1848–9
National Museums Liverpool (the Walker)

of student drawing clubs such as the Cyclographic Society, which circulated members' drawings for mutual criticism and discussion and was a forerunner of the Pre-Raphaelite Brotherhood.[10]

The Pre-Raphaelite Brotherhood

The young Rossetti was self-possessed, articulate, passionate and charismatic, and attracted interesting people to his circle. He played a principal part in the foundation of the Pre-Raphaelite Brotherhood (PRB) in 1848. There were originally seven members, but of these the leading roles were taken by Hunt, Millais and Rossetti. It cannot be said with any certainty whether any one of them was responsible for bringing the Brotherhood into being, but each made a contribution; according to his brother, Rossetti 'had an abundance of ideas, pictorial and also literary, and was fuller of "notions" than the other two, and had more turn for proselytising and "pronunciamentos"... the fact is that not one of the three could have done much as an innovator without the other two.'[11]
It was a joint enterprise, a loose alliance of like-minded young men, who shared certain ideas and enthusiasms and enjoyed each others' company, but it was not an organized, focused group. The aims of the Brotherhood were never defined; none of the members could even recall the exact date when the Brotherhood came into being; and the circle included a few who were not formally members, such as Ford Madox Brown and Walter Deverell. The title they adopted, originally a term of jokey abuse, implied a defiant admiration for the art of the early Italians, then considered primitive and archaic in the pejorative sense. But the Brotherhood was not a revivalist group. It was born out of dissatisfaction with the current state of art, represented by the Royal Academy, its Schools, its Members and its Summer Exhibitions. The PRB considered the art of the Academy to be shallow, stale and repetitious and wanted to make art that was challenging and different. Thus Rossetti allied himself early on with innovation and with attacking the establishment.

Rossetti's chief works produced during the brief period when the PRB was a coherent group, were his two oil paintings *The Girlhood of Mary Virgin* (fig. 9) and *Ecce Ancilla Domini!* (fig. 10) and his drawing *The first anniversary of the death of Beatrice* (fig. 6). All of them appear startlingly original in the context of their time, but their originality cannot be attributed to Rossetti alone. For the first few years after 1848, the Brotherhood was a genuinely collaborative enterprise; the artists exchanged ideas and worked together closely. The Pre-Raphaelite drawing style, flat, linear and angular, without shadows or modelling, is seen not only in Rossetti's drawing (fig. 6) but also in contemporaneous drawings by Hunt (fig. 8) and Millais. All had studied the same visual sources — Lasinio's engravings of the Campo Santo at Pisa, German outline engravings by Moritz Retzsch and Flaxman's outlines. All wanted their art to appear archaic, not to reproduce early art but as a way of purifying their style of academic convention. They made their figures deliberately awkward, as a challenge to the graceful and carefully modelled drawing style taught at the Academy. The Pre-Raphaelite drawing style

fig. 8
William Holman Hunt
Lorenzo and Isabella
1849
Musée du Louvre, D.A.G. (Fonds Orsay),
Paris

fig. 9
The Girlhood of Mary Virgin
1848–9
Tate. Bequeathed by Lady Jekyll 1937
cat. 12

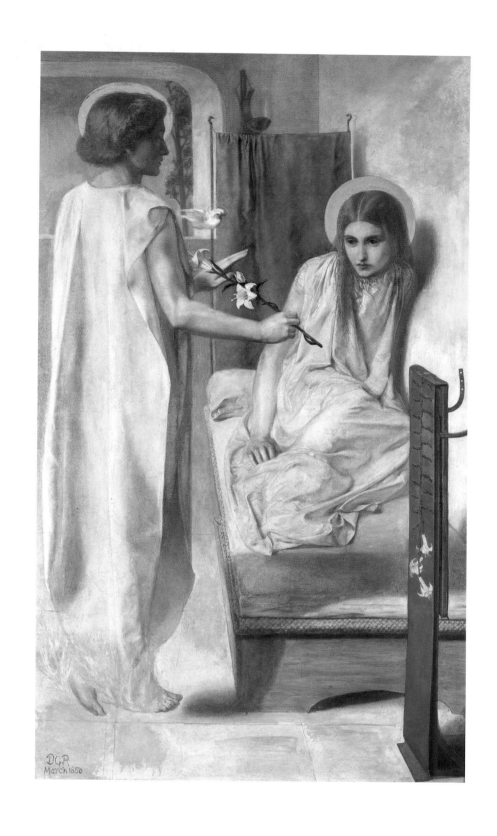

fig. 10
Ecce Ancilla Domini!
1849–50
Tate. Purchased 1886
cat. 13

appears to be a genuine 'group' style, evolved by all three artists together.

Like their drawings, the first exhibited oil paintings by chief members of the PRB – Hunt's *Rienzi* (private collection), Millais's *Isabella* (fig. 7) and Rossetti's *The Girlhood of Mary Virgin* (fig. 9) all of 1848–9, and Hunt's *A Converted British Family* (Ashmolean Museum, Oxford), Millais's *Christ in the House of his Parents* (Tate) and Rossetti's *Ecce Ancilla Domini!* (fig. 10) all of 1849–50, share a sense of common purpose. They all display deliberate archaisms and a novel use of bright colour and minute detail. The Brothers experimented in varying degrees with painting thinly over a white ground to achieve purity of colour; their treatment of detail was influenced more by Flemish than by Italian painting. Rossetti and Hunt studied Van Eyck's *Arnolfini Portrait* in the National Gallery, London, and visited Bruges and Ghent in 1849, particularly admiring the work of Memling.[12] The Pre-Raphaelites also shared an interest in Tractarianism, a contemporary movement within the Church of England, which sought to bring dignity and solemnity to the act of worship through the use of vestments, precious objects, incense, colour and the revival of medieval symbolism in church decoration and ritual; but they tried to make the symbols in their pictures appear natural and realistic. In addition, these early Pre-Raphaelite works were produced with a certain amount of mutual collaboration: for example, Ford Madox Brown advised Rossetti about the background and accessories in *Ecce Ancilla Domini!* and Deverell helped him finish painting it.

Nevertheless, each of these paintings has its original aspect, and as a group they appear less coherent than Pre-Raphaelite drawings of the period. In many respects Rossetti's *Ecce Ancilla Domini!* (fig. 10) was a more extreme statement than the oil paintings by the other Pre-Raphaelites. In the first place, only Rossetti included a supernatural phenomenon that could not be explained in realistic terms, the Angel Gabriel floating above the ground, feet aflame. Rossetti, alone amongst the PRB, was moving away from naturalism, from the imitation of external appearance. As his brother William Michael remarked, *Ecce Ancilla Domini!* was a 'vehicle for representing ideas.'[13] And in the second place, only Rossetti used colour symbolism in such a radically simplified manner, limiting himself to the three primaries, blue for the Virgin, red for Christ's Passion and yellow for holiness, with white, for purity, predominating. Remove the symbolism, which is of course crucial to what Rossetti wanted to say, and the painting can be seen to contain the embryo of Whistler's *Symphony in White* (1862, National Gallery of Art, Washington) and Mondrian's pure abstraction.[14]

When Rossetti's first painting, *The Girlhood of Mary Virgin* (fig. 9), was exhibited in 1849, it was praised. 'Every allusion gives evidence of maturity of thought,' wrote the *Athenaeum*, inspired with 'the expectation that Mr. Rossetti will continue to pursue the lofty career which he has here so successfully begun.'[15] But the following year, the same journal was highly abusive about *Ecce Ancilla Domini!* (fig. 10), accusing Rossetti of 'ignoring all that has made the art great in the works of the greatest masters.'[16] Rossetti was caught up in the increasingly hysterical critical reaction

that greeted Pre-Raphaelitism in 1850, a reaction that was bound up with accusations of blasphemy, covert Catholicism and artistic revivalism, which was misunderstood as wilful imitation of the mannerisms of earlier art. Following this unfavourable reception, Rossetti became deeply suspicious of exhibiting in public for the rest of his life. After showing three watercolours at the Old Watercolour Society's Winter exhibition (December–January 1852–3) he virtually stopped exhibiting, only allowing his work to be shown very occasionally, mainly in private exhibitions open only to friends and sympathizers.

Anti-naturalism

Rossetti was never comfortable with the detailed naturalism that soon became a hallmark of Pre-Raphaelitism and struggled with perspective and 'correct' drawing. According to his brother, he was conscious that they were 'required in order to make a picture comformable to the modern standard,' but nevertheless felt that they should not usurp 'the place of the main idea or of human emotion and expressional force.'[17] Rossetti seems to have felt that the Academy, which valued correctness and rule above inner truth, would never understand his work or exhibit it sympathetically. 'It is the intention of the RA [Royal Academy] to keep down everything at all chargeable with new principles in art,' he wrote on 7 May 1853. 'Whenever, or if ever, I exhibit again, I shall be very careful how I submit anything to their mercies.'[18]

fig. 11
William Holman Hunt
The Awakening Conscience
1853–4
Tate. Presented by Sir Colin and Lady Anderson
through the Friends of the Tate Gallery 1976

In a world where the chief way of making one's reputation was by exhibiting a major statement at the Academy, it was a bold move to go his own way, and Rossetti was lucky in that he found a circle of sympathetic patrons, including the great art critic John Ruskin, who supported him, bought his work and recommended it to other like-minded collectors. Whilst not entirely free from financial problems, and certainly not free from the attempts of Ruskin to direct his work, Rossetti could pursue his own ideas without the need to pander to public taste or submit to the lottery of open exhibitions. He could be more personal and experimental in his work than most of his contemporaries. As the others besides Rossetti went their separate ways in the early 1850s, the Brotherhood disintegrated. Hunt, Brown and Millais continued to produce and exhibit large, naturalistic figure compositions as the vehicle for their ideas. Rossetti for the most part worked on a small scale and in a more personal manner. His most important, powerful and innovatory works of the middle 50s were watercolours and drawings on paper, subverting the hierarchy of media and scale favoured by the Academy as well as the hierarchy of subjects. In these works, Rossetti paid less attention to the imitation of superficial appearance and more to his own interior world of ideas.

Two telling examples of Rossetti's difficulties with oil paintings show him moving away from the detailed naturalism adopted by Hunt and Millais in paintings like *The Hireling Shepherd* (1851–2, Manchester City Galleries) and *Ophelia* (1851–2, Tate). The first example is his attempt at a Pre-Raphaelite landscape. In 1850 Rossetti was at Knole Park, Sevenoaks, working on the background

for an oil painting of a Dante subject, *The Meeting of Dante and Beatrice in Paradise*, painted from real trees in the open air in accordance with the approved method for Ruskinian 'truth to nature'. He soon abandoned the painting. (Much later he was to reuse the same canvas, incorporating the unfinished landscape into the background of the dreamlike *Bower Meadow* of 1872, fig. 68). He wrote to a friend, 'The fact is, between you & me, that the leaves on the trees I have to paint here, appear red, yellow &c to my eyes; and as of course I know them on that account to be really of a vivid green, it seems rather annoying that I cannot do them so: my subject shrieking aloud for Spring.'[19] It was not just that he lacked the technique to paint in oils or the patience to represent naturalistic detail; it was because he wanted something different from landscape. He wanted symbolic colour – the vivid green for Spring that is evident in watercolours such as *The Meeting of Dante and Beatrice in Paradise* (fig. 14) and *The Annunciation* (fig. 30). When he needed a landscape for the background of *Writing on the sand* (fig. 19) in 1859, he simply borrowed two sketches from his friend the watercolour painter George Price Boyce and copied them.

The second example is his attempt to paint a subject of contemporary life, set in a London street, *Found* (fig. 13), a modern moral subject in oils that was to be dense with symbolic realism. Its theme, that of a fallen woman confronted by her innocent past, was similar to Holman Hunt's *The Awakening Conscience* (fig. 11). Hunt's conception dates from January 1853, whereas the first explicit references to Rossetti's subject date from slightly later.[20] The theme of the fallen woman was a frequent subject for

fig. 12
W. and D. Downey
Fanny Cornforth
photograph
Delaware Art Museum,
Samuel and Mary R. Bancroft Archives

fig. 13
Found
1854–5 / 1859–81
Delaware Art Museum,
Samuel and Mary R. Bancroft Memorial,
1935
cat. 57

fig. 14
**The Meeting of Dante
and Beatrice in Paradise**
c. 1853–4
Syndics of the Fitzwilliam Museum,
Cambridge
cat. 43

fig. 15
The first anniversary
of the death of Beatrice
1853
Visitors of the Ashmolean Museum, Oxford.
Bequeathed by Mrs Thomas Combe 1894
cat. 42

fig. 16
Giotto painting the portrait of Dante
1852
Collection Lord Lloyd-Webber
cat. 40

fig. 17
Dante's Vision of Rachel and Leah
1855
Tate. Bequeathed by Beresford Rimington
Heaton 1940
cat. 45

fig. 18
Paolo and Francesca da Rimini
1862
Trustees of the Cecil Higgins Art Gallery,
Bedford
cat. 44

fig. 19
Writing on the sand
1859
The British Museum, London
cat. 58

contemporary debate and featured in novels published in 1852, but in any case Rossetti's poem 'Jenny', about a fallen woman, was started in the late 1840s, showing he had been interested in the idea for many years.[21] Even so, when *The Awakening Conscience* appeared at the Academy in 1854, Rossetti was worried that because he was taking so long to make any progress, *Found* would be considered an imitation of Hunt's picture.[22] Rossetti continued with it, however, taking his painting up and laying it aside many times throughout his life. Even with the help of studio assistants, he never completed it, finding the difficulties of composition and technique too much for him. One could argue that *Found* was an aberration in Rossetti's work, a leftover from the early days of the Pre-Raphaelite Brotherhood, and that it confirmed his defects as a painter. But the fact that he persisted so long (he declared his intention of taking it up again as late as 1880) suggests that it was the idea — the repentant female — that was important to him, rather than the technical problems or the contemporary setting.

Radiant colours and vibrant surfaces

Rossetti may not have been able to paint in a conventionally acceptable manner, but the styles and techniques he developed for himself were innovatory. The vivid, singing quality of the colour in Rossetti's watercolours of the 1850s is one of his most powerful and original achievements. He created his own way of painting in watercolour, using thick pigment, often minutely stippled, hatched and scumbled, to give a vibrant surface, sometimes mixing paint with gum to give a richer effect. The surfaces seem to glow with inner light, like stained glass windows. This technique worked on a small scale and was consciously based on the pages of medieval illuminated manuscripts. Rossetti had long admired them, but his interest in them had been stimulated by Ruskin, who collected them enthusiastically and showed Rossetti examples from his collection.[23] Rossetti also seems to have achieved something similar but on a much larger scale in the Oxford Union murals; when Pauline Trevelyan saw them, she wrote that 'the colour is like flowers of fresh fruit with the bloom on',[24] and Coventry Patmore, too, noted 'colouring so brilliant as to make the walls look like the margin of a highly-illuminated manuscript.'[25]

Patmore's article goes on to discuss how Rossetti achieved this startling effect, describing Rossetti's colour as 'a voluptuous radiance of variegated tints'. It appeared 'sweet bright and pure... and yet if closely looked into, there is scarcely a square inch of all those hundred square feet of colour which has not half-a-dozen tints in it. The colours coming from points instead of from masses, are positively radiant, at the same time that they are wholly the reverse of glaring. An indefiniteness of outline ...is a necessary result of Mr. Rossetti's manner of colouring.'[26] This suggests that Rossetti used his stippling technique on a large scale, in a way that has something in common with pointillism, mixing points of different colours. But it is no longer possible to see how the paint was applied, because, notoriously, the murals rapidly faded, due to Rossetti's technical inexperience and thoughtless naivety in neglecting to prepare the wall surfaces.

Equally novel was Rossetti's ink drawing technique. An early example of how fine his workmanship could be is *Hesterna Rosa* (cat. 52), but his draughtsmanship is seen at its best in *Mary Magdalene at the door of Simon the Pharisee* (fig. 32) and *Hamlet and Ophelia* (fig. 21), both of 1858–9 and said to be based on a study of Dürer's engravings.[27] The drawings are more personal and original than this implies. They are distinguished by a dense network of finely drawn lines, describing in minute detail the rich patterning of fabrics, the sheen of flowing hair, the grain-ing of wood and the textures of brick. The effect is however the reverse of naturalistic – the figures in the *Mary Magdalene* drawing are ranked in size according to their importance, the architecture is simplified after the manner of structures in illuminated manuscripts, and the figures are crowded together in a shallow claustrophobic space, to powerful effect.

The power of love

An overview of Rossetti's subject matter up to and beyond 1860 shows the depth and originality of his vision even when compared to his erstwhile Pre-Raphaelite colleagues Hunt, Millais and Brown, all of whose pictures were more complex and deeply thought than those of most Academ-icians. Central to Rossetti's art was the celebration of woman, and through her the power of love. He believed that woman enshrined the mystery of existence, and all of his work concerns woman in different aspects. Female excellence was exemplified by the Virgin; ideal love by Beatrice; female sensuality by Gretchen, Francesca, Guenevere, Mary Magdalene and Lady Lilith; female beauty in the paintings of the 1860s; the power of woman over man in *Venus Verticordia* (fig. 53) and *Astarte Syriaca* (fig. 66). He was interested in pairs and opposites: love and death, virtue and vice, innocence and repentance, spiritual and carnal love. *Ecce Ancilla Domini!* (fig. 10) was intended to be one half of a diptych, with a companion, never completed, showing the Death of the Virgin; *Paolo and Francesca da Rimini* (fig. 18) is in three parts, as is the Llandaff altarpiece (fig. 26), and many other paintings were intended to have pendants or to be part of pictures with several panels that were never finished (see cat. 69). He often included opposites within one work, contrasting life and death in *The Raven* and *The Sleeper* (fig. 4, cat. 5), good and evil in *Retro me Sathana* (cat. 7), and virtue and vice in *Borgia* and *Hesterna Rosa* (fig. 23, cat. 52). In *Found*, *Arthur's Tomb* and *Hamlet and Ophelia* (figs. 13, 25, 21) he expressed the opposites in particularly dramatic and elo-quent form, an intense moment of confrontation between a man and a woman.

Though Rossetti's paintings are not strictly autobio-graphical, they were closely linked to his personal experi-ence. Around 1850, Elizabeth Siddal was introduced to Rossetti, and her features began to appear in his work. At first she modelled to Deverell, who had introduced her to the Pre-Raphaelite circle, and then she sat to Hunt and Millais; she also began to sit for Rossetti (see cats. 31, 39, 49, figs. 20, 56), and soon she sat for no one else. The two

fig. 20
**Head of Elizabeth Siddal full face,
looking down**
1855
Visitors of the Ashmolean Museum, Oxford
cat. 28

fig. 21
Hamlet and Ophelia
c. 1858–9
The British Museum, London
cat. 88

fig. 22
The First Madness of Ophelia
1864
Gallery Oldham, Charles Lees collection
cat. 91

grew close, though they were never formally engaged, but for Rossetti this was no ordinary love relationship: he later said that when he first saw her 'he felt his destiny was defined'.[28] Likewise, for him she was no ordinary model: she came to personify his ideas about the mystery of woman, appearing in his paintings as Delia, Beatrice, Francesca, the Virgin Mary. In the early and mid 1850s, drawing her became compulsive, 'like a monomania' as Ford Madox Brown noted.[29] The extended series of drawings of her is like a sequence of love poems and has no precedent in British art. In the later 1850s, Rossetti's attitude to woman changed and became more complex. The change took place around the time he met Fanny Cornforth, a model who may also have become his mistress (figs. 12, 59, 97). His obsession with Elizabeth Siddal became less single-minded; he was now becoming more at ease with his sexuality, and the emphasis in his work on moral exemplars and contrasts lessened. In *Borgia* (fig. 23) the treatment of vice was no longer condemnatory, but celebratory, leading to the paintings of the 1860s rejoicing in female beauty and sensuality.

Other worlds

Rossetti's works contain opposing shapes as well as opposing ideas — mirrors, mirror images and balancing figures recur many times. These are not mere compositional devices but have powerful emotional effects that give depth to his art. In *The Meeting of Dante and Beatrice in Paradise*, *Dante's Dream* and *The Blue Closet* (figs. 14, 60, 61, 35) the

fig. 23
Borgia
1851 / 1854 / 1858–9
Tullie House Museum and Art Gallery,
Carlisle
cat. 51

paired figures create a slow rhythm, which sets the scene in another world, as if in a dream. A similar effect, like a trancelike vision, is created in *Beata Beatrix* (fig. 57) by the hazy way in which the paint is applied, as well as by the opposing figures on either side of the central figure. The effect of conjuring up another world is seen at its most uncanny in *The Maids of Elfen-Mere* and *How They Met Themselves* (cats. 74-5, fig. 33) where the pairs and three-somes are supernatural beings placed in shocking con-frontation with mortals. Rossetti was fascinated by tales of the supernatural and by the myth of the world beyond the grave, bridged by love, as in *Dante's Dream* or *The Blessed Damozel* (figs. 61, 69). Later in life, when he was beset by illness and paranoia, he became interested in spiritualism and attended séances; much earlier, in a letter of 1855, he had expressed disbelief.[30] Nevertheless, dreams and supernatural worlds are an important element in his art. The musical rhythms set up by opposing pairs and mirror images continue in later works such as *The Bower Meadow* and *Astarte Syriaca* (figs. 68, 66), and he recreated the effects in real life, filling his house at Cheyne Walk with mirrors, creating ghostly reflections wherever one looked.

The central position of woman and of the interior or dream world in Rossetti's art extended beyond the 1850s into his later work; his vision of the Middle Ages was shorter-lived, though equally important. Though medi-eval subjects were present in his art from the beginning, his vision of the Middle Ages was at its most intensely ori-ginal in the series of watercolours depicting a 'Froissartian' world of chivalry and courtly love. These date from 1857, also the year when his Tennyson engravings were

fig. 24
**Sir Launcelot
in the Queen's Chamber**
1857
Birmingham Museums & Art Gallery.
Presented by subscribers
cat. 93

fig. 25
Arthur's Tomb
1854–5
The British Museum, London
cat. 73

published and when the Oxford Union murals of Arthurian subjects were painted. By this time, Rossetti had been exposed to Ruskin's interest in illuminated manuscripts and had met the young Burne-Jones and William Morris, also enthusiasts for all things medieval. They refocused Rossetti's interest in the period and may have contributed some of the visual sources, but Rossetti's medieval vision was his own, quite unlike the more literal approach to recreating the Middle Ages seen in paintings by Victorian Academicians such as Maclise or Landseer,[31] or the romantic sketches of knights and ladies of Rossetti's juvenilia (s 5, 9).

In the Tennyson engravings (cats. 76–83) Rossetti did not always literally illustrate the texts but took Tennyson's poems merely as his point of departure, evoking the Middle Ages in miniature, with quaint detail and intricate decoration, but limited to black and white. The medieval watercolours (figs. 31, 35, 36) develop this vision in colour. Rossetti places his figures in imaginary settings without conventional perspective or logic. The figures are crammed together in a narrow zone at the front of the scene; the furnishings and spaces are defined by rectangular lines and planes parallel to the picture surface. The costumes and furnishings take elements from medieval sources but do not copy them literally: they are freely combined for decorative effect, without concern for historical accuracy. The musical instruments and furniture are impossible inventions; Rossetti delights in the patterns of tiles, textiles and fanciful heraldic devices, all of which contribute to the general effect of destroying recession and emphasizing surface. The scale of these

fig. 26
The Seed of David
1858–64
Llandaff Cathedral, Cardiff
cat. 64

fig. 27
The Passover in the Holy Family
1854–5
Tate. Presented by Charles Ricketts
in memory of Henry Michael Field 1916
cat. 61

fig. 28
Mary Nazarene
c. 1855
Tate. Purchased 1911
cat. 69

fig. 29
Mary Magdalene
leaving the house of feasting
1857
Tate. Purchased 1911
cat. 70

works is modest, but they look detailed and busy; they are unreal, playful and wilful. It is this quality that Ruskin came to dislike, acknowledging that he himself was 'answerable for a good deal of this fatal medievalism ... for the stiffness and quaintness and intensity as opposed to classical grace and tranquillity,' and declaring he was 'sickened of all Gothic by Rossetti's clique.'[32] Compared to earlier watercolours such as *The first anniversary of the death of Beatrice* of 1853 (fig. 15), with its more fully modelled, carefully lit figures placed in a more realistic space, the 'Froissartian' watercolours present a very different style. Yet they have one thing in common – in them, Rossetti creates an interior world of art, drawn from memory and imagination, a private realm apart from everyday life.

The exact meanings of *The Blue Closet* and *The Tune of Seven Towers* (figs. 35, 31) are not known. Rossetti himself, when asked why he had included some inexplicable object in a picture replied, 'To puzzle fools, boy, to puzzle fools,'[33] suggesting they indeed contain a strong element of playful fantasy. But it would be a mistake to regard these two watercolours as simply evoking a generalized world of medieval colour and chivalry. They may well have had personal significance for Rossetti; other watercolours in the group, not in the exhibition, such as *The wedding of St George and the Princess Sabra* (1857, Tate, S 97) and *The death of Breuse sans Pitié* (1857, private collection, S 107) are based on very specific narratives, and *Sir Galahad at the ruined chapel* (fig. 36) is an ingenious realization of particular features of Tennyson's text. Nevertheless, it is in this group of watercolours of 1857 that can be seen the

seeds of the Aesthetic Movement: the painting not as a copy of reality or as a realistic narrative but as an object of beauty in itself. The seeds were to bear fruit in the paintings of the 1860s, hymns to the beauty and sensuality of women, showing them luxuriously arrayed, surrounded by flowers and jewels: 'beautiful women with floral adjuncts'.[34]

fig. 30
The Annunciation
1855, retouched 1858
private collection
cat. 62

44

fig. 31
The Tune of Seven Towers
1857
Tate. Purchased with assistance through
the National Art Collections Fund from
Sir Arthur Du Cros Bt and Sir Otto Beit
1916
cat. 87

fig. 32
Mary Magdalene
at the door of Simon the Pharisee
1858–9
Syndics of the Fitzwilliam Museum,
Cambridge
cat. 68

fig. 33
How They Met Themselves
1851 / 1860
Syndics of the Fitzwilliam Museum,
Cambridge
cat. 89

fig. 34
St Catherine
1857
Tate. Bequeathed by Mrs Emily Toms in
memory of her father, Joseph Kershaw, 1931
cat. 85

fig. 35
The Blue Closet
1857
Tate. Purchased with assistance through
the National Art Collections Fund from
Sir Arthur Du Cros Bt and Sir Otto Beit
1916
cat. 86

'Beautiful women with floral adjuncts'

ROSSETTI'S NEW STYLE

Elizabeth Prettejohn

Around 1860, everything about Rossetti's practice in painting changed abruptly. We can see this at once if we compare a work of 1859, such as *Sir Galahad at the ruined chapel* (fig. 36), with one of 1861, such as *Fair Rosamund* (fig. 38). *Sir Galahad* is a watercolour, intricately worked in Rossetti's characteristic 'dry brush style' and crowded with small-scale figures, who enact a complex narrative drawn from a poem by Tennyson. The minutely detailed medieval accessories, such as Galahad's armour and the ritual trappings of the forest shrine, help to tell the story, as does the complicated spatial arrangement: Galahad dominates the centre, while his horse waits in the background at top right, and singing angels are concealed at bottom left beneath the intricately crafted shrine (this device neatly illustrates the poem, in which Galahad hears the voices of angels he cannot see). The complicated arrangement, so cleverly adapted to its subject matter, is by the same token unique to *Sir Galahad*; other works from before 1860 are as ingenious and detailed, but necessarily diverse in composition. *Fair Rosamund*, on the other hand, is instantly recognizable as a typical Rossetti of the period after 1860, one of the type William Michael Rossetti called 'beautiful women with floral adjuncts'.[1] In other respects, too, it differs from *Sir Galahad*. It is an oil painting and makes full use of the glossiness of that medium, for instance in the lustrous waves of the red hair and the gleaming bottle-glass roundels of the window, as well as its capability for blending tones, seen in the gradual modulation of the flesh colours, from the brightly lit left shoulder over the collarbone and shadowed right shoulder, and up the neck to the vivid pink of the cheek and the gentle cleft of the chin. The figure is large relative to the picture surface, and she appears alone, in startling close-up: this is a study of the figure rather than the dramatization of a story or event. The accessories are relatively few in comparison to those of *Sir Galahad*, and strangely repetitive. The rose repeats the figure's name (Rosamund, 'rosa mundi', rose of the world); as an emblem of love, it also echoes her status (beloved of King Henry II). The rose in natural form adorns her hair; in gold metal it decorates her necklace and makes an ornament on the parapet; it is woven into the fabric of her dress, and reappears in the decorative roundels of the parapet; the figure holds a rose-branch, and her lips and complexion partake of the colour of the rose. Thus all of the symbols and details, which in *Sir Galahad* complicate and elaborate the story, in *Fair Rosamund* converge on one idea: love, the rose, the woman are equivalents, signs for one another.

This was the third time Rossetti had made a radical reform to his own pictorial style and practice, and again the reform was to have repercussions not only on the artists of his immediate circle, but much more widely as well. Its most conspicuous result was a concentration on female beauty as the prime subject matter for visual art, and it is easy enough to trace the sequence of iconic images of female figures through Rossetti's own later work to that of other English artists such as Edward Burne-Jones, and eventually to that of continental Symbolists such as Fernand Khnopff and Gustav Klimt (see pp. 120-9). But the change was not limited to subject matter, and we should miss its radicalism if we were to understand it

fig. 36
Sir Galahad at the ruined chapel
1859
Birmingham Museums & Art Gallery
cat. 84

merely as a new approach to the representation of the female figure. As in Rossetti's previous reforms, the new kind of subject appeared in the context of a wholesale reconfiguration of the practice of painting, from the most basic level of materials and techniques up to the most abstract or conceptual level of the meanings and ideas that can be embodied in visual form. And again, as in the previous cases, Rossetti achieved this reconfiguration not by adapting the practices of his contemporaries, but rather by immersing himself in a more distant and alien pictorial mode. In 1848, at the beginning of the Pre-Raphaelite movement, the mode was that of Van Eyck and the artists of the Early Renaissance; in the watercolours of the 1850s, it was that of medieval manuscripts. Now, in the 1860s, Rossetti departed decisively from these 'primitive' or archaic modes, to identify his art, instead, with that of the Venetian High Renaissance, of Titian and Veronese.

This might be described as a willed progression to artistic maturity. Rossetti's ambition to succeed, to become a major painter, is evident from his earliest correspondence, but there is a new note in the letters of the late 1850s and early 1860s. Repeatedly he expresses his desire to work on a large scale, and to be classed as an oil painter, not a mere watercolourist.[2] The commissions for the Llandaff altarpiece in 1856 (cats. 63-6, fig. 26) and for the Oxford Union murals in 1857 (cats. 92-3, fig. 96) gave the first hints that he might be regarded as a credible practitioner in large-scale mural decoration for public buildings, widely seen as a more exalted field of artistic activity than the more commercialized production of easel paintings for exhibition and sale to private buyers. At the same time, other artists in his extended circle were making forays into large-scale mural painting; in 1859 Rossetti wrote of his admiration for G.F. Watts's monumental fresco, *Justice: A Hemicycle of Lawgivers*, in the Hall at Lincoln's Inn in London.[3] An important article by the critic Tom Taylor, published in 1863, called vigorously for high art in public buildings, as opposed to commercialized art for private buyers, and named Rossetti among the English painters of 'proved power for large work' of this kind.[4]

But the two commissions, at Llandaff and Oxford, required capabilities that Rossetti had not yet had the opportunity to develop. The Oxford murals were dogged from the start by technical problems (see cats. 92–3). The Llandaff altarpiece was to be in oils, a medium in which Rossetti had only the experience of his two early paintings, *The Girlhood of Mary Virgin* (fig. 9) and *Ecce Ancilla Domini!* (fig. 10). Both of those pictures had been executed in the small-scale brushwork of early Pre-Raphaelitism. To cover a surface the size of the Llandaff altarpiece with the tiny, meticulous brushstrokes of early Pre-Raphaelite practice would be a labour of almost impossible proportions, and Rossetti began to have doubts, too, about the aesthetic effect of the Pre-Raphaelite style in a large-scale work. On a trip to Paris in early 1860 he was bowled over by a work in the Louvre: the vast canvas by the Venetian painter Paolo Veronese, *The Marriage Feast at Cana*. In letters about the Louvre written on a previous visit, in 1849, Rossetti had never mentioned this work. Now, though, he calls it 'the greatest picture in the world beyond a doubt'.[5]

fig. 37
Regina Cordium
1860
Johannesburg Art Gallery

fig. 38
Fair Rosamund
1861
National Museums and Galleries of Wales,
Cardiff
cat. 96

On his return to London, he criticized William Holman Hunt's large painting, *The Finding of the Saviour in the Temple* (1854–60, Birmingham Museums & Art Gallery), recently completed and placed on exhibition. Hunt's picture is an extraordinary tour-de-force of painstaking Pre-Raphaelite detail elaborated over a large surface, but Rossetti calls it a 'wooden puppet-show of enlarged views'. Significantly, Rossetti contrasts Hunt's picture with 'Veronese's flesh, blood, and slight stupidity'. 'Give me the latter however,' he continues, 'or even Millais's, when Veronese's is not to be had. But O that Veronese at Paris!'[6]

Veronese's *Marriage Feast at Cana* seems, then, to have impressed Rossetti as a successful approach to painting at vast scale, something for which he now felt the Pre-Raphaelite technique inadequate. Moreover, it was not just the design, but the breadth and lusciousness of Veronese's paint handling that seemed to answer his search for a pictorial mode appropriate to the large-scale work he now wanted to make. Indeed, he had been worrying about this problem before the trip to Paris. In 1859, he wrote to his friend William Bell Scott of an experiment he was making in the painting of flesh. This was the first of his pictures of single female figures, the painting eventually known as *Bocca Baciata* (fig. 39). The letter, though, does not give the picture a title, but presents it as a technical exercise in cultivating a broader style: 'I have painted a little half-figure in oil lately which I should like you to see, as I have made an effort to avoid what I know to be a besetting fault of mine – & indeed rather common to PR [Pre-Raphaelite] painting – that of stipple in the flesh. I have succeeded in quite keeping it at a distance this time,

and am very desirous of painting, whenever I can find leisure & opportunity, various figures of this kind, chiefly as a rapid study of flesh painting. I am sure that amid the many botherations of a picture, where design, drawing, expression & colour have to be thought of all at once (and this perhaps in the focus of the four winds out of doors, or at any rate among somnolent models, ticklish draperies & toppling lay figures), one can never do justice even to what faculty of mere painting may be in one. Even among the old good painters, their portraits & simpler pictures are almost always their masterpieces for colour & execution; and I fancy if one kept this in view, one might have a better chance of learning to paint at last.'[7] Many of the characteristics of Rossetti's images of women seem to be in place in this description: the elimination of dramatic or narrative incident, the concentration on beautiful paint handling, the invocation of the old masters. But in this context they are presented as an exercise in learning to paint in oils. In another letter, to the watercolour painter George Price Boyce, who had commissioned the picture, Rossetti describes it as having 'a rather Venetian aspect'.[8] This helps to explain the reference, in the letter to Scott, to 'the old good painters'; Rossetti evidently means the Venetian painters, celebrated for their richly coloured half-length portraits.

No doubt Rossetti is thinking, above all, of the half-lengths of beautiful women by Venetian painters such as Titian and Palma Vecchio, in which the draperies often slip from the shoulders to reveal voluptuous flesh (figs. 40, 54). But as Alastair Grieve has suggested, Rossetti may also have studied the half-length portrait of the male *St Dominic*

fig. 39
Bocca Baciata
1859
Museum of Fine Arts, Boston.
Gift of James Lawrence 1980.261
cat. 94

by the Venetian artist Giovanni Bellini, which had recently entered the collection of the South Kensington Museum (fig. 41).[9] The placement of Rossetti's figure, in a compressed space between a flat floral background and a foreground parapet, seems to echo the Bellini. In *Bocca Baciata* Rossetti is not, then, merely borrowing the idea for a subject, a sensual woman, from the Venetian artists; he is exploring and recreating, in his own work, a Venetian way of composing and painting a compelling picture. The beauty of the painting, and even its sensual appeal, are matters not merely of the desirability of the represented woman, but also of the richness of the paint handling and colour and of the immediacy with which the figure in its shallow space addresses the viewer.

It seems that the picture was not given its title, *Bocca Baciata*, until after it had been completed and exhibited in 1860 at the Hogarth Club (a private exhibiting society formed by associates of Rossetti's).[10] In other words, the visible form of the picture was established before its literary reference — the exact opposite of the conventional procedure, in which a picture is made to 'illustrate' a literary text. In this respect, too, Rossetti is radically altering his earlier procedures (as we have seen, he frequently illustrated passages from Dante and other authors in the 1850s). But it does not follow that the literary reference becomes less important to the work — far from it: the reference is ingeniously chosen not only to reflect the visual character of the picture but to extend and deepen its implications. The title derives from the end of a tale in *The Decameron*, by the 14th-century Italian writer Boccaccio, in which a woman takes eight lovers in succession and finally

fig. 40
Titian
Woman with a mirror
c. 1513–15
Musée du Louvre, Paris

marries a ninth, to their mutual joy. In the tale, the woman is not censured for her promiscuity, but rather celebrated for her sensuality and capacity for love: '*Bocca baciata non perde ventura, anzi rinnuova come fa la luna*' ('the mouth that has been kissed does not lose its fortune, rather it renews itself just as the moon does').[11] The fragmentary quotation of this line in Rossetti's title elaborates the visible sensuality of the woman and resonates with the faraway look in the woman's eyes; is she remembering past loves or imagining future ones?

Bocca Baciata may have begun as a technical exercise, undertaken with a view to self-education in the handling of oil paint. But in the process of working it became something quite different: the first experiment in a simultaneous exploration of Venetian style and female beauty that would develop in significance and complexity over a remarkable series of subsequent pictures.

The 'Venetian' pictures

Bocca Baciata is a small work, in a distinctive, nearly square, format that measures only about 30 centimetres in either dimension, and the works that immediately followed it are similar. *Fair Rosamund* of 1861 (fig. 38) is slightly larger, but *Regina Cordium* of 1860 (fig. 37), *Girl at a lattice* of 1862 (fig. 42) and *Helen of Troy* of 1863 (fig. 43) remain small, and all of these works are tightly framed around the figure's head and shoulders. *Fazio's Mistress* of 1863 (fig. 51) begins to expand, presenting the figure at half length, and from 1864 the half-length figure is life-size, in formats of 80

fig. 41
Giovanni Bellini
St Dominic
1515
National Gallery, London

fig. 42
Girl at a lattice
1862
Syndics of the Fitzwilliam Museum,
Cambridge
cat. 97

fig. 43
Helen of Troy
1863
Hamburger Kunsthalle
cat. 99

centimetres or more in height. All of these paintings place the figure in a shallow, constricted space, and most deploy a ledge or parapet at the bottom edge, as in Venetian portrait formats (see figs. 40, 41); in *Venus Verticordia* of 1863–8 (fig. 53) a dense mass of honeysuckle, and in *The Beloved* of 1865–6 (fig. 52) a black child holding a burnished vase of roses take the place of the parapet. Thus the picture-type is of extraordinary consistency, and this is also true of the handling of paint, the colour harmonies, the organization of space, the way the figure addresses the viewer, the deployment of literary titles, and the evocation of Venetian Renaissance art. These characteristics are so tightly bound together that it is difficult to speak of any one of them without reference to the others. Yet it is worth making the attempt to analyze the components that, together, make these pictures so compelling, and at times disturbing.

It may be appropriate to begin with the obvious: the close-up concentration on a woman's face. The faces are nearly devoid of expression, particularly in comparison with other Victorian pictures that dramatize a strong emotion; we may think, for example, of the startled expression of the female figure in William Holman Hunt's *The Awakening Conscience* of 1854 (fig. 11). Rossetti's *Lady Lilith* (fig. 44) inhabits a composition that has certain elements in common with Hunt's picture (including the figure's carefully painted white dress), but her expression is deadpan. As Rossetti's friend, the poet Algernon Charles Swinburne (fig. 55) put it, in an article of 1868 that reviewed several of Rossetti's recent works: 'Of evil desire or evil impulse she has nothing; and nothing of good. She is indifferent, equable, magnetic; she charms

and draws down the souls of men by pure force of absorption....'[12] Swinburne captures the strange tension between the remoteness of the figures' expressions and the viewer's sense of immediate involvement. Many of the figures seem to make eye contact with the viewer, others look to the side, but there is often a sense of distraction, or a lack of focus in the eyes. The figures are so close and vivid that the sense of engagement is strong, yet this is partly frustrated by our inability to fathom their psychology.

This effect is closely related to the unconventional perspective of the pictures. As we have seen, Rossetti had, since the beginning of his career, refused to design internal picture spaces that conformed to the ordinary rules of post-Renaissance perspective. The shallow spaces of the new single-figure pictures – bounded in *The Blue Bower* (fig. 47), for instance, by the insistent blue ceramic backdrop, or in *Venus Verticordia* by the wall of roses – can be said in one sense to obviate the need to represent a recession into perspectival depth. Yet the abundant volumes of the figures are at odds with this: the figures seem to burst from their spaces, just as they crowd the edges of the picture surface. The effect is peculiarly unsettling in *Lady Lilith*, in which the background roses and the bright foliage reflected in the rear mirror seem no more distant than the arm of the chair and the vase in the foreground. As a result, the figure's fleshy corporeality turns in a seemingly impossible gyration, echoed by the rippling curves of her hair and fur robe. Again, the figures seem too close to us for comfort. This is particularly apparent when they are at life size, that is, at the same scale as ourselves: we encounter another human being but we seem to stand

fig. 44
Lady Lilith
1868
Delaware Art Museum, Samuel
and Mary R. Bancroft Memorial, 1935
cat. 107

closer to her than propriety should allow. By eliminating the conventional recession of perspective space internal to the picture, and bringing the figure so close as apparently to intrude on our own space, outside the picture, Rossetti disrupts the conventions that had operated in Western painting since the Renaissance. There is no categorical distinction or measurable distance between us, as spectators, and the space within the picture. It is as if the perspective had been turned inside out, projecting into our space rather than receding safely into the illusionistic depth within the picture. The contrast between *Lady Lilith* and Hunt's *The Awakening Conscience* is instructive. Hunt, too, introduced a mirror, reflecting a sunlit exterior scene, on the rear wall at the top left, but in the Hunt we easily read the space as projecting backward into the room, as well as out into the garden seen in the mirror. *Lady Lilith* negates any such spatial illusionism, and we wonder whether the mirror reflects a view from the depicted room at all, or whether it is perhaps a magic mirror presenting a scene from some remote place or time (a few years after painting this picture Rossetti wrote a poem, 'Rose Mary', about such a magic mirror).

The elimination of pictorial depth is not merely a matter of design; it is also an effect of the colour, as insistent in the background as in the foreground, so that the rear backdrops seem to start forward. In *The Blue Bower* the blue of the background, fancifully composed of Chinese blue-and-white ceramic pieces,[13] matches in intensity the bright blue cornflowers that spill over the ledge at the front of the picture. The relief of the figure against the background, here as in other cases, is attained entirely by colour contrast, not by any sense of atmospheric distance. Rossetti learned this procedure largely from studying the management of colour in Venetian paintings. In the first volume of *Modern Painters*, published in 1843, Ruskin had dwelt upon an analogous treatment of foreground and background blues in Titian's *Bacchus and Ariadne*, a painting in the National Gallery in London (fig. 46). For Ruskin Titian had sacrificed truth of atmospheric perspective in the interests of colouristic 'splendour', by making the blue of the distant mountains as intense as that of Ariadne's robe in the foreground: 'it is difficult to imagine anything more magnificently impossible,' he wrote.[14] Perhaps Rossetti 'corrects' Titian's error, by closing the space in *The Blue Bower*, so that no great distance is represented. Nonetheless, the picture derives its special intensity from the seeming nearness of everything in it, from the Japanese *koto* on which the woman plays to the passion flowers and convolvulus, placed behind the figure, but equally vividly coloured.

We have seen how, in *Bocca Baciata*, Rossetti wished to experiment with a broader method of laying on paint, to escape the 'stippled' effect of the individual brushstrokes in Pre-Raphaelite painting. In the series of paintings that followed, he emphasized the capacity of the oil painting medium to produce deep, lustrous and velvety colours through layering, blending and glazing; the new method is as different as possible from the Pre-Raphaelite practice of laying colours thinly and preserving their distinctness and purity. Moreover, he integrated the colour harmonies over the whole surface of the picture, as in the blues of *The Blue Bower*. In *Fair Rosamund* the colour of the

fig. 45
Sibylla Palmifera
1865–70
National Museums Liverpool
(Lady Lever Art Gallery, Port Sunlight)
cat. 108

rose is also a flesh-tint. In *Helen of Troy* the yellow-gold colours of the figure's hair, robe and complexion are linked with the raging fire in the background, connecting Helen's visible appearance with the destruction of Troy for which her beauty is responsible. White tints weave through *Lady Lilith*, from the dress and fur to the background roses; white, associated traditionally (and in *Ecce Ancilla Domini!*, fig. 10) with innocence and purity, makes an ironic or perhaps sinister keynote in this picture of Lilith, the evil first wife of Adam before the creation of Eve.

The picture that came to be called *Lady Lilith* may have begun simply as a picture of a woman making her toilette, like *Fazio's Mistress* of 1863 and the watercolours of 1864, *Morning Music* and *Woman combing her hair* (figs. 50, 49). All of these pictures clearly relate to Titian's *Woman with a mirror*, on display at the Louvre under the title *La femme à sa toilette* at the time of Rossetti's visits to Paris (fig. 40; at some point, Rossetti also acquired a photograph of this Titian).[15] Even after *Lady Lilith* acquired its present title, Rossetti stressed that it represented a *modern* woman making her toilette.[16] In some cases, such as *Bocca Baciata*, Rossetti is known to have painted the picture first and assigned it a title later; in others he changed the title long after it was painted. Thus *Fazio's Mistress* was later called *Aurelia*, with reference to the red-golden colour of the figure's hair.[17] Were the titles, then, somewhat arbitrary, given perhaps to satisfy Victorian patrons' expectations that a picture ought to have a nameable subject? That can scarcely be the case, since Rossetti frequently wrote poems to accompany the pictures, elaborating the resonances of the figure's name

fig. 46
Titian
Bacchus and Ariadne
1523
National Gallery, London

fig. 47
The Blue Bower
1865
The Trustees of the Barber Institute of Fine
Arts, The University of Birmingham
cat. 105

in different ways; such a poem was written for *Lady Lilith* (see cat. 107), while *Fazio's Mistress* is related to a poem by the early Italian poet Fazio degli Uberti describing the beauty of his beloved, translated by Rossetti for his volume published in 1861, *The Early Italian Poets* (see cat. 100). Nonetheless, the relationship between Rossetti's pictures and their literary or poetic titles is quite unlike the traditional one (used by Rossetti himself in many works of the 1850s), in which a visual image is designed to 'illustrate' a pre-existing text. Rather as he reversed the usual terms for pictorial perspective, Rossetti in his pictures of the 1860s often reversed the usual relationship between the visual image and its literary 'source'— the visual image came first and the literary association later.

As we have already seen in the case of *Bocca Baciata*, that does not mean that the literary association is adventitious or unimportant. Each of the pictures of female figures draws powerfully on the association, indicated in the title, with ideas of female beauty or love, often with a frank sexual dimension. *Fair Rosamund* is the mistress of King Henry II, hated by his lawful wife Queen Eleanor. *Helen of Troy* is the woman whose surpassing beauty led to the most famous war in literary history, that of Homer's *Iliad*. *Fazio's Mistress* is the beloved of one of the important poets of the early Italian tradition of courtly love poetry. *The Beloved* (fig. 52) represents the Bride of the Song of Solomon, the Biblical love poem. *Lady Lilith* is the legendary first wife of Adam and appears in Goethe's *Faust* as a seducer of men, imprisoning them in her beautiful hair. *Venus Verticordia* is the ancient goddess of love. Rossetti chose the title 'Venus, turner of hearts' to indicate how

the goddess could turn men's affections away from their lawful or rightful lovers. Later he discovered that the epithet 'verticordia' was used by Latin authors to mean something like the opposite — it designated Venus's role in turning women's hearts away from infidelity (see cat. 104). He contemplated changing the title, and in 1870 published the sonnet he wrote to accompany the picture simply as 'Venus'; later, though, he returned to his original title, *Venus Verticordia*, perhaps because he thought the alliterative sound preferable. Certainly the rhythm and sound of the words are always important in Rossetti's titles, as well as any intellectual connotations they might suggest.

In none of these cases does the picture 'illustrate' the story associated with the woman named in the title. The pictures move resolutely away from Victorian conventions for narrative painting. There is no action, and no specific emotion is dramatized; the figures do not even inhabit a particular moment in time. The allusiveness of the titles functions differently. Rather than referring back to some event in history, legend or literature, the titles set off a train of associations in the viewer's mind. *Lady Lilith* is the oldest woman in legend, preceding even the birth of Eve, but she is also, in Rossetti's words, a 'modern Lilith' who can stimulate thoughts of vanity or self-absorption in the world of the present day. The figure in *The Beloved* is Solomon's bride, but both the title and the picture's visual address to the spectator allow us to imagine the woman more generally, as our own, or anyone's, beloved. The first owner of the picture, George Rae, responded vividly to this suggestion, writing of the 'electric shock of beauty'

fig. 48
A Christmas Carol
1867
Executors of the late Lord Leverhulme
cat. 109

fig. 49
Woman combing her hair
1864
private collection
cat. 102

fig. 50
Morning Music
1864
Syndics of the Fitzwilliam Museum,
Cambridge
cat. 101

that thrilled him every time he looked at it, and musing that he 'might have fallen in love with the lovely central figure, as that old Greek sculptor did with his statue' (with reference to the myth of Pygmalion).[18] Thus the literary or poetic associations of the pictures, hinted in the titles, are flexible and allow the viewer to take a role in constructing their meanings (hence the possibility that a picture's title could be changed, to spur a different set of associations, as when *Fazio's Mistress* became *Aurelia*). This can be seen as analogous to the way the unconventional perspective reorients the viewer's relationship to the figure in the picture. Intellectually, as well as visually and spatially, the pictures call into question the traditional ways in which viewers respond to pictures. They break down the barrier between the viewer's world and the internal world of the pictures in a variety of ways: by cancelling the conventional illusion that there is a self-contained space within the boundaries of the picture frame, by putting the viewer into a close-up encounter with a painted figure as large as life, by inviting the spectator to invent or imagine poetic connotations.

Above all, the pictures encourage the spectator to respond romantically or erotically to what she or he sees and imagines in the contemplation of the work. There is an obvious issue about gender here: the figures are invariably female, and some recent writers have argued that they therefore imply that the responding spectator is male.[19] This argument has considerable cogency; certainly some female viewers of Rossetti's pictures have felt themselves excluded from the experience the pictures seem to offer. Yet these are works of the imagination, not living people,

however immediate they appear. There is no reason why a spectator who does not, in real life, desire women should refuse to respond to the exploration of erotic desire that is surely central to the distinctive power of these paintings. Interestingly, some viewers, both in the Victorian period and more recently, have experienced the figures as masculine or androgynous.[20] The massive throats and limbs of many of the figures can scarcely be described as conventionally feminine; the bodies and heads are heroic in scale and presence, never dainty or fragile. Certainly the figures are defiantly at odds with ordinary Victorian notions of female prettiness.

In Rossetti's own time, not only the female figure-type but, above all, the pictures' exploration of erotic desire was altogether new, and in flagrant defiance of the standards for decency or propriety espoused by many (although by no means all) Victorian art critics. Some of the pictures' first viewers found them horrifying or revolting. That is not to say that Rossetti was the first to paint sensual pictures, which would clearly be nonsense. Indeed it can be said that Rossetti learned each of the techniques he used to produce his pictures' eroticism from the Venetian Renaissance painters, and indeed that each of them was already associated with sensualism. Since the Renaissance itself, the Venetian school had been seen as distinguished for colour rather than drawing or design. Colour had been seen as closely associated with the pleasures of the senses, whereas design was characterized as more intellectual and conceptual. Sensuous pleasure need not always, of course, be understood as sexual or erotic, and Venetian colour could be described as sensuous even when it was

fig. 51
Fazio's Mistress (Aurelia)
1863
Tate. Purchased with assistance through
the National Art Collections Fund from
Sir Arthur Du Cros Bt and Sir Otto Beit
1916
cat. 100

fig. 52
The Beloved
1865–6
Tate. Purchased with assistance through
the National Art Collections Fund from
Sir Arthur Du Cros Bt and Sir Otto Beit
1916
cat. 106

fig. 53
Venus Verticordia
c. 1863–8
Russell-Cotes Art Gallery and Museum,
Bournemouth
cat. 104

used in subjects that had no erotic resonance (for example fig. 41). But the linkage between sensuousness and eroticism was certainly present, with varying degrees of emphasis, in accounts of Venetian art from the Renaissance to the Victorian period. In his earlier writings John Ruskin often expressed reservations about Venetian art, particularly in the context of religious painting, and it was with great effort that he taught himself to admire the physicality, both of the representation of the human body and of the handling of colour, in the work of Titian, Veronese and the other Venetians. Ruskin's change of heart in 1858, and his new willingness to appreciate Venetian art, must have been one important influence on Rossetti, who at this period was a close friend.[21]

Rossetti's pictures of the 1860s presented a particular interpretation of Venetian colour and style, one that emphasized their erotic potential. In this sense his pictures are a kind of commentary on Venetian painting, just as his translations of Dante and the early Italian poets were, as he wrote, a form of commentary on that poetic tradition.[22] In Rossetti's scenes of women at their toilette, the reference to Titian's *Woman with a mirror* (fig. 40) is overt. But Rossetti brings his figures closer and curtails the surrounding space, to emphasize the immediacy of the viewer's encounter with the figure. His treatment of the flesh is more specific and perceptibly enhances the sense of its materiality or tactility. The Titian, with its attendant figure and the play of the two mirrors, can be interpreted as an allegory of vanity, but in Rossetti's toilette scenes there is no question of a moral message. The viewer of the Titian can stand back to observe a narrative *about* the contemplation of physical beauty, set in a space of its own, but the viewer of Rossetti's *Fazio's Mistress*, *Woman combing her hair*, or *Lady Lilith* is irrevocably implicated in the act of contemplating beauty. The changes to the Titianesque formula are slight, but in each case they emphasize the erotic address of the picture and bring it closer to the viewer.

For Rossetti's old friend Ruskin, this was an unacceptable interpretation of Venetian art. In a series of letters written in 1865 Ruskin offers a devastating critique of Rossetti's current practice; it is also a perceptive one. Ruskin sees clearly that Rossetti has abandoned his former technical methods, based on the study of Van Eyck, but insists that Rossetti does not understand the only acceptable alternative, the method of Titian and Correggio: 'No great painter ever allowed himself, in the smallest touch, to paint ill — *i.e.*, to daub or smear his paint'.[23] In a subsequent letter Ruskin mentions the painting of the flowers in *Venus Verticordia*, which he insists on calling *Flora*, doubtless with reference to Titian's sensual *Flora* in the Uffizi (fig. 54; in Titian's painting the garment falls away to reveal the figure's left breast, also nude in the Rossetti). At the same time, Ruskin's deliberate mistitling of the work calls attention to the flowers: 'I purposely used the word "wonderfully" painted about those flowers. They were wonderful to me, in their realism; awful — I can use no other word — in their coarseness: showing enormous power, showing certain conditions of non-sentiment which underlie all you are doing — now ...'[24] Ruskin's emphasis on the flowers, rather than the overt eroticism of the figure in *Venus Verticordia*, may seem a strange displacement.

As the younger artist Graham Robertson wittily commented when he heard of the incident: 'What does that extraordinary Ruskin mean when he speaks of the 'coarseness' of the flowers? He can't be referring to their execution, as they are painted with Pre-Raphaelite delicacy. I suppose he is reflecting upon their morals, but I never heard a word breathed against the perfect respectability of a honeysuckle. Of course roses have got themselves talked about from time to time, but really if one were to listen to scandal about flowers, gardening would become impossible.'[25] The honeysuckle can of course be interpreted as a sexual symbol, *pace* Robertson, and the hot reds Rossetti uses perhaps emphasize the connotations of its shape. But Ruskin's objection is not limited to the sexual coding of the flowers. He had understood Rossetti's project, even if he judged it harshly. The eroticism of *Venus Verticordia*, like that of Rossetti's other pictures of this period, is not simply a matter of the figure's nude flesh, of the subject matter or of the symbolism; it is, as Ruskin clearly saw, woven throughout the style and technique of the picture.

It is notable that *Venus Verticordia* is the only nude among Rossetti's pictures of this period. The eroticism of Rossetti's pictures is never a matter of overtly sexual content (even *Venus Verticordia* reveals only one breast), but it is unmistakable nonetheless. As early as 1860, when he first saw *Bocca Baciata*, William Holman Hunt had responded much as Ruskin would five years later: '... I will not scruple to say that it impresses me as very remarkable in power of execution — but still more remarkable for gross sensuality of a revolting kind peculiar to foreign prints.... I would not speak so unreservedly of it were it not that I see Rossetti is

fig. 54
Titian
Flora
c. 1516–18
Uffizi, Florence

advocating as a principle the mere gratification of the eye and if any passion at all — the animal passion to be the aim of art …'[26] Hunt, like Ruskin, acknowledges the power of Rossetti's painting at the same time as he denounces its sensuality; he too senses the indivisibility of the picture's handling of paint and its erotic address. Indeed the reference to 'foreign prints' likens the picture to pornography — that is, it suggests that the picture titillates or excites the viewer physically, as pornography does, rather than permitting the distanced contemplation appropriate to fine art.

Both Hunt and Ruskin, then, clearly perceive the way the images break down the barrier between picture and viewer, to elicit a response more intense than that normally considered appropriate to high art. Both were determined to resist the pictures' allure, but most of Rossetti's friends and patrons fell willingly under their spell. Rossetti's artist-friend Arthur Hughes reported that Boyce, the owner of *Bocca Baciata*, was liable to 'kiss the dear thing's lips away', so strongly did its beauty affect him.[27] George Rae, as we have seen, felt an 'electric shock of beauty' every time he beheld *The Beloved*. In both cases the experience of the picture does not stop at contemplation from a distance, but elicits a physical response or action from the viewer. Interestingly, Rae's wife also responded performatively to *The Beloved*: 'It is my belief,' wrote Rae, 'that she spends half the day before the picture as certain devout Catholic ladies had used to do before their favourite shrines in the days of old.'[28] Here the intensity of the experience is likened to religious fervour rather than sexual arousal. This idea would recur in later

accounts of the impact of Rossetti's work, such as that of the poet and critic F.W.H. Myers, who described Rossetti's images of women as 'the sacred pictures of a new religion', in an essay of 1883 entitled 'Rossetti and the Religion of Beauty'.[29]

Since Rossetti did not exhibit except on rare and controlled occasions, there is no way of knowing how his pictures would have fared had they come under the scrutiny of contemporary art critics. No doubt the responses would have varied, but it is likely that some critics would have found their eroticism improper; his *Poems* of 1870 (cat. 161) met with violent antipathy from some quarters. But Rossetti's experiments in 'Venetian' painting, although unseen by the general public, were occasionally reported in the press, in articles by associates of Rossetti who had seen the pictures in his studio. Thus Rossetti's reputation as a painter of unconventional pictures began to grow, even in the absence of the pictures themselves. In 1865 F.G. Stephens, one of the original members of the Pre-Raphaelite Brotherhood and now the art critic for the *Athenaeum*, published an account of Rossetti's recent work, presented as a radical new departure in English art. A painting by Rossetti, Stephens writes, 'is of the nature of a lyrical poem, which aims at effect quite as much by means of inherent beauty and melodious colouring as by the mere subject, which is superficial. Titian and Giorgione produced lyrics of this sort in abundance; many of their pictures are nothing if not lyrical. In this direction English Art has not yet ventured far.'[30] Stephens thus emphasizes the unconventionality of Rossetti's new approach, in contrast to the predominance of narrative and anecdote in most English painting of this date. Moreover, he clearly indicates Rossetti's procedure for innovation: to break away from current conventions in English art, Rossetti associates his work, instead, with the art of the Venetian Renaissance. Stephens goes on to offer rapturous descriptions of *The Blue Bower*, *Venus Verticordia* and *The Beloved*. Of *The Blue Bower* he writes: 'The green and chestnut-auburn, the pallid roses of the flesh, and the firmamental blue of the background, are as ineffable in variety of tint as in their delicious harmony.... More subtle harmonies than the above are indescribable. The woman is beautiful in no common way; but her air more powerfully entrances us to sympathy with her act of slowly drawing luxurious music from the strings, so that the eyes and the ear of fancy go together. Then we have the marvellous fleshiness of the flesh; the fascinating sensuousness of the expression, which is refined, if not elevated, by the influence of the music.'[31] Stephens, ordinarily a matter-of-fact writer, here struggles to find adequately rich language to convey the impact of the picture (the words 'ineffable' and 'indescribable' suggest how difficult this was). No doubt Rossetti had carefully schooled him in the message he was to deliver, but Stephens learned his lesson well. His account captures the complex mixture of elements in Rossetti's new style of the 1860s.

Stephens's article places Rossetti firmly in the vanguard of current English painting and clearly adumbrates the ideas that would become associated, by the later 1860s, with the term 'art for art's sake'.[32] Rossetti's pictures of women played a leading role in the innovative art practices of the 1860s that elevated visual beauty and sensuous pleasure above the narrative and moralizing concerns of earlier Victorian art, and made a crucial impact on the work of other artists, such as Edward Burne-Jones, James McNeill Whistler, Frederic Leighton, George Frederic Watts, Simeon Solomon and Frederick Sandys. Once again Rossetti was a leader in a controversial new development in English art.

The extreme reactions provoked by Rossetti's works among his contemporaries have persisted up to the present day, when his pictures of women are alternately attacked as misogynist and adored as emancipatory. These extremes are appropriate; the 'beauty' of Rossetti's pictures is too passionate and too powerful to elicit a moderate reaction. Moreover, it is part of Rossetti's project to present the extremes of love and beauty, for instance in the pairing of *Lady Lilith* and its accompanying sonnet, 'Body's Beauty', with *Sibylla Palmifera* and its sonnet, 'Soul's Beauty' (cats. 107–8). Swinburne, in his article of 1868, writes of the complexity of beauty: 'Beauty may be strange, quaint, terrible, may play with pain as with pleasure, handle a horror till she leave it a delight; she forsakes not such among her servants as Webster or as Goya.'[33] Or Rossetti, Swinburne might have added (indeed the context of the article encourages the reader to supply the missing name). Rossetti's project in the pictures of women is not to idealize or sanitize either physical beauty or love. Instead the pictures unflinchingly confront love and beauty in their most intense phases, terrifying as well as rapturous, destructive as well as creative.

Beata Beatrix

One painting stands apart from the rest of Rossetti's work of the 1860s: *Beata Beatrix* (fig. 57). Like other paintings of the mid-1860s (figs. 44, 47, 53), it represents a half-length female figure at life size. But a glance is enough to show that it is not in Rossetti's 'Venetian' mode. The colour is more subdued. The handling is not built into lustrous, sensuous layers but seems to trace an evanescent film over the canvas. The background is not vivid and close, but dimly suggests an abstracted, atmospheric space with shadowy indications of a distant city, and spectral figures. The title refers to a woman renowned for her beauty and for the love she inspires, like others of the 1860s, but with a difference: this is Beatrice, the beloved of Dante and, imaginatively, of Dante's namesake Rossetti. The love of Dante belongs to the Florentine Middle Ages, not the Venetian High Renaissance. Its affinities are with death and spiritual transcendence, not with the earthy sensual pleasures of this life.

The upturned face of the figure, with eyes closed to contemplate a spiritual rather than an earthly vision, represents Beatrice as she appears in the closing lines of Dante's *Vita Nuova*, as Rossetti explained in a letter to the picture's first owner: 'She sees through her shut lids, is conscious of a new world, as expressed in the last words of the *Vita Nuova*.'[34] The title, *Beata Beatrix* or 'blessed Beatrice', derives from those 'last words' – in Rossetti's translation, 'that blessed Beatrice who now gazeth continually on His countenance *qui est per omnia saecula benedictus*' ('who is blessed throughout all ages').[35] But the face is also

that of Elizabeth Siddal, with the lifted chin and closed or half-closed eyelids seen in so many of Rossetti's drawings of her (cats. 21–38, fig. 56). Rossetti had always identified Siddal with Beatrice, since the watercolour of 1851, *Beatrice meeting Dante at a marriage feast, denies him her salutation* (cat. 39), and in numerous other works of the 1850s. This identification, however, took a chilling turn when Siddal died in February 1862, repeating the fate of Beatrice herself. It is painful to imagine the agony of grief and guilt that Rossetti must have felt: by consistently casting Siddal in the role of Beatrice it was as if he had willed her to her early death. Perhaps it was by way of expiation that Rossetti made this picture, elaborating the parallel between Siddal and Beatrice from the new perspective of Siddal's death and combining symbols associated with Siddal with Dantesque references. At the same time, the picture assimilates the imagery of love with that of death. This is a *Liebestod*, like that of Wagner's *Tristan and Isolde*, first produced in 1865 while Rossetti was at work on this picture, although there is no evidence that he knew of it at this date.[36]

The dove, which Rossetti used as a symbol for Siddal, now appears as the messenger of death, but it shares the colour red with the figure of Love in the upper left corner (the dove is a standard symbol of love, associated with the goddess Venus). It bears a white poppy, symbol of sleep or death, but perhaps also a reference to opium; Siddal had died as the result of an overdose of laudanum (it is unknown whether this was inadvertent or deliberate). Immediately above the dove, and to the right of the figure, is a symbol of Beatrice's death: the sundial, pointing to

fig. 55
Algernon Charles Swinburne
1861
Syndics of the Fitzwilliam Museum,
Cambridge
cat. 116

the number nine, associated with Beatrice in the *Vita Nuova*. The moody light that illuminates the sundial also creates an aureole behind the figure's head, suggesting a halo. As the title suggests, the picture can be taken to represent the beatification of Beatrice; the dove wears a tiny halo as if to show that it comes from God. Behind the figure the forms dissolve in the glowing light, but a bridge is dimly discernible in the distance; this has often been identified as the Ponte Vecchio, in Dante's Florence, but it is vague enough to double for a London bridge, perhaps even Blackfriars Bridge next to which Rossetti and Siddal lived during their brief marriage. The two background figures are those of Dante on the right turning to gaze at Love, on the left, bathed in heavenly light and holding a flame.

Beata Beatrix is singular within Rossetti's oeuvre, in the exceptionally close correspondence between the subject matter (the death of Dante's Beatrice) and an event in Rossetti's personal life (the death of Siddal). But this raises important questions about the interpretation, not only of *Beata Beatrix*, but of all of Rossetti's work. Should we see the picture primarily as a personal document about Rossetti's love for Siddal and his grief at her death, enriched by the allusion to the ideal love of Dante for Beatrice? Or should we see it as a representation of the end of the *Vita Nuova*, a work Rossetti had revered long before he ever met Siddal, to which he was able to give specially compelling visual form by drawing on his own personal experience? In short, what was the relationship of Rossetti's life to his art?

This question may, of course, be asked of any artist, but it is particularly urgent in the case of Rossetti.

fig. 56
Study of Elizabeth Siddal as Delia
c. 1855
Birmingham Museums & Art Gallery.
Presented by subscribers
cat. 31

fig. 57
Beata Beatrix
c. 1863–70
Tate. Presented by Georgiana, Baroness
Mount-Temple in memory of her husband,
Francis, Baron Mount-Temple 1889
cat. 98

Throughout his career he followed the Pre-Raphaelite practice of representing his models as faithfully as possible, and he drew his more important models from his family and closest friends. Thus his pictures are, on one level, portraits of the real people with whom his relationships were most intimate. It is tempting, then, to explain the major developments of his artistic career in terms of events in his personal life. At the very beginning of his career, when he was barely twenty, he used family members as models for his two oil paintings; thus his sister, Christina Rossetti (cats. 14, 121), appears as the model for the Virgin Mary in both *The Girlhood of Mary Virgin* and *Ecce Ancilla Domini!* (figs. 9, 10). In the early 1850s, when he fell deeply in love with Elizabeth Siddal, he used her more and more exclusively as his only model; by casting her as Beatrice, the beloved of his own namesake Dante, he affirmed his love for her. Towards the later 1850s, for unknown reasons, Rossetti and Siddal drew apart, or perhaps quarrelled, and at this point other women begin to appear as models for his work (for example, Annie Miller, fig. 58). By 1858 he had met Fanny Cornforth (figs. 59, 97), who appears as the model for *Bocca Baciata* of the following year and for many of Rossetti's most sensual subsequent pictures. Although it is not known whether Rossetti and Cornforth had a sexual relationship, many students of Rossetti's works have assumed that this must have been the case, and that Rossetti's new experience of sexual love was an important motivation for the newly sensual representation of women initiated by *Bocca Baciata*.[37] In 1860, Siddal became seriously ill, and a *rapprochement* ensued; she and Rossetti were married, and Rossetti

fig. 58
Annie Miller
1860
The L.S. Lowry Estate
cat. 114

painted her as *Regina Cordium*, 'Queen of Hearts' (fig. 37, cat. 95). But the marriage was a tragic one; Siddal remained ill, gave birth to a stillborn child in 1861, and died of an overdose early the following year; as we have seen, *Beata Beatrix* represents a memory of Siddal after her death. The widowed Rossetti moved later in 1862 to Tudor House, in Cheyne Walk in Chelsea; there Fanny Cornforth reappeared almost immediately as a constant companion and model. Again there is no way to tell whether their relationship was sexual, apart from the eroticism of the many pictures for which she modelled in this period, among them *Fair Rosamund* of 1861 (when Rossetti was still married to Siddal), *Fazio's Mistress* of 1863, *The Blue Bower* of 1865, and initially *Lady Lilith* as well (later the figure was repainted from another model). In the second half of the 1860s, as we shall see, Rossetti began to draw and paint from Jane Morris, née Burden, the wife of William Morris, and her face dominates his later work (cats. 122–30, 139–47, 153-5). Again it is unknown whether their relationship was sexual, but it was certainly a friendship of great intensity. Rossetti continued to provide for Cornforth, with whom he clearly maintained an affectionate relationship.

This biographical narrative is so dramatic, and so full of human interest, that it has dominated accounts of Rossetti's work. But much of it remains highly conjectural; Rossetti's letters and the reminiscences of his friends provide an account of his life that is partial in both senses of the word. Moreover, it does not really answer the question posed at the outset — what was the relationship of Rossetti's life to his art? — except to show that the two were closely related. But that we already knew, for, as we have

fig. 59
Fanny Cornforth
c. 1860
Visitors of the Ashmolean Museum, Oxford.
Bequeathed by John N. Bryson 1977
cat. 113

seen, the 'Venetian' pictures of women insistently push at the boundary between the distanced representations of fine art and the urgent feelings of real life. What we still do not know, however, is why this is important. Does Rossetti's art continue to matter, long after the death of all of its models as well as the artist himself and the social world they all inhabited, primarily as a human story, vividly, and sometimes disturbingly, exploring the problems of sex, love and death that we must all at some time confront? Or does it matter because it shows how 'real' life, in all its mundane and material particularity, is not inconsistent with the greatest art, and can indeed become identical with it?

These are precisely the questions that the Dantean subject matter of *Beata Beatrix* proposed. The final vision of Beatrice, in the *Vita Nuova*, not only records the end of the story of Dante's earthly love for her, but also hints at Dante's intention to translate that love into another realm altogether – that of divine revelation, or alternatively that of the greatest art, the threefold vision of Hell, Purgatory and Heaven that would make up the *Divine Comedy*. Rossetti would have been acutely aware of the controversy, in which his own father, the Dante scholar Gabriele Rossetti, played a prominent role, about whether Beatrice had ever been a real person, or whether she was always an allegorical figure to represent an abstraction, Love, Poetry, Faith or (for Gabriele Rossetti) 'an allegory of political harmony'.[38] *Beata Beatrix* offers an answer to that question: Beatrice is a real person, reincarnated in the full physical sense of the word as Elizabeth Siddal. But she does not cease to be Dante's Beatrice, and that might lead the spectator's

thoughts almost anywhere – to thoughts of beauty, of love, of religion, of philosophy, of political harmony, or of the greatest art.

Dante's Dream

Rossetti's half-length pictures of women turned out to be much more important artistic explorations than could have been imagined when he first embarked on *Bocca Baciata*. But throughout this period Rossetti never relinquished his ambition to make large-scale paintings of important subjects with multiple figures, male as well as female. Repeatedly he tried to interest his patrons in commissioning such works, which would be worked up to large scale from existing designs, some dating from years ago, others new; the subjects of *Mary Magdalene at the door of Simon the Pharisee* and *Cassandra* (cats. 67, 68, 60, fig. 32), for example, were repeatedly offered to patrons for large-scale treatment in oils in the 1860s and beyond. However, these commissions invariably proved problematical. Some patrons baulked at the high prices Rossetti asked; others felt they had inadequate room in their houses; still others embarked on commissions but abandoned them later. In 1867 C.P. Matthews, proprietor of a brewing firm, agreed to commission a new design called *Aspecta Medusa*, which represented Perseus holding up the severed head of Medusa over a well, so that Andromeda could see its reflection in the water (looking at the head itself, according to the ancient legend, caused the viewer to turn into stone). But Matthews eventually withdrew the commission on the grounds that the severed head would be too horrible an image to hang in a domestic setting.[39]

Only in one case did Rossetti push through a commission of this kind, and even so it was fraught with problems: *Dante's Dream*, the largest independent picture he ever painted, more than two metres high by three metres wide (fig. 61). Rossetti's involvement with this subject was profound and persisted throughout his career. He first explored it in the late 1840s in the course of translating Dante's *Vita Nuova*. The dream occurs while Dante is ill; his debility brings on a fear of mortality, and it strikes him that some day Beatrice must die. Falling into a disturbed sleep, he sees a succession of images culminating in a vision of Beatrice lying dead, while ladies cover her with a white veil. As he was finishing his translation, in 1848, Rossetti made a list of subjects from the *Vita Nuova* that he planned to represent in pictorial form: *Dante's Dream* is the sixth of these.[40] From the beginning, then, Rossetti thought of his exploration of the *Vita Nuova* as a double project, involving both a verbal form (the translation) and a visual one (the series of pictures of *Vita Nuova* subjects). In 1856, when given a commission from a friend of Ruskin's, Ellen Heaton, Rossetti offered the subject of *Dante's Dream*, which he executed in watercolour (fig. 60). But his interest in the subject was not exhausted. From 1863 onwards he repeatedly mentioned his intention of executing it as a large-scale oil painting, and he suggested it in 1868 to C.P. Matthews in lieu of the aborted *Aspecta Medusa*.[41] Matthews did not, however, take this up, and the work was finally commissioned the next year by William Graham, who specified that the

dimensions should be no more than 3½ by 6 feet (about 100 by 180 cm).[42]

Rossetti set to work with delight, and in August 1870 wrote to an artist-friend: 'A big picture is glorious work, really rousing to every faculty one has or ever thought one might have, and I hope I am doing better in this than hitherto.'[43] He worked obsessively on the painting, refusing to show it to visitors. In his enthusiasm he expanded the work considerably, so that when finally finished late in 1871 it covered well over three times the surface area Graham had been expecting. Graham had nowhere to hang it but on his staircase, where it was difficult to see; understandably, he returned it to Rossetti and asked for a smaller replica, which Rossetti made later in the 1870s with the help of his studio assistant Henry Treffry Dunn. Meanwhile, the large version was resold to another patron, but returned in 1878, again because its size made it difficult to hang in a private residence. Finally, in 1881, it was sold to the Liverpool Corporation for the Walker Art Gallery, one of the grandest of the public art galleries that were springing up in English cities in the later 19th century. Thus the painting finally, although by an exceptionally circuitous route, realized Rossetti's longstanding desire to make a great work for a public building.

The large *Dante's Dream* must, then, be accounted the work in which Rossetti most fully realized his professional ambitions as a painter. It is not difficult to see why Rossetti expanded the canvas so far beyond his patron's wishes. In the final version the figures are life-size, which would have been impossible at a scale any smaller, unless the composition established in the watercolour of 1856 were changed

substantially. The impact of the life-size figures is crucial: the viewer confronts figures as large as real human beings, in a scene that is at the same scale as reality. At this scale the picture fills the viewer's whole visual field and opens out, like the vision of an alternative reality, more sumptuous than the everyday world but no less immediate. It may be possible to resist this fantasy, to refuse its invitation to depart from mundane reality, but it is impossible to condescend to it, as one might to a smaller work.

This kind of effect, cancelling the distance between the viewer and the picture space, is characteristic, as we have seen, of Rossetti's work after 1860. Moreover, the painting is very much in Rossetti's later style, with red, green and gold colour harmonies woven throughout the surface and fully rounded figures in voluminous draperies, very different from the thin, angular figures of the earlier watercolour. Beatrice has the face of Jane Burden Morris (with her dark hair changed to reddish-gold when the picture was retouched before going to the Walker), and the models for the two female attendants, Alexa Wilding and Marie Spartali Stillman, are also highly characteristic of Rossetti's later work. The poses, too, have become mellifluous, perhaps slightly mannered; together with the curvilinear folds of the draperies, they create a mesmeric rhythm across the canvas, like a solemn procession or ritual dance. If the effect is otherworldly, that is wholly appropriate: this is, after all, a dream.[44]

Rossetti was able, then, to make all of the resources of his later style tell in the realization of the subject matter. Nonetheless, the composition remains unchanged, in all of its essentials, from the scene Rossetti first imagined in

fig. 60
Dante's Dream
watercolour version
1856
Tate

fig. 61
Dante's Dream
1871
National Museums Liverpool (the Walker)
cat. 147

1856, or perhaps even earlier. Indeed, the design is typical of the watercolours of the mid-1850s, with foreground figures rising to the full height of the canvas and intriguing glimpses through to distant scenes, winding staircases and fragments of cityscape (in the *Vita Nuova* Dante describes the city of Florence mourning at Beatrice's death). Thus the large *Dante's Dream* is both a wholly new work, in which the visual appearance of every detail is seen afresh in the guise of Rossetti's later style, and fundamentally the same as the earlier one. This is the most dramatic example of Rossetti's inveterate habit of making replicas of his works, and it suggests that the motive was not always commercial; in this case, as with the multiple versions of the famous *Proserpine* (figs. 62, 104), it was Rossetti himself who wished to repeat the subject. Indeed, replication was central to Rossetti's practice, and it was carried out in a variety of ways.[45] In his translations of Dante and the Early Italian poets he created what might be called replicas of the original poems; the translations repeat the design of the original works in a new language, as the later *Dante's Dream* repeats that of the earlier one in a new style and medium. As we have seen, Rossetti frequently wrote a poem to accompany a painting, thus creating what has been called a 'double work of art';[46] the two versions are, of course, different in medium but can nonetheless be described as alternative forms of the same artistic idea. Moreover, he returned again and again to certain compositional types, such as the Titianesque toilette scene or, more broadly, the picture-type of the half-length female figure. Sometimes the assemblage of interrelated works becomes exceedingly complicated: *Lady Lilith* is in one sense a repetition of

Titian's *Woman with a mirror*; it is doubled by its own poem, 'Body's Beauty'; and it is also the inverted double of its pictorial alter ego, *Sibylla Palmifera*, with *its* poem, 'Soul's Beauty'. It is as if one work of art constantly demanded the creation of another, in a series of replications that need never end.

Dante's Dream is a replica in several of these ways. The oil painting repeats the composition of the earlier watercolour. At the same time, the pictorial works are replications both of the episode in the *Vita Nuova* and of Rossetti's translation of it. But the scene in the *Vita Nuova* is itself doubled, like all of the events in that work. The structure of the *Vita Nuova* involves a prose narrative punctuated by verses that retell and reflect upon the same events. Thus the dream, like other events in Dante's life, is described twice in succession, first as it happens in Dante's life, then as he recasts it in verse.[47] Rossetti's composition can be taken to relate to either of the two tellings, but in a letter to Ellen Heaton, the purchaser of the watercolour version, he relates the pictured scene to the second, verse retelling.[48] In his own translation this reads:

> These 'wildering phantasies
> Then carried me to see my lady dead.
> Even as I there was led,
>   Her ladies with a veil were covering her;
> And with her was such very humbleness
> That she appeared to say, 'I am at peace.'[49]

Perhaps it is significant that Rossetti associates the picture with the second, verse description: it is here that the event,

fig. 62
Proserpine
1882
Birmingham Museums & Art Gallery.
Purchased by the Public Picture Gallery
Fund
cat. 155

experienced in life, is transmuted into artistic form.
In this respect, as in so many others, the *Vita Nuova* seems
to contain a significant key to Rossetti's artistic project.
Rossetti's own pictures can always, like the prose passages
in the *Vita Nuova*, be interpreted as representations of
events in his life, but their meaning never stops there.
They also, like the verse passages, recast those events in
to the form of independent or autonomous works of art.

Jane Burden Morris

The most striking case of replication in Rossetti's work is,
of course, the series of images that represent Jane Burden
Morris. She first appears in 1857 as Guenevere, in studies
and drawings related to the project to decorate the Oxford
Union with Arthurian subjects (cat. 93, fig. 96). At this
time she was just seventeen, the daughter of a worker in
an Oxford livery stable; her strange, dark beauty caught
the attention of Rossetti and his friends. Then, after
her marriage to William Morris, she appears as Mary, the
mother of Christ, in the Llandaff altarpiece (cats. 64–5,
fig. 26). For a time, while the Morrises were living at Red
House in Kent, outside London, she disappears from
Rossetti's art. In 1865, the Morrises returned to London,
and that summer Rossetti commissioned a series of photographs of her, posed in a marquee in the garden behind
his house in Chelsea (cats. 131–8, figs. 67, 90, 99). From
1868, when Rossetti painted her portrait in a sumptuous
blue silk dress, which she made for the occasion (fig. 63),
her face returns again and again: as *La Pia de' Tolomei* from

Dante's *Purgatorio* (figs. 80, 100), *Mariana* from Shakespeare's *Measure for Measure* (fig. 64), *La Donna della Finestra* ('The Woman of the Window') from Dante's *Vita Nuova* (fig. 81, 101), and as a series of figures from ancient mythology, *Pandora* (figs. 72, 102), *Proserpine* (figs. 62, 104), *Astarte Syriaca* (fig. 66). Other representations of her have evocative invented titles: *Reverie, Silence, The Day Dream, Water Willow* (figs. 79, 77, 71, cat. 129). How could a face so idiosyncratic that it is instantly recognizable, in the work of other artists as well as that of Rossetti, convincingly impersonate so diverse a range of literary, legendary and allegorical figures?

As early as 1869, the American writer Henry James visited Rossetti's studio, where he saw some of these works in progress, as well as a variety of studies. When he then met Morris herself, he was astonished, not only at her own appearance but at the uncanny way she seemed to resemble her own portraits: 'A figure cut out of a missal – out of one of Rossetti's or Hunt's pictures – to say this gives but a faint idea of her, because when such an image puts on flesh and blood, it is an apparition of fearful and wonderful intensity. It's hard to say [whether] she's a grand synthesis of all the pre-Raphaelite pictures ever made – or they a "keen analysis" of her – whether she's an original or a copy. In either case she is a wonder. Imagine a tall lean woman in a long dress of some dead purple stuff, guiltless of hoops (or of anything else, I should say,) with a mass of crisp black hair heaped into great wavy projections on each of her temples, a thin pale face, a pair of strange, sad, deep, dark Swinburnish eyes, with great thick black oblique brows, joined in the middle and tucking

themselves away under her hair, a mouth like the "Oriana" in our illustrated Tennyson, a long neck, without any collar, and in lieu thereof some dozen strings of outlandish beads – in fine Complete. On the wall was a large nearly full-length portrait of her by Rossetti [fig. 63], so strange and unreal that if you hadn't seen her, you'd pronounce it a distempered vision, but in fact an extremely good likeness.'[50]

James is, of course, gently satirizing the self-conscious 'artiness' of the circle that surrounded Rossetti and the Morrises, but his observations are nonetheless acute. He shows how Morris herself fashioned her own image, ignoring contemporary fashion to wear loose, unstructured dresses, like the draperies in paintings.[51] Her presence was compelling partly because of her unusual height; in group photographs she is taller than other people, even than most men. The long, flowing lines of her gowns emphasized her height. Since she did not wear the hoops and stays that were standard undergarments for women of the period, her carriage may have been less stiff and formal. The photographs taken in Rossetti's garden in 1865 are, of course, carefully posed. Nonetheless, photographs and contemporarary descriptions of Morris suggest that she carried herself in a distinctive, pliant or loose-limbed manner; in paintings she never sits bolt upright, as usual in contemporary portraits and portrait photographs of other women, but allows her back and neck to curve. In contrast to the characteristic pose of Siddal, with upturned face, Morris's head is often inclined. Her 'outlandish' jewellery, the way she dressed her hair, and the colours of her dresses all seem to have emphasized the dark colouring and abundance of wiry hair that looked 'foreign', 'medieval', or non-Caucasian to contemporary observers. The compelling image of Rossetti's later pictures, then, is not entirely of the artist's creation: it was a collaboration between his own imagination and that of Morris herself.

This is one reason for James's uncanny sense that it is Morris, the woman, who is the work of art — that there is some kind of bizarre reversal of the usual relationship between the sitter and the pictures that represent her. But James is also responding to the distinctive character of Rossetti's pictures, the way they too seem to transgress the boundary between art and life. This cannot be explained as simply as James implies when he describes the portrait as 'an extremely good likeness'. Indeed, Morris's appearance in Rossetti's later works is increasingly abstract or symbolic: the repetitive waves of her hair, the exaggerated bow-curve of her lips, the elongated and mannered pose of her fingers, like the gestures of a ballet dancer, all fall into stylized configurations, as decorative as the pattern-designs of the Morris firm or of Eastern pottery. Nonetheless the pictures give the strongest possible sense of encountering a powerful human presence — or, at times, a superhuman one, for instance in *Astarte Syriaca* (fig. 66).[52]

In these works from the end of the 1860s onwards, Rossetti continues to use many of the techniques he had developed in the earlier series of half-lengths for intensifying the viewer's encounter with the figure in the picture: the presentation of the life-size figure, too close for comfort, in a shallow space that seems to open out towards the viewer rather than receding into the distance. But his style changes, not as drastically, perhaps, as in the years around 1860, but perceptibly nonetheless. Again the picture size increases. Since the figures in the half-lengths are already life-size, the increase in picture size means representing more of the figure, so many of the pictures of Morris are at three-quarter-length (figs. 62, 64, 66, 71, 102, 104). In such cases the canvas is often tall and thin, to maintain the tight fitting of the figure within the frame; this emphasizes the 'tall lean' physique that James observed. Moreover, it introduces a subtle change in the viewer's relationship to the figure, no longer seen head-on as in the half-lengths. With the face removed to the top of the tall canvas, the viewer feels abject or subordinated, like a kneeling worshipper before a religious image. This effect is particularly evident in *Astarte Syriaca*.

There is also a change in paint handling, as Rossetti moves away from the lustrous, glowing or glossy use of the oil medium in the 'Venetian' pictures, to introduce a drier, crumblier touch, in which the striations of the brush are more evident. There is more texture, but less silky sensuousness. Towards the end of the 1860s, and in many works representing Morris (as well as other sitters), Rossetti began to use coloured chalks or pastels, usually on a very pale green paper; these are at the same scale as the paintings and could serve either as independent works or as preparatory studies, or both (figs. 72, 77, 79-81).[53] The matt, slightly rough or grainy textures of these media may have helped him to develop analogous effects in his oil paintings. The colours are still harmonized, but with a greater preponderance of cool greys and

fig. 63
Jane Morris (The Blue Silk Dress)
1868
The Society of Antiquaries of London
(Kelmscott Manor)
cat. 125

fig. 64
Mariana
1870
Aberdeen Art Gallery & Museums
Collections
cat. 141

greens. Perhaps the new colour range is organized around the range of blue-green tints Rossetti uses to represent Morris's eyes, which are more salient than the eyes in most of the earlier pictures of single female figures. Although they remain slightly unfocused or distracted, the eyes have a special lustre that makes them seem to rivet the viewer's gaze, sometimes with uncomfortable power, as if the painted image could see into the viewer's mind.

This new prominence of the eyes is achieved partly, perhaps, by increasing their size relative to the whole face, rather narrower and thinner than the models Rossetti had used earlier, but it is principally the result of an adept management of colour: the eyes are keyed into the colour scheme of the picture so that they seem to ring out. This is necessary in purely practical terms, because Rossetti also emphasizes, or even exaggerates, the deep red of the large lips — the eyes would disappear if they did not shine brightly enough to hold their own. It is worth stressing the technical complexity of Rossetti's achievement in making this extraordinary face appear coherent, for his later work has often been accused of becoming overly coarse or crude. The treatment is emphatic, certainly, and often uncomfortably so, but in fine examples (such as the important pictures for which Morris was the model) it is judged with extraordinary precision. Otherwise the face would become flat and inert like a comic strip; indeed this is exactly what happens in poor contemporary copies of Rossetti's work by other hands, perhaps including some from his own studio in which the work of assistants is probably dominant.[54]

fig. 65
Jane Morris
1865
private collection
cat. 124

fig. 66
Astarte Syriaca
1877
Manchester City Galleries
cat. 153

Furthermore, there may be a reason for the simultaneous overemphasis of the eyes and mouth. Theodore Watts, a lawyer and aspiring writer (later called Watts-Dunton), met Rossetti in 1872 and remained a close friend for the rest of the artist's life (he is pictured with Rossetti in Henry Treffry Dunn's watercolour drawing of the sitting room in Tudor House, fig. 109). After Rossetti's death he published an article purporting to clear up common misconceptions about the artist. According to Watts, Rossetti considered the human body 'rich in symbol': 'To him the mouth really represented the sensuous part of the face no less certainly than the eyes represented the spiritual part; and, if in certain heads the sensuous fulness of the lips became scarcely Caucasian, this was a necessary correction to eyes which became on their part over-mystical in their spirituality.'[55] Watts was, of course, defending Rossetti against charges that the facial features in his pictures were mannered and exaggerated. But William Michael Rossetti, too, believed that in his later work, and particularly in the pictures that represented Jane Morris, Rossetti was trying to achieve a balance between the sensual and spiritual aspects, which had remained separate in much of his earlier work — between the 'Body's Beauty' of *Lady Lilith* (as well as *Bocca Baciata*, *Venus Verticordia* and others) and the 'Soul's Beauty' of *Sibylla Palmifera* (as well as the Dantesque watercolours, *Beata Beatrix* and others).[56] The conspicuous intensification of both eyes and mouth, at once, in the images of Morris may then represent one way of balancing the sensual and the spiritual.

As we have seen, the drier handling and cooler colour harmonies, as well as the greater physical and psychological remoteness of the three-quarter-length figures, also tip the balance back from the extreme sensuality of the 'Venetian' pictures. In the late works, too, Titian and the Venetians are no longer the presiding models. Early in 1873 Rossetti became interested in Michelangelo's sonnets, which he proposed to translate.[57] Although he never did so, he evidently began to look at Michelangelo's work in visual media, primarily, no doubt, in reproduction, since he never visited Italy and, by this date, seldom ventured out to galleries or exhibitions. In the early 1870s Burne-Jones, too, was exploring Michelangelo's body-types, to which Ruskin strenuously objected for what he saw as an overemphasis on anatomy and on the physicality of the body. In a lecture of 1871 Ruskin delivered a powerful attack on Michelangelo, initiating a controversy about the artist that called forth responses from Walter Pater, Edward John Poynter and John Addington Symonds.[58] Despite his increasing isolation from the London art world, Rossetti responded to this contemporary debate about Michelangelo's art in his own painting. Michelangelo is a clear point of reference for the powerful limbs, commanding figure-type and serpentine poses of the paintings representing Morris. However, Rossetti was also interested in the spirituality of drawings by Michelangelo, thought to represent the revered friend of his old age, Vittoria Colonna, and saw a resemblance between these faces and that of Jane Morris.[59] Perhaps Rossetti saw in Michelangelo the kind of struggle to reconcile body with spirit that haunted his own work.

fig. 67
John Robert Parsons
Jane Morris
1865
photograph
Victoria & Albert Museum, London
cat. 131

Between heaven and earth

Rossetti continued to use models other than Jane Burden Morris in the period after the 1860s. These pictures are diverse in subject and approach; perhaps, indeed, the only feature that links them is that they do not present the image of Morris. However, they show that Rossetti was still experimenting with new ideas in the final decade of his life, even though persistent insomnia, increasing addiction to the drugs he used to help him sleep, and other health problems both physical and psychological made his work more erratic than before. If he had been able to regain his physical and mental health, instead of dying in 1882 at the early age of fifty-four, one or other of these experiments might have led to another major shift in his art, analogous to those of 1848, the mid-1850s, and 1860. That did not happen. Nonetheless, a number of Rossetti's works of the 1870s point in intriguing new directions.

In some cases this meant returning to earlier interests or reflecting anew on issues raised in his own art. Even in his self-imposed isolation, Rossetti increasingly cultivated his reputation as a painter-poet – like Michelangelo, a new enthusiasm of the 1870s, or William Blake, who had always fascinated Rossetti and his close associates. For years friends and patrons had tried to induce him to make a painting to correspond to his most famous poem, 'The Blessed Damozel', first drafted before the formation of the Pre-Raphaelite Brotherhood and published in an early form in *The Germ* in 1850. A revised version appeared as the opening poem in the long awaited collection of

Rossetti's original verse that finally appeared in 1870, and for many critics, both at the time and subsequently, it seemed to capture the essence of Rossetti's art better than any other single work. But in Rossetti's 'double works of art' – paired poems and pictures – it was always the picture that came first, while the poem was written later. Never before had Rossetti worked the other way around. However, in 1871 he agreed to attempt a pictorial version for one of his most faithful patrons, William Graham, and shortly afterwards began a second painting of the same composition (figs. 69, 103).

Does it make a difference, then, that in this sole case Rossetti devised the visual composition after the verbal form of the work? At first glance, no: the composition is more elaborate than many of the other pictures of half-length female figures, but recognizably of the same type. Yet this demonstrates an interesting reflection on Rossetti's career: the painting argues, retrospectively, that the pictorial type of the late paintings is thoroughly consistent with his earliest poem – that one imaginative impulse connects Rossetti's earliest thoughts with his latest work. The poem describes a woman in Heaven who longs for her lover, still alive on earth. Thus it involves the relationship between heavenly and earthly, or soul and body, that was an increasing preoccupation in Rossetti's work of the 1870s. The pictorial composition represents both worlds, with the Damozel in a large upper canvas, surrounded by angels, and the lover, at much smaller scale, in a narrow horizontal predella underneath; the frame both unites and separates the two scenes. The organization is like that of a Renaissance altarpiece, in which individual panels are juxtaposed within an elaborate frame. Conventional perspective operates in the predella scene, a landscape with a river and trees receding into the distance, but Heaven in the upper scene is a place where space does not function as it does on earth. The Damozel and angels have fully modelled bodies, but there are no spaces between them, and the interstices are filled with lush flowers. This Heaven is not dematerialized and its inhabitants are not disembodied; in it, however, the isolation or alienation characteristic of the earthly landscape, with its perspective distances, is annulled. In the poem Heaven is also free from earthly time, and it is the place where lovers can be united forever; perhaps this suggests, in retrospect, one element of Rossetti's lifelong fascination with non-perspectival spaces. It remains uncertain, in the poem as in the separated scenes of the paintings, whether this Heaven is attainable; but it is imaginable in both painted and poetic forms.

In *The Bower Meadow* (fig. 68) there is a different experiment with perspective and another kind of return to Rossetti's earlier work. The landscape background had been made long ago, in the autumn of 1850, in Rossetti's one attempt to practise Pre-Raphaelite outdoor painting. In a sense Rossetti had always remained faithful to the Pre-Raphaelite principle of painting from nature; he went to extravagant lengths to obtain roses and honeysuckle, for instance, from which to paint the flowers in *Venus Verticordia* — but he brought them into the studio (see cat. 104). Since he was unwilling either to work out of doors or to abandon the practice of painting from nature, he was unable to paint landscape scenes.[60]

Now, in 1872, he returned to the landscape he had painted more than twenty years earlier and finished it by adding groups of figures.[61] Thus the picture reviews the history of Rossetti's career, recasting it in spatial terms, from the Pre-Raphaelite past in the distant background to the new style of the 1870s in the foreground. The swift perspective recession, highly unusual in Rossetti's work, represents this temporal progression by recasting it in terms of pictorial space. The dizzying changes in figure size, from the large-scale half-length figures in the foreground, through the dancing figures in the middle distance, to the tiny background figure, is matched by the diminishing scale of the brushstrokes, from the confident, sweeping strokes of Rossetti's later style in the foreground through to the intricate, finely detailed brushwork of the background trees. The organization is deliberately formalized, not only in the perspective diminution, but also in the uncannily symmetrical disposition of the figures. In the foreground one figure turns towards the spectator, the other turns away; one has dark hair and the other red; one is dressed in pink, the other in green. The middle pair is positioned exactly between the heads of the first pair; again one figure faces forwards, the other back; one is fair and the other dark; one is in green and the other in pink — but they switch sides. Thus the poses and colours set up crossing rhythms, like a visual equivalent of the literary figure of chiasmus. In his poetry of this period, Rossetti was exploring highly structured forms such as the sonnet, and ballad forms with fixed refrains. Like other poets and artists of his circle he was interested in notions of formal order associated with the slogan 'art for art's sake'.

fig. 68
The Bower Meadow
1872
Manchester City Galleries
cat. 148

fig. 69
The Blessed Damozel
c. 1871–8
Fogg Art Museum,
Harvard University Art Museums.
Bequest of Grenville L. Winthrop

In *The Bower Meadow*, as in contemporary works by artists such as Burne-Jones, Leighton, Whistler and Albert Moore, such ideas are explored alongside evocations of other art forms, music and dance, but without a narrative or dramatic subject. Both in its highly ordered symmetrical organization and in its reference to the art of music, the work recalls Rossetti's watercolour of 1857 *The Blue Closet* (fig. 35), an important early exploration of the ideas surrounding 'art for art's sake'. Now Rossetti returns to these ideas in the context of the artistic practices of the 1870s.

Rossetti had not, then, lost touch with developments in contemporary art, despite his increasing seclusion. In *Roman Widow* of 1874 (fig. 70), he combines his own single-figure picture-type with the classicism seen in the contemporary work of artists such as Leighton and Moore. He even draws on the interest of artists such as Lawrence Alma-Tadema in incorporating archaeologically precise artefacts; the widow sits beside a cinerary urn with a Latin inscription copied from an actual example,[62] and the motif of playing on two musical instruments is borrowed from a Pompeian wall-painting. The next year Rossetti made a design for a more important subject from classical mythology, *Orpheus and Eurydice* (cat. 151). He had not, then, given up the idea of executing large-scale compositions with many figures; another example from this period is his design for a picture of *The Death of Lady Macbeth* (cat. 150).

The diversity of these works of the 1870s suggests that Rossetti was still searching for new directions in his art, but circumstances meant that they remained isolated experiments. It was the series of images of female figures, and particularly those for which the model was Jane Burden Morris, that made the most striking – for some, disturbing – impact when his work was finally revealed to the public in the memorial exhibitions that followed his death, at the Royal Academy and the Burlington Fine Arts Club in the winter of 1882–3. The critic for *The Times* observed that opinions varied about the 'type of female loveliness which in the history of art will remain identified with his name': 'Admirers of the "Keepsake" style of beauty object to the melancholy cast of features, darkened by wavy masses of hair, the fully-developed lips, the gray eyes "deeper than the depth of water stilled at even," the long, slender throat, affected by Rossetti; others see in these attributes the very embodiment of ideal womanhood.'[63] The 'keepsake' images to which the critic refers had been highly popular in the 1830s and 1840s, when they were circulated in the form of engraved reproductions; like Rossetti's paintings they presented single female figures as types of beauty, but with diminutive facial features and dainty poses altogether unlike Rossetti's powerful images.[64] Thus the critic is emphasizing the unconventionality of Rossetti's conception of beauty. Although a wide range of Rossetti's pictures was on display, the critic's description suggests that it was the representations of Jane Morris that made the strongest impact, and this was true of most of the critical accounts of 1882–3.

The French art critic Théodore Duret, reviewing the exhibitions in the important Parisian art journal the *Gazette des Beaux-Arts*, noted that Rossetti was known to have used several women as models, but again the figure-

fig. 70
Roman Widow (Dîs Manibus)
1874
Museo de Arte de Ponce, Puerto Rico
cat. 149

type he described as typical of Rossetti is that of Morris: 'The woman imagined by Rossetti is a colossal being, having, on a great neck, a strongly accentuated face, with salient lips and an enormous, luxuriant head of hair. This creature, a kind of sibyl, or siren, or melusine, has none of the delicate aspects of woman; she is nonetheless very much alive and, when one has gazed at her for a long time, she becomes unforgettable; she exercises a kind of fascination, but one mixed with disquiet; one would be afraid to draw too near to her, one senses that she would seize you in her arms, she would crack your bones.... And in the different subjects which he has treated, borrowed ... from poems, legends, ballads, Rossetti has wished to fix on her features everything that dreaming, ecstasy, mystic vision can awaken, and pass from images into the human mind.'[65] Where the critic for *The Times* noted the antithetical responses, either disapproving or laudatory, of different viewers, Duret implies that the pictures elicit both kinds of response at once; for him the pictures are simultaneously fascinating and repellant. Examples might be multiplied, but the critics' conclusions are consistent, not only with one another but with subsequent estimates of Rossetti's art, up to the present day. The pictures were found to be exceptionally powerful, but never easy to contemplate. Their 'beauty' is not something quickly enjoyed or easily forgotten; rather it is difficult to fathom and often as disturbing as it is pleasurable.

Most reviewers of the memorial exhibitions attributed the strange power of Rossetti's art to the presentation of a particular female type, and recent debates about Rossetti's art have followed suit. For some observers Rossetti's pictures present a positive image of women, powerful and arresting rather than subservient or demure; for others they are misogynistic, presenting women either as mere sex objects or as irrational beings, threatening to men. But it is wrong to see the pictures too exclusively in terms of the sexual politics either of the Victorian period or of our own day. As the passage from Duret suggests, it is not just the stock type of the *femme fatale* in Rossetti's work, but the simultaneous sense that, like Dante's Beatrice, the figure can mean much more, that makes the pictures so compelling. Walter Pater, who placed less emphasis on Rossetti's representation of women than other critics, perhaps grasped something more important about Rossetti's art: 'One of the peculiarities of [the poem] *The Blessed Damozel* was a definiteness of sensible imagery, which seemed almost grotesque to some, and was strange, above all, in a theme so profoundly visionary.'[66] For Pater it is the union of extreme material or physical specificity with the most abstract or 'visionary' ideas that distinguishes Rossetti's art, in both poetry and painting; in this respect Pater compares Rossetti to Dante, who presented the highest spiritual insights in the form of a vision actually seen and experienced.

Thus it is important that Rossetti presents the female figure in the most vivid and immediate physical form, but this should not be taken too literally to represent mundane ideas about the role and status of women in the world, still less to signify merely the representation of the historical women who played a role in Rossetti's personal life. In pictures such as *Proserpine*, *Astarte Syriaca*, *The Day Dream*, we *see* Jane Burden Morris, but the paintings

fig. 71
The Day Dream
1880
Victoria & Albert Museum, London
cat. 154

do not simply *represent* her. The subject matter — the ancient Greek goddess of the underworld and of death, the still more ancient Syrian goddess of love, or the world of dreams and reverie, in these three examples — makes possible a leap of the imagination from the most specific and individual characteristics of a particular human being to the most abstract and general ideas we can conceive. As Duret succinctly put it, the pictures move from being mere 'images' to exploring 'the human mind' in the fullest sense. Perhaps, then, it can be said that the pictures of women realize, after all, Rossetti's ambition to paint major works with important subjects, for they lead to thoughts of the ultimate issues facing human beings: death, love, and the imagination. Moreover they do so, as Pater says, without relinquishing 'definiteness of sensible imagery' in the representation of a particular human individual. In that sense Rossetti, even though he became increasingly a visionary painter, also remained a true Pre-Raphaelite to the end of his life.

fig. 72
Pandora
1878
National Museums Liverpool
(Lady Lever Art Gallery, Port Sunlight)
cat. 146

Sensual eroticism

ROSSETTI'S REPUTATION AROUND 1900   Edwin Becker

or empty tranquil-lity

Appreciation for the work of Rossetti increased dramatically at the end of the 19th century – a remarkable phenomenon, considering that the artist had rarely exhibited his work either in England or on the Continent.[1] His poetry was read and translated, and the essence of his artistic views was therefore familiar, but the paintings, drawings and watercolours were known only, if at all, from engravings and reproductions. An admirer of his work would have had to make a great effort and visit numerous private collectors in England to obtain a clear impression of Rossetti's talent as a painter. This inaccessibility, as well as the intriguing stories about his bohemian life style, contributed to the mythologizing of Rossetti's art. Both art critics and *fin-de-siècle* painters, despite never having seen the original works of art, fell under Rossetti's spell. Some emphasized the provocative, erotic aspects of his art, while others tended to stress his poetic tranquillity.

**Infinite images of the soul:
the growth of recognition for Rossetti in France**

During the 1860s many French art critics had considered the Pre-Raphaelite Brotherhood, of which Rossetti was a co-founder, to be an outmoded movement. They felt that the artists lacked technical innovation, while their application of countless minute details obscured the overall effect of their canvases.[2] Composition and other formal aspects of a painting were generally considered of prime critical importance, and most commentators found the art of the Pre-Raphaelites too literary and too over-

burdened with overt symbolism. However, this point of view applied mainly to the highly detailed, almost photographic, paintings of the 'early' Pre-Raphaelites, and as the work of the so-called 'second group', centred around Rossetti, Edward Burne-Jones and William Morris, became better known, it met with greater appreciation. Burne-Jones's paintings, in particular, which were regularly hung in exhibitions in Paris, were greeted with enthusiasm. For instance, in 1882 the French critic Ernest Chesneau in his influential book on 19th-century English painting, *La Peinture anglaise*, stated that the pre-eminence of painstaking Pre-Raphaelite naturalism (according to John Ruskin's credo) was in Burne-Jones's case placed at the service of a higher imaginative power. Thus this English artist instilled his art with an emotion, a poetic dimension, seldom seen in French painting.[3] Chesneau might have characterized Rossetti's work in a similar way, were it not for the fact that at this time he had still not seen any of the latter's canvases.[4] Rossetti himself, just before he died in 1882, had sent Chesneau a list of his most important works, but in his book the critic could do no more than provide a simple list of them, although he did include an engraving after *Dante's Dream* (fig. 61), the monumental painting that had been purchased in 1881 by the Walker Art Gallery, Liverpool.

Another leading French critic, Robert de la Sizeranne, responded to the Pre-Raphaelites with mixed feelings. He recognized that these British artists showed great dedication, but at the end of his book *La Peinture anglaise contemporaine 1844–1894* he wrote: 'Let us never abandon those fine French qualities of logic, composition, harmony, simplicity and proportion,'[5] and he concluded: 'The English painters are great seducers: let us admire them but not follow them.'[6] Nevertheless, de la Sizeranne, who was a fervent supporter of the cause of 'art for art's sake', did show great respect for the mystical paintings of George Frederic Watts, whose creations gave form to the most mysterious powers that govern mankind.[7] One can only guess at his views on Rossetti, since he did not know his work well. The only one of his paintings that de la Sizeranne discussed at length in his book was the watercolour *Lucrezia Borgia* (s 124, 1860–8, Tate), which was included as one of the few illustrations. He was enthralled by a few fascinating details, such as the scene in the mirror in the background, and he tried to decipher the code as if he were attempting to solve a puzzle. He clearly did not know how to approach Rossetti's layered 'symbolism', and he tried to interpret it using one-to-one comparisons, in which everything had a defined, non-subjective meaning, and drawing on his own historical knowledge about the Borgia family.

The Pre-Raphaelites (the name was often used quite broadly and included many names who did not belong to the original Brotherhood) were fully recognized only in the circle of decadent literature, particularly after the publication in 1884 of a key work by the French writer Joris-Karl Huysmans, *A rebours* (Against Nature), about the aesthete Des Esseintes, who withdraws into his own world of art(ifice). In this 'bible' of the decadents, several remarkable paintings by Watts are described as mysterious, or even obsessive.[8] At that time it was impossible to view Rossetti's most important works together. In the same year

that *A rebours* was published, the French writer and critic Paul Bourget reported his disappointment that even in London, at the epicentre, it was desperately hard to form a clear impression of Rossetti's work, as it was divided among several private collections. Of the 395 works catalogued by William Sharp he was able to see only twenty.[9] Bourget, whose lyric poetry focuses on the dramas of spiritual life and the crises of love, was naturally very curious about the paintings of his literary soulmate, Rossetti.

In this respect the collector and critic Théodore Duret had been more fortunate a year earlier. He had written a review of the two retrospective exhibitions of Rossetti's oeuvre held in London. These memorial exhibitions did of course offer at long last an exceptional opportunity to see the work of this 'cryptic, not easily accessible' artist, whose work only circulated among the initiated. Duret went to the exhibitions at the Royal Academy and Burlington Fine Arts Club, as well as the auction at Christie's of Rossetti's studio drawings. He was particularly impressed by Rossetti's pictures of women and described his imagined woman as 'a colossal being, having, on a great neck, a strongly accentuated face, with salient lips and an enormous, luxuriant head of hair.' He saw her as a typical example of the *femme fatale*: she was a kind of sibyl or seductive siren and exercised a kind of fascination and awe, but at the same time aroused feelings of anxiety. It was this dichotomy between repulsion and attraction that characterized Rossetti's pictures. Duret even went so far as to say that it was difficult to get the pictures off your mind, as they continued to obsess you like a dream or an ecstatic or mystical vision.[10] He praised Rossetti above all for the fact that the artist had enriched the art of painting with new sensations that had never been portrayed before.

The poet Gabriel Sarrazin published two articles in 1884 about 'The Aesthetic School in England', in which he argued that Rossetti was their leader. He also made a distinction between Rossetti's poetry and painting, calling his poetry 'mystical' but without 'carnal eroticism', and his paintings 'sensual'. Just like Duret, he thought that Rossetti had created a new type of woman, a seducer who used her body as an instrument of flirtation: *The Blessed Damozel* (figs. 69, 103) was described by Sarrazin as an angelic siren who displayed her peerless beauty with appropriate pride; and he thought the *Venus Verticordia* (fig. 53) was flaunting her seductive breasts.[11] Sarrazin's translation of the poem 'The Blessed Damozel' by Rossetti was used in 1887 by the French composer Claude Debussy as a source of inspiration for his 'lyric poem' *La Damoiselle élue*. The first edition of this piece of music for choir and orchestra appeared in 1893 with a colour lithograph by Maurice Denis (fig. 73) on the cover. Inspired by the image of the unattainable mistress in Rossetti's poem, Denis gave his own symbolic interpretation in large contrasting areas of colour: a lady with wavy hair looks down at the terrestrial world from a starry sky full of blessed souls.

It was the *fin-de-siècle* writers, devotees of Symbolism, who continued the discovery of Rossetti as a painter, although what they saw were mainly reproductions — because it was so difficult actually to get to see the real thing. In 1887 the French-Swiss writer Edouard Rod fell completely under Rossetti's spell: he applied himself to

fig. 73
Maurice Denis
La damoiselle élue
(The Blessed Damozel)
1893
Van Gogh Museum, Amsterdam

learning English in order to be able to read Rossetti's poems, and he translated a few of them himself, but he had misgivings about the poetry, uncertain whether it would make the same impression on him as the astonishing paintings had done. 'We find ourselves, as the poet himself so magnificently put it, in the "sphere of the infinite images of the soul".... The figures in his paintings have an immobility, a silence, a pose almost suspended, a hesitation in their rare movements, which make them resemble those figures in dreams who remain long fixed in the imagination, without ever entirely taking shape.'[12] The dreamlike and spiritual were key concepts in the Symbolist movement, and they were the characteristics that Rod ascribed to Rossetti.

At the same time Rod was critical of Rossetti's technical ability. He considered Rossetti's technique (in the field of linear perspective) to be mediocre, with obvious mistakes, such as hands that were too big and bodies that were ill-proportioned, but 'the colourist who can use and harmonize such magnificently subtle shades exonerates the shortcomings of the draughtsman... one understands so well that the goal he is seeking to attain allows him to disregard the niceties of technical perfection'.[13] Rossetti understood very well, Rod claimed, that the 'plastic' period of art (concentrating on technique and pure form) was over, and that in the 'intellectual' period (Symbolism) that lay before them, painting would have to aspire to a different ideal: expressing the innermost soul.

Portraits of women as projections of tranquil longing: Rossetti's influence on the Salons de la Rose + Croix

The flamboyant Sâr Péladan, a representative of the French decadent movement at the end of the 19th century, was, like the Pre-Raphaelites, an admirer of the Flemish Primitives and early Italian painters and an opponent of traditional history painting and trivial genre pieces. Péladan wanted to re-establish the cult of the Ideal in all its glory, with Tradition as the basis and Beauty as the means of achieving it. Between 1892 and 1897 he organized six exhibitions showing idealist, Symbolist, art, in order, as he put it, to save Western culture from ruin. Realist and Impressionist art, in Péladan's view, had to be rejected, because it was not capable of representing great ideas; it could only handle the superficial and the anecdotal.

Rossetti conformed perfectly to Péladan's ideals, which underlined above all the mystical aspect of art. In May 1887 Péladan wrote several letters to Rossetti's brother William Michael because he was planning to publish an introduction to the French translation of Rossetti's volume of poetry *The House of Life*. This edition, translated by Mme Clémence Couve as *La Maison de Vie*, did indeed appear that same year with an introduction by Péladan. In it he praised Rossetti's Neo-Platonic vision: the outside world is merely a reflection of eternal truth. As with Gustave Moreau, so Péladan stated in his foreword, Rossetti's art was not about physicality but above all about rendering conceptions of the soul. And Rossetti's charm was the same as a woman's appeal: one should succumb to it without trying to explain it. This was all according to the Symbolist maxim that it is much more exciting and mysterious to suggest something than to give a plain description of it.[14] The eccentric Péladan wanted to exhibit original works by Rossetti at his notorious and much criticized Salons de la Rose + Croix, but he had to settle for photographic reproductions.[15] These did not pass unnoticed by artists such as Louis Welden Hawkins, Fernand Khnopff, Edmond Aman-Jean and Maurice Denis, who participated in Péladan's Salons. Although stylistically their work is extremely varied, as Symbolists they all placed the Idea above the concrete form, what is suggested above what is directly perceived.

The influence of Rossetti on Louis Welden Hawkins is immediately apparent. Hawkins, who was friendly with Symbolist writers such as Stéphane Mallarmé and Jean Lorrain, made an exact miniature copy on ivory of Rossetti's *Fair Rosamund* (fig. 38).[16] Hawkins had learnt the technical skills for miniature painting early in his career when he had worked as a painter on porcelain. The inspiration for this little gem was possibly Jean Lorrain's series of legends *Princesses d'ivoire et d'ivresse* (Princesses of ivory and ecstasy).[17] Rosamund, the mistress of King Henry II of England, who was eventually murdered by his jealous wife Eleanor, was the embodiment of forbidden and fatal love.

A freer interpretation of Rossetti's work can be seen in Hawkins's *Innocence* (fig. 74). The painting represents the dualism of women, in one aspect devout and virtuous as the *femme fragile*, in the other devilish like the *femme fatale*. The modelling of the bodies of the half-figures,

fig. 74
Louis Welden Hawkins
Innocence
c. 1895
Van Gogh Museum, Amsterdam

116

who seem to be standing in front of a balustrade, the flat (golden) background and the overlapping of the figures call to mind paintings by Rossetti such as *Sancta Lilias* (s 257, 1874, Tate), *The Beloved* (fig. 52) and *Venus Verticordia* (fig. 53). *Innocence* is stylistically strongly related to Hawkins's *Les auréoles* (whereabouts unknown), whose original frame had a scroll bearing the inscription: 'They sing the songs of the angels with lips still tainted by earth', in the same way that Rossetti often added incidental fragments of poetry to his paintings.[18] The sparing use of colour in both of Hawkins's works contrasts strongly with the lavish colour harmonies of Rossetti, but they do have the same golden sheen that can be seen in the icon-like *Sancta Lilias*. We should bear in mind that Hawkins probably knew Rossetti's paintings only through black-and-white reproductions.

The Dutchman Johan Thorn Prikker was also invited by Péladan to exhibit at the Salon de la Rose + Croix. In March 1893 Thorn Prikker wrote to his good friend Henri Borel, the author and translator from the Chinese, that one of the things he was working on was a large drawing, 'after that poem by Dante Gabriel Rossetti, "The Blessed Damozel". It is a figure of a woman staring downwards, with lilies coiled around her arm'.[19] Unfortunately, the drawing was never completed, but from a sketch and a description of it we know that Thorn Prikker was planning to represent a woman standing, wearing a white robe (probably in the style of his most famous work, *The Bride*, 1893, in the Kröller-Müller Museum, Otterlo), elevated above a circle of figures and surrounded by flames ascending to heaven, embellished with saints, lilies and passion

fig. 75
Lucien Lévy-Dhurmer
Eve
1896
private collection

flowers. Thorn Prikker was not interested in imitating Rossetti's painting but in capturing the essence of the picture: the distinction between the Ideal (the heavenly) and Reality (the worldly) beneath it.

In Holland, too, admiration for Rossetti's work gradually increased in the 1890s, although this was true more of his poetry than of his paintings. In 1895 a number of articles appeared in *De Kroniek*, one of the most important journals for the artistic and literary avant-garde, devoted to Rossetti's recently published biography, written by his brother William Michael and termed 'a literary work of uncommon value'.[20] The portrait artist and art reviewer Jan Veth (who himself made a lithographic portrait of Rossetti) admired the portrait drawings that illustrated the publication and was enraptured by the face of Elizabeth Siddal, 'fine and tranquilly painted, and seldom have I seen more soulful eyes staring from a more enigmatic face'.[21] The most enthusiastic praise came that same year from the artists Richard Roland Holst and his wife Henriëtte. As supporters of 'socialist' community art, they saw the introverted and individualistic Rossetti as an example of a person who had withdrawn from modern, capitalist society. They acknowledged Rossetti's 'Beauty as an absolute power, existing above and beyond humankind, deferring only to poetry…'.[22] Furthermore, they did not so much emphasize the sultry sensuality in Rossetti's painting, but rather the immobility of the figures: they appeared as if seen in a dream or memory, as Rod had also remarked, and yet, in apparent contrast, they could conjure up feelings in lifeless things. 'A poetic memory, a fading noise, he weaves them into his compositions and

fig. 76
Fernand Khnopff
Silence
1890
Musée royaux des Beaux-Arts de Belgique, Brussels

fig. 77
Silence
1870
Brooklyn Museum of Art, New York.
Gift of Mr Luke Vincent Lockwood 46.188
cat. 142

gives them shape, so that the depiction of inanimate things reflects the conscious life that has passed them by...'.[23] This introverted aspect of 'the secrets of the soul' was cherished by many Symbolist exhibitors at Péladan's Salons.

Even though the artist Lucien Lévy-Dhurmer never exhibited at the Salon de la Rose + Croix, he felt a great sense of allegiance to the artists whose work was on show there. Titles such as *Circe*, *Mystery*, *Eve* and *Medusa* are evidence of his Symbolist themes. Despite such aspects of sensuality as the red, loosely flowing hair draped over her naked body, his *Eve* (fig. 75) remains an 'aloof' dream figure. The almost square shape of the canvas, the emphasis on the gestures made by her finely shaped hands, the wealth of flowing red hair and the detailed background call to mind paintings by Rossetti such as *Venus Verticordia* (fig. 53). Furthermore, Lévy-Dhurmer's *Eve*, like Rossetti's *Venus*, shows the ambivalence between eroticism and aloofness, whose outcome is a restrained sensuality. One of Lévy-Dhurmer's most famous works, most of which were executed in pastels, is his portrait of the Belgian Symbolist writer Georges Rodenbach (c. 1895, Musée d'Orsay, Paris), author of poems such as 'Du Silence' (1888) and 'Bruges-la-Morte' (1892). Rodenbach's 'Du Silence' was undoubtedly a source of inspiration for Lévy-Dhurmer's *Silence* of 1895, to which the artist must have been very attached, as it hung in his room throughout his entire life.[24] The critics labelled this work a human sphinx shrouded in a black veil, whose eternal silence instilled fear, evoking the same kind of physical response as Rossetti's paintings (see p. 78). The traditional gesture for enjoining silence,

fig. 78
Edmond Aman-Jean
Portrait of Thadée Caroline Jacquet
c. 1891–2
Van Gogh Museum, Amsterdam

fig. 79
Reverie
1868
private collection
cat. 139

fig. 80
La Pia de' Tolomei
1868
private collection
cat. 140

fig. 81
La Donna della Finestra
1870
Bradford Art Gallery
cat. 143

a finger in front of the lips, had already been represented in 1842–3 by the sculptor Auguste Préault in a mask for a monumental tomb, and it appeared in various later interpretations by artists such as Henri Martin, Odilon Redon and Fernand Khnopff (fig. 76).[25] There is also a large-format drawing entitled *Silence* in Rossetti's oeuvre (fig. 77). This, however, derives from an entirely different iconography, as Rossetti himself indicated in a letter to Jane Morris, who posed for his drawing: 'Silence holds in one hand a branch of peach, the symbol used by the ancients; its fruit being held to resemble the human heart and its leaf the human tongue. With the other hand she draws together the veil enclosing the shrine in which she sits'.[26] With his use of this symbol and in the absent gaze of the woman, Rossetti is closer to the hushed and secretive atmosphere of Khnopff than the dark mysteries of Redon or Lévy-Dhurmer. But all the works link Silence to the Supernatural (which is indicated in the Rossetti by the enclosed shrine and in the Lévy-Dhurmer by the starry sky), to make a metaphor for Eternal Silence. In this sense Rossetti's *Silence* could also be called Symbolist.

The poster for the first Salon de la Rose + Croix was designed by Edmond Aman-Jean and was inspired by the Rossettian theme of Beatrice, who was carried off by an angel whilst looking around for an imaginary Dante. The general theme has been summarized concisely as Inspiration. Aman-Jean is better known for his delicate portraits of women (fig. 78), who appear calm and enigmatic and are often surrounded by flowers. In 1895 the art critic Roger Marx gave an apt characterization of Aman-Jean's female portraits: 'He unravels the secrets of the soul, reveals intimate feelings' and creates around these 'delicate creatures [an atmosphere] of calm and silence conducive to meditation. Their gestures show a partial lassitude; the hands, with their elongated fingers, indicate indolent abandon. Aman-Jean renders a restful glance, a unique reflection of undulating hair with the comprehensive intuitive tenderness of a poet.'[27] This characterization of Aman-Jean's work could be applied to pictures by Rossetti such as *Reverie* (fig. 79): the elongated hands, the apparent lassitude of the gestures and the air of calm emanating from the portrait are all there. Perhaps the most apt analogy between Rossetti's fascinating ladies and the women in *fin-de-siècle* art was provided by Camille Mauclair when he wrote in 1901 that a female portrait is not a likeness of a woman but the image of a desire evoked by the woman: it is a setting, a frame, within which we project our dreams (which is why the composition and cropping of the portrait are so important). The woman is never seen directly, but in a vague half-light. At the same time, he goes on to say, the portrait has decorative qualities, and it is partly due to this that one feels that the subject is distanced and so becomes a hieratic or priestly figure, not a woman of flesh and blood but an Idea. It is not surprising that Mauclair dedicated this essay to Eugène Carrière, the painter who turned all his human characters into dream figures that loom up like ghostly shapes emerging from the gloom.[28]

The Woman as Idea: from fashionable imitation to free interpretation

The pre-eminent Belgian decadent Fernand Khnopff was one of Péladan's favourite artists; and, as a true anglophile, he was more influenced by Rossetti than the other *fin-de-siècle* painters. The most direct reference to Rossetti is to be found in Khnopff's essay on works of art inspired by Dante, in which he mentions *Beata Beatrix* (fig. 57), *Dante's Dream* (fig. 61) and *The Lady of Pity* (*La Donna della Finestra*; figs. 81, 101): three of Rossetti's most remarkable works. Khnopff has particular praise for *Beata Beatrix*: 'Never has the idea of death been rendered more beautifully. Nothing in the work makes us think of physical decay, only of moral calm, with an underlying Christian idea of final bliss for the chosen few. The painting is so intensely emotional that it seems enchanted in the same way as the "Oval portrait", described in the story of Edgar Allan Poe.'[29] It is noteworthy, though not surprising, that Khnopff refers here to a favourite poet of Rossetti's, Poe. In Poe's short story an artist becomes so obsessed with his model that the painting, once completed, destroys her. The model, who hates Art because it is her rival, tastes defeat, and Art — the more elevated form — triumphs and takes the place of reality. Here the immortality of art is contrasted with the transience of love: Elizabeth Siddal would die, yet her portrait as Beata Beatrix would still live on.

fig. 82
Fernand Khnopff
I lock my door upon myself
1891
Bayerische Staatsgemäldesammlungen,
Neue Pinakothek, Munich

The subtle similarities between Rossetti and Khnopff had already been pointed out in 1890 by Walter Shaw Sparrow, who called Khnopff's *The Caresses* (1896, Musées royaux des Beaux-Arts de Belgique, Brussels) a 'pictorial distillation of Rossetti's art'.[30] But perhaps the most visible example is Rossetti's influence on *I lock my door upon myself* (fig. 82), exhibited at the Salon de la Rose + Croix of 1893 and inspired by the poem 'Who shall deliver me' by Rossetti's sister Christina. In this poem the first-person narrator tries to escape all the tumult of the outside world and become more inward-looking. In his exaggeratedly horizontal painting Khnopff combined Rossetti's ideal of beauty with tranquillity. The position of the model, bending downwards, is comparable to *The Blessed Damozel* (figs. 69, 103), as are the dreamy gaze, staring into space, and the long hands with their slender fingers. Identical too is the positioning behind a kind of balustrade, a demarcation that is once again meant to indicate to the observer the conscious distance between fantasy and reality. Khnopff's work exudes a cool silence, an alienated atmosphere, and the melancholy woman, just like Rossetti's female figures, complies with the idea of a deliberately chosen and cherished isolation. But it was not only Christina Rossetti who provided the source for Khnopff's *I lock my door upon myself*, because earlier Dante Gabriel had also pithily summarized Khnopff's narcissistic, introverted theme when he wrote: 'I shut myself in with my soul, And the shapes come eddying forth'.[31]

As correspondent of the English journal *The Studio*, Khnopff had probably seen Rossetti's original paintings in London on several occasions. In any case, in Brussels there were many photographic reproductions of Rossetti's work available through the publisher and art bookshop, Maison Dietrich. A list of photo-engravings was published as an appendix to Georges Destrée's publication on the Pre-Raphaelites,[32] and the reproductions of works after Rossetti by Maison Becker-Holemans, which were announced on the poster of the Salon de l'Art Idéaliste, were also undoubtedly much praised.[33] Avant-garde circles in Brussels were greatly impressed by the Pre-Raphaelite Brotherhood in general. In her review of late 19th-century Belgian art, Madeleine Octave Maus, wife of a great art patron, reported that Rossetti's photo-engravings, along with those of Burne-Jones, attracted the attention of a sophisticated and modish public, dressed according to the aesthetic, Pre-Raphaelite fashion in green velvet or mauve silk, sometimes carrying lilies in their hands.[34] And Belgian *fin-de-siècle* authors such as Emile Verhaeren, Charles van Lerberghe and Maurice Maeterlinck found all their poetic ideals in the art of the Pre-Raphaelites. For them the flight into the mystical dream was an attempt to escape their strait-laced provincial backgrounds.

Rossetti's influence reached further than France, Holland and Belgium: in Germany and Austria, too, critics and artists had become fascinated by his 'beauties'. The Austrian writer and cultural philosopher Rudolf Kassner, a friend of the poet Rainer Maria Rilke, had read Rossetti's sonnets, seen reproductions of his portraits of women ('... pictures that nowadays are known throughout the entire world...') and was familiar with Muther's *History of Modern Painting*. He was surprised, then, when he saw a small pencil drawing of Elizabeth Siddal, leaning against

fig. 83
Elizabeth Siddal standing at a window
1854
Victoria & Albert Museum, London
cat. 24

a window (fig. 83), in the Victoria & Albert Museum in London.[35] It was undoubtedly a beautiful drawing, but it did not live up to the myth of the Siddal figure. It seemed to him too subtle, modest and worldly. In his book, Muther had presented an ideal with its principal emphasis on the sensual side of Rossetti's work: the splendid white hands sliding flirtatiously over a gold chain or dreamily fingering roses, where the magnificent display of colour still further intensified the glowing, sensual effect.[36] In Kassner's view, Woman is really Rossetti's theme.[37] It makes no difference in what shape or form she appears, whether as *Venus Verticordia*, *Fazio's Mistress*, or *Lady Lilith*; all epitomize the idea in Rossetti's imagination of woman as a combination of desire and lust.

These portraits of women are artificial; not only in terms of their well-considered, effective structure, but also in theme. Kassner argued that Rossetti's 'metaphors' are often as dry as embossed metal flowers. Furthermore, he considers many portraits to be literary and contrived. Still more to the point is his remark that you look at Rossetti's portraits of women as if you are looking at them through a mirror.[38] The wide range of meanings that can be attributed to mirrored reflections is an important point of departure in Rossetti's art, as is also the case with Khnopff:[39] the decorative, non-perspectival composition, the golden frame with symbolic references and the added, dual, meaning achieved by the addition of verse; all these aspects throw light on different sides of the same imaginary person, who is more of an abstract idea, like 'Body's Beauty' or 'Soul's Beauty', than a true-to-life representation. In everyday life, too, Rossetti quite literally liked

fig. 84
Franz von Stuck
Innocentia
1889
private collection

reflection: his house in Cheyne Walk was full of mirrors of all shapes and sizes, working as reflections of reality.

Sensual eroticism, which in the art critic Richard Muther's view characterizes Rossetti's art, was explicitly rendered by Franz von Stuck, the 'artist prince' from Munich. In 1889 he painted his *Innocentia* (fig. 84), making clear reference to Rossetti's *Venus Verticordia* (fig. 53). Although Stuck's image-type derives from Christian iconography (in this case the Immaculate Conception of the Virgin Mary), the actual subject is quite different: a young teenage girl becoming conscious of her awakening sensuality, expressed in the hazel eyes, the red lips and the sprig of lilies, pointing unashamedly at the genitals. Unmistakably, Rossetti's Venus with her bright red lips, pale skin and her diagonally pointing arrow, has been used here as a source of inspiration, and the poem 'Innocentia' by Otto Julius Bierbaum dedicated to Stuck, completes the comparison with the English poet-artist.[40]

There were to be many more examples in European art of Rossetti's influence after 1900, from weak, superficial imitators to idiosyncratic interpreters such as Gustav Klimt, whose elite, sophisticated Viennese ladies are enveloped in the same sort of decorative surroundings, their slender hands conjuring up the same sort of nervous tension and their faces suffused with the same cool aloofness. And for Klimt, too, Woman is an icon, with a strange mixture of magnetic appeal and chilliness, of sensual eroticism and empty tranquillity, just as in Rossetti's work.[41] Nothing of any importance appears to be happening, as if time has stood still and we have landed in a different era, and yet there is the feeling of an exciting stimulus, a voluptuous emanation, an almost physical confrontation. This dual significance continues to fascinate us, and it is here that the power of Rossetti, who was able to inspire so many artists, lies hidden.

Notes

Full titles of all works referred to will be found in the **Bibliography**, pp. 239–43.

'The most startlingly original living'

Julian Treuherz

1   Patmore 1857, p. 584.
2   Muther 1896, p. 597.
3   Fry 1916, p. 100.
4   Ainsworth 1976.
5   Erdman 1973.
6   Browne 1994, pp. 31-2, 41-3.
7   Grieve 1973d, p. 142.
8   Parris 1984, p. 53, cat. 6 (entry by Mary Bennett)
9   F, I, p. 6.
10 Fredeman 1975, pp. 108–12.
11 W.M. Rossetti 1895, I, p. 128.
12 F, I, pp. 128–9.
13 Quoted in Grieve 1973b, p. 24.
14 Ibid., pp. 18–24
15 W.M. Rossetti 1895, I, pp. 147–8.
16 Ibid., p. 162.
17 Ibid., p. 159–60.
18 F, I, p. 254.
19 Ibid., p. 156.
20 Parris 1984, pp. 120–1, cat. 58 (entry by Judith Bronkhurst); F, I, pp. 263, 270.
21 Grieve 1976, pp. 10–16, 35–6.
22 Letter from Ruskin cited by Grieve 1976, p. 11.
23 Treuherz 1984, pp.158, 163–4.
24 Surtees 1979, p. 277.
25 Patmore 1857, p. 584.
26 Ibid.
27 Parris 1984, p. 284, cat. 223 (entry by Alastair Grieve).
28 Brown 1981, p. 126.
29 Ibid., p. 148.
30 Dunn 1984, pp. 55, 62; F, II, p. 148.
31 Banham and Harris 1984, pp. 83–9.
32 Quoted by Banham and Harris 1984, p. 93.
33 Robertson 1933, p. 88.
34 W.M. Rossetti 1895, I, p. 203.

'Beautiful women with floral adjuncts'

Elizabeth Prettejohn

1   W.M. Rossetti 1895, I, p. 203.
2   See for example F, II, pp. 101, 155; D & W, II, pp. 487, 576–7. On 25 June 1864, in a letter to his aunt Charlotte Lydia Polidori, he announces his intention 'henceforward to do almost exclusively large works in oil' (D & W, II, p. 509).
3   F, II, pp. 273, 278.
4   Taylor 1863, p. 26.
5   F, II, p. 298.
6   F, II, p. 306.
7   F, II, p. 276.
8   F, II, p. 269.
9   Grieve 1999, pp. 22-3.
10 The first extant reference to the title is in a letter of 12 September 1860 to George Price Boyce, the picture's owner (F, II, p. 310). Previously Rossetti had referred to the picture simply as a 'portrait' (F, II, p. 269) or 'a little half-figure in oil' (F, II, p. 276).
11 See Grieve 1999, p. 22.
12 In Swinburne 1868, p. 46.
13 The blue-and-white hexagons on the back wall are adorned with the prunus blossom motif (which Rossetti called 'hawthorn') found on Chinese pots. They have often been described as tiles, but the hexagonal shape is not found on Chinese tiles. Perhaps Rossetti based them on the hexagonal lid of a jar or a hexagonal plate, repeated and cleverly fitted together to make a continuous surface.
14 Ruskin 1903-12, III, pp. 268-9.
15 See Grieve 1999, pp. 24–5. In 1866 Rossetti refers to *Lady Lilith* simply as 'the Toilette picture' (D & W, II, p. 602).
16 D & W, II, p. 850.
17 W.M. Rossetti 1889, p. 69.
18 Quoted in Macleod 1987, p. 339.
19 Among the most thoughtful feminist explorations of Rossetti's work are Pollock 1988, pp. 120–54; Psomiades 1997, pp. 94–133; Pearce 1991, pp. 31–58.
20 As Colin Cruise has argued, Rossetti's close associate at this date, Simeon Solomon, transformed the Rossettian pictorial type into images representing male figures; see Cruise 1996.
21 See Grieve 1999, pp. 23–9.
22 In the preface to the first edition of *The Early Italian Poets* (1861), repr. in D.G. Rossetti 1911, p. 283.
23 Ruskin 1903–12, vol. XXXVI, p. 490.
24 Ibid., p. 491; the title *Flora* appears on p. 489.
25 Quoted in S, p. 99, no. 173.
26 Quoted in Grieve 1999, p. 22.
27 Quoted in F, II, p. 278, n. 2 to letter 59.44.
28 Quoted in Macleod 1987, p. 339.
29 Myers 1883, p. 325.
30 Stephens 1865, p. 545.
31 Ibid., p. 546.
32 For a brief history of the term and its implications see Prettejohn 1999, pp. 1–14; for Rossetti's role in 'art for art's sake' see Alastair Grieve's chapter in the same volume, Grieve 1999, pp. 17–35.
33 Swinburne 1868, p. 50.
34 Quoted in S, p. 94, no. 168.
35 D.G. Rossetti 1911, p. 346.
36 He would, of course, have heard of the opera from Franz Hüffer, the German music critic and Wagner scholar who married Ford Madox Brown's daughter Catherine in 1872. He was a close friend of Rossetti at least by 1871, when he arranged for the publication of a German edition of Rossetti's *Poems*.
37 For an investigation of the extant historical data that is available about Cornforth, which demonstrates that there is no basis for much of the traditional story about her, see Drewery, Moore and Whittick 2001.
38 This political allegory would apply to Italian freedom and unification in the present as well as to the cessation of factional strife in Dante's time. See Milbank 1998, p. 103; and pp. 102–16 for a more general discussion of the debate about Beatrice's historical existence.
39 S, pp. 106–7, no. 183; D & W, II, pp. 642–3, 647–51.
40 F, I, p. 76.
41 D & W, II, pp. 648–50.
42 W.M. Rossetti 1889, pp. 65–6.
43 D & W, II, p. 898.

44 For an interesting exploration of ideas of dreaming in Rossetti's work see Roberts 1974.

45 For a compelling account of these practices see McGann 2000.

46 See Ainsworth 1976.

47 In fact there is a third repetition, as each of the poems within the *Vita Nuova* is also given a prose explication. After Beatrice's death, the order is reversed, so that in each case the explication precedes the poem, so that (as Dante explains) the poem 'may seem to remain the more widowed at its close' (D.G. Rossetti 1911, p. 336). Like the *Divine Comedy*, the *Vita Nuova* can be read as a meditation on the art of poetry and its interpretation; this was certainly one of the ways in which Rossetti read it.

48 Quoted in s, p. 42, no. 81.

49 D.G. Rossetti 1911, p. 330.

50 James 1974, pp. 93–4.

51 For a detailed account of Morris's self-fashioning, see Mancoff 2000.

52 For an important reading of *Astarte Syriaca* see Pollock 1988, pp. 149–54.

53 Rossetti's friend, the artist Frederic Shields, left a detailed account of his working procedure, Shields 1890, pp. 70–3.

54 Walter John Knewstub worked for Rossetti as a pupil-assistant for several years beginning in 1862 (see D & W, II, p. 453). Henry Treffry Dunn, who was with Rossetti from 1867 until the end of his life, played a large share in routine replicas and may have helped even with

important works; see Dunn 1984. Charles Fairfax Murray, Frederic Shields and others may also have assisted Rossetti. The use of studio assistants was common at the time (Burne-Jones, for example, used assistants extensively).

55 Watts 1883, p. 412.

56 W.M. Rossetti 1889, p. 99.

57 D & w, III, pp. 1120-2.

58 See Østermark-Johansen 1998, pp. 75–139.

59 As he wrote to Jane Morris, Rossetti contemplated entitling a drawing of her *Vittoria Colonna*, 'who I find was *certainly* the original of those heads by [Michelangelo] which are portraits of you; but I thought it would not do to tackle Mike' (B & T, p. 54). See also Østermark-Johansen 1998, pp. 160–1.

60 See for example his letter to W.B. Scott, quoted above, in which he mentions the 'botheration' of working 'in the focus of the four winds out of doors' (F, II, p. 276).

61 He may have used only a part of the earlier canvas, which a letter of 1850 describes as 7 feet wide (F, I, p. 156). Perhaps he had finished only part of the landscape and later cut the canvas down to its present size.

62 W.M. Rossetti 1889, p. 92.

63 The Times 1883. The quotation is from Rossetti's 'The Blessed Damozel' (see cat. 152).

64 See Grieve 1999, pp. 26–7 and plate 8.

65 Duret 1883, p. 54.

66 Pater 1889, p. 230.

Sensual eroticism or empty tranquillity

Edwin Becker

1 For a review of the history of the American reception of Rossetti, which will not be dealt with here, see Casteras 1984.

2 Jacques Lethève, 'La connaissance des peintres préraphaélites anglais en France (1855–1900)', *Gazette des Beaux-Arts* 53, 6th series, May–June 1959, p. 317.

3 Ernest Chesneau, *La Peinture anglaise*, Paris 1882, p. 238.

4 Dubernard-Laurent 1996, II, pp. 153–4: there is serious doubt whether Chesneau and Rossetti ever actually met.

5 Robert de la Sizeranne, *La Peinture anglaise contemporaine 1844–1894*, Paris 1922, p. 281.

6 Ibid., p. 284.

7 Wilton and Upstone 1997, p. 26.

8 J.- K. Huysmans, *A rebours*, Paris 1897 (original edition 1884), pp. 173–4.

9 Paul Bourget, 'Lettre de Londres', in *Le Journal des Débats politiques et littéraires*, 24 September 1884, republished in *Etudes et portraits*, Paris 1889, II; Dubernard-Laurent 1996, II, p. 173.

10 Duret 1883, p. 54.

11 Dubernard-Laurent 1996, II, pp. 169–70.

12 Edouard Rod, 'Les pré-raphaélites anglais', *Gazette des Beaux-Arts* 36, 2nd series, November 1887, p. 405.

13 Ibid., pp. 412–13.

14 Mme Clémence Couve, *La Maison de Vie*, with an introduction by Joséphin Péladan, Paris 1887, pp. L, LII.

15 For a general introduction to the Salons de la Rose + Croix see Jean da Silva, *Le Salon de la Rose + Croix 1892–1897*, Paris 1991.

16 Lucas Bonekamp, *Louis Welden Hawkins*, exh. cat., Amsterdam (Van Gogh Museum) 1993, p. 58, no. 19.

17 Ibid.

18 Ibid., pp. 36–7.

19 Joop M. Joosten (ed.), *De Brieven van Johan Thorn Prikker aan Henri Borel en anderen 1892–1904*, Leiden / Nieuwkoop 1980, p. 112

20 W.M. Rossetti 1895. See also: Smit 1998, p. 77.

21 Smit 1998, p. 78.

22 Henriëtte and Richard Roland Holst, 'Dante Gabriel Rossetti als dichter en schilder (1828–1882)', in E.D. Pijzel (ed.), *Mannen en vrouwen van beteekenis in onze dagen*, Haarlem 1898, p. 289.

23 Ibid., p. 320.

24 *Autour de Lévy-Dhurmer. Visionnaires et Intimistes en 1900*, exh. cat., Paris (Grand Palais) 1973, p. 42, no. 58.

25 Charles W. Millard and Andreas Blühm (eds.), *Auguste Préault 1809–1879. Romanticism in bronze*, exh. cat., Amsterdam (Van Gogh Museum) 1997–8, pp. 28–9, no. 4.

26 B & T, p. 71.

27 Roger Marx, 'Edmond Aman-Jean – Les Salons de 1895', *Gazette des Beaux-Arts*, I May 1895, p. 446, cited in Henri Dorra (ed.), *Symbolist Art Theories*, Berkeley, Los Angeles & London 1994, p. 257.

28 Camille Mauclair, 'Sur le portrait de la femme', in *Art en Silence*, Paris 1901, pp. 308, 310, 312.

29 Fernand Khnopff, 'Les œuvres d'art inspirées par Dante', *Le Flambeau* 7, 31 July 1921, cited in *Fernand Khnopff 1858–1921*, exh. cat., Paris (Musée des Arts décoratifs), Brussels (Musées royaux des Beaux-Arts de Belgique), Hamburg (Hamburger Kunsthalle) 1979–80, pp. 231–2; Jeffrey W. Howe, *The Symbolist Art of Fernand Khnopff*, diss. Ann Arbor (Michigan) 1979, p. 18.

30 Walter Shaw-Sparrow, 'Fernand Khnopff', *The Magazine of Art* 14 (1890), p. 40, cited in Casteras 1995, p. 39.

31 D.G. Rossetti 1999, p. 476.

32 Olivier Georges Destrée, *Les Préraphaélites. Notes sur l'art décoratif et la peinture en Angleterre*, Brussels 1894, p. [114].

33 Laurence Brogniez, 'Les préraphaélites en Belgique : d'étranges rêveurs…', in *Splendeurs de l'Idéal. Rops, Khnopff, Delville et leur temps*, exh. cat., Liège (Musée de l'Art Wallon de la Ville de Liège) 1997, pp. 125–39, ill. p. 65.

34 Madeleine Octave Maus, *Trente Années de Lutte pour l'Art : 1884–1914*, Brussels 1926, pp. 113, 178.

35 Kassner 1900, p. 140.

36 Richard Muther, *Geschichte der Malerei*, Berlin 1922 (4th edition), vol. III, p. 365.

37 Kassner 1900, p. 137.

38 Ibid., p. 142.

39 Jeffrey Howe, 'Mirror Symbolism in the Work of Fernand Khnopff', *Arts Magazine*, September 1978, pp. 112–18.

40 Edwin Becker, *Franz von Stuck. Eros & Pathos*, exh. cat., Amsterdam (Van Gogh Museum) 1995–6, p. 38.

41 Richard Muther, *Studien*, ed. Hans Rosenhagen, Berlin 1925, p. 287.

fig. 85
Charles Lutwidge Dodgson (Lewis Carroll)
**Dante Gabriel, sister Christina,
mother Frances and brother William
Rossetti**
1863
photograph
National Portrait Gallery, London

fig. 86
Charles Lutwidge Dodgson (Lewis Carroll)
Dante Gabriel Rossetti
1863
photograph
National Portrait Gallery, London

fig. 87
W. and D. Downey
**Rossetti with Algernon Swinburne
(left), Fanny Cornforth
and William Rossetti (right)**
1863
photograph
National Portrait Gallery, London

fig. 88
W. and D. Downey
Rossetti with William Bell Scott (left)
and John Ruskin (right)
1863
photograph
National Portrait Gallery, London

fig. 89
Emery Walker
Tudor House, 16 Cheyne Walk
photograph
National Portrait Gallery, London

fig. 90
Jane Morris seated, full length
albumen print by Emery Walker from the
original photograph by John Robert Parsons
Birmingham Museums & Art Gallery
cat. 132

Notes to catalogue

The order in which entries appear in the catalogue is a compromise between chronological and thematic arrangement: strict chronology is not possible owing to the artist's habit of working on paintings over long periods, often laying them aside and finishing them long after they were first started.

Catalogue entries have been written primarily to explain the often complicated subject matter of the works. Questions of dating, provenance, stylistic development and critical history have not been treated in detail but are discussed where they affect the understanding of the subject matter.

We have preferred the spelling of Elizabeth Siddal's surname with one l. Though she was born Elizabeth Siddall, and her family continued to use this spelling, the form Siddal was adopted when she entered the Pre-Raphaelite circle. Rossetti spelt it Siddal in the first mention of her in one of his letters (September 1850, F, I, p. 151). Though others continued to use the spelling Siddall (for example Ford Madox Brown: Brown 1981, p. 101), she was generally known as Elizabeth Siddal until her marriage to Rossetti.

Dimensions are given in centimetres, height before width.

Full titles of all literature referred to will be found in the **Bibliography**, pp. 239–43.

Catalogue

Early work to Pre-Raphaelitism

As a young man Rossetti could not decide whether to become a poet or a painter. He lacked the application to study art and never completed his course at the Royal Academy Schools. He persuaded Ford Madox Brown to teach him, and attended life classes, but never learned academic drawing or perspective. Despite, or perhaps because of this, his work showed originality from the start. His early drawings, inspired by romantic poetry, dwelt on supernatural and moral themes. At first heavily shaded, his technique became progressively lighter, flatter and more linear. In 1848, the Pre-Raphaelite Brotherhood was formed, with Rossetti, John Everett Millais and William Holman Hunt as its leaders. They wished to bring back to English art the seriousness of purpose, contact with reality and originality that they felt it had lost. Jointly they created a new, simplified style, deliberately archaic and expressive. It was inspired by the art of the early Italian Renaissance, hence the title of the Brotherhood, but the revival of complex symbolism and fine detail also derived from late medieval and early Flemish art. Rossetti's first two exhibited oil paintings (cats. 12, 13) were startlingly original treatments of the early life of the Virgin Mary, emphasizing her purity. They helped to define the new style.

1
Self-portrait
(s 434)
dated bottom right: March 1847
pencil with white heightening on paper,
19.7 x 17.8 cm
National Portrait Gallery, London
figure 2

Showing Rossetti aged eighteen. 'Thick, beautiful, and closely curled masses of rich brown much-neglected hair, fell about an ample brow, and almost to the wearer's shoulders; strong eyebrows marked with their dark shadows a pair of rather sunken eyes, in which a sort of fire, instinct of what may be called proud cynicism, burned with a furtive kind of energy.... His rather high cheekbones were the more observable because his cheeks were roseless and hollow enough to indicate the waste of life and mid-night oil to which the youth was addicted; close-shaving left bare his very full, not to say sensuous, lips and square-cut masculine chin....Rossetti came forward...with an *insouciant* air which savoured of defiance, mental pride and thorough self-reliance.' (recollection of a fellow student of Rossetti in 1846, quoted by Stephens 1894, p. 10)

2
The Raven
(s 19)
signed and dated bottom right: GCDR (monogram) / June / 46
brown ink on paper, 33.8 x 23 cm
private collection

cat. 1

cat. 2

cat. 3

3
The Raven
(S 19 C)
c. 1848
ink and wash on paper, 23 x 21.6 cm
Wightwick Manor, The Munro Collection
(on loan to The National Trust)

4
The Raven
(S 19 B)
c. 1848
ink and wash on paper, 22.9 x 21.6 cm
Victoria & Albert Museum, London
figure 4

These three drawings show Rossetti's
fascination with Edgar Allan Poe's
poem *The Raven*, first published in 1845.
The poet, haunted by memories of his dead
love Lenore, is startled by a tapping at his
chamber door. A raven flies in, perches
on a bust of Pallas Athene, and answers the
poet's tormented questions about his lost
love with the unchanging refrain 'Never-
more'. The theme of lovers parted by death
fascinated Rossetti from the beginning of
his career, and recurs throughout his work
(Grieve 1973d).

The first drawing (cat. 2) shows the poet
leaping up from his chair, startled by a circle
of ghostly spirits and goblins, some holding
censers:

'Then, methought the air grew denser,
    perfumed from an unseen censer
Swung by seraphim whose foot-falls tinkled
    on the tufted floor'

The stylized drawing technique is influenced
by contemporary French printmakers and
illustrators such as Delacroix and Gavarni.
Rossetti may also have taken the motif of the
circle of spirits from a painting by Theodor
von Holst, whom he regarded as 'in some sort
the Edgar Poe of painting' (Grieve 1973d,
fig. 2; Gilchrist 1863, I, pp. 379–80).
The second and third drawings in the
sequence (cats. 3 and 4) show the poet
seated by lamplight, as described by Poe. These two
later drawings are less mannered, and the
treatment of the ghostly seraphim shows
Rossetti moving towards a more linear style.

5
The Sleeper
(S 29)
c. 1848
inscribed top left: E.A.POE; top right:
D.G.ROSSETTI; below: The Sleeper
ink with border of pink bodycolour on paper,
26.5 x 17.3 cm
The British Museum, London

Illustrating 'The Sleeper' by Edgar Allan
Poe, first published 1831, which describes
a lady asleep by a lattice window, open to the
night air. The poem draws on the ambiguity
between sleep, death and the supernatural,
and ends by suggesting that she is not asleep
but dead.

'I pray to God that she may lie
Forever with unopened eye,
While the pale sheeted ghosts go by.'

6
Ulalume
(S 30)
c. 1848
brown and black ink and pencil on paper,
20.7 x 19.7 cm
Birmingham Museums & Art Gallery.
Presented by subscribers

Another drawing on the theme of lovers
separated by death, this one illustrates a
poem of 1847 by Edgar Allan Poe. The poet
and his soul, in the form of a winged figure,
wander amongst cypress trees in 'the ghost-
haunted woodland of Weir' and discover
the tomb of Ulalume, the poet's lost love,
on the anniversary of her death. Rossetti
shows two episodes from the poem, one with
the poet leading the soul and the other when
the soul speaks, desperately begging the poet
not to go further. The kneeling position
of the soul 'letting sink her Wings till they
trailed in the dust' shows how literally Rossetti
interpreted the text.

7
Retro me Sathana
(S 37)
signed and dated bottom right:
DGR / JULY 1848
ink on paper, 24.5 x 17.5 cm
Bolton Museums, Art Gallery & Aquarium,
Bolton Metropolitan Borough Council

cat. 4

cat. 5

cat. 6

'Get thee behind me Satan' is a quotation from the New Testament (Luke 4:8). A priest holds a crucifix to which a young girl is praying, with 'the devil slinking behind them baffled' (W.M. Rossetti 1895, I, pp. 99–100). The theme of opposition between good and evil is suggested by the shield divided into two halves, black and white. The motto below the shield, *Ex Nocte Dies* (out of the night comes the day), hints that the girl may be a sinner in repentance. This links the drawing with the theme of *Faust: Gretchen in Church* (cat. 8). Rossetti began an oil painting of *Retro me Sathana* in 1847 but abandoned it after showing it to Charles Eastlake, Keeper of the National Gallery, who did not approve of the subject, probably because of its satanic links and its Catholic overtones.

8
Faust: Gretchen in Church
(s 34)
signed and dated bottom left:
GCDR (monogram) / JULY 1848
ink on paper, 27.3 x 21 cm
private collection

An incident from Goethe's *Faust*. Gretchen is praying in church after she has succumbed to Faust's advances and caused the deaths of her mother and her brother. As the choir sings the *Dies Irae* the devil appears and taunts her; she falls forward in a swoon. Rossetti may have known prints of this subject by the German artists Peter Cornelius and Moritz Retzsch.

The drawing gains in meaning when it is compared to *The Girlhood of Mary Virgin* (cat. 12). The two works, begun at approximately the same time, have many visual parallels, though they are thematically opposed to each other. Gretchen, the devil and the standing figure behind are in the same compositional relationship as the Virgin, St Anne and Joseph; the girl in prayer is the counterpart to the child-angel; the flaming sword in the foreground, emblematic of Gretchen's inner conflict, is in the same position as the palm and thorn branches in the painting, symbolizing the sorrows and joys of the Virgin (Grieve 1973b, pp. 5–6). The drawing was made for the Cyclographic Society, a forerunner of the Pre-Raphaelite Brotherhood; drawings by members on a given theme were circulated amongst them for their criticisms. In this case Millais approved of the originality and expressive quality but criticized the poor perspective and proportions of some of the figures (W.M. Rossetti 1895, I, p. 121).

9
Genevieve
(s 38)
inscribed bottom left: Genevieve; signed and dated bottom right: GCDR (monogram) / AUGUST 1848
pencil and ink on paper, 27.7 x 14.7 cm
Syndics of the Fitzwilliam Museum, Cambridge

Illustrating the poem 'Love' by Coleridge, first published 1799. Coleridge tells how a

medieval poet won the love of Genevieve after singing a song about a knight winning the love of his lady. Rossetti considered the drawing 'the best thing I have ever done' (F, I, p. 71). Like the previous item, this was drawn for the Cyclographic Society, but it is in a more linear style of outline drawing, inspired by Flaxman and by German illustrators such as Moritz Retzsch (Grieve 1973b, p. 13).

10
Taurello's first sight of fortune
(s 39)
c. 1850–2
inscribed below drawing:
Frederic G. Stephens – from his
P.R. Brother / Dante G. Rossetti
brown ink on paper, 27.9 x 27.9 cm
Tate. Bequeathed by H.F. Stephens 1932
figure 91

The subject of the drawing was suggested by a brief passage from *Sordello*, a long narrative poem by Robert Browning (1840) set during the wars of the Guelphs and the Ghibellines. Taurello, the young man on the left, recalls how, when newly arrived at court, he was asked in jest by King Heinrich to rule instead of him. The King invested him with 'the silk glove of Constance'. Rossetti shows her taking off the glove, and delights in the details of medieval costume and townscape, derived from his admiration of the world depicted by Van Eyck and Memling. He had seen their work on his visit to Bruges and Ghent in 1849; on this trip he had taken with him a

cat. 7

cat. 8

cat. 9

Frederic G. Stephens – from his P.R Brother
Danti G. Rossetti

fig. 91
Taurello's first sight of fortune
c. 1850–2
Tate. Bequeathed by H.F. Stephens 1932
cat. 10

copy of Browning's poem (F, I, p. 114). The angular gestures, unsettling facial expressions and abrupt perspective are characteristics of the early phase of the Pre-Raphaelite style, emulating the 'primitive' qualities of early Italian and Flemish art.

11
The first anniversary of the death of Beatrice
(S 42)
signed and dated bottom left: Dante G. Rossetti / P.R.B. 1849; inscribed top right: Dante G. Rossetti / to his P R Brother / John E. Millais; above the curved top: Florence, 9th June 1291: The first anniversary of the death of Beatrice; by the window: Beata Anima bella, chi te vede, 9 Giugno / 1290; by the statue: FLORENTIA (on flag) and S Reparata, O:P:NS (below)
ink on paper, 40 x 32 cm
Birmingham Museums & Art Gallery. Presented by subscribers
figure 6

Below the drawing is an extract from Rossetti's recently completed translation of Dante's *Vita Nuova* (The New Life), giving the subject – Dante, absorbed in drawing an angel on the first anniversary of the death of Beatrice, is interrupted by the unexpected arrival of friends. The extremely flat and linear style, with harsh shading and hardly any modelling, is characteristic of early Pre-Raphaelitism, and is intended to evoke the archaism and purity of early Italian art. Every stroke of the pen is carefully controlled and Rossetti

includes tiny details and inscriptions to convey the exact location and time. Beatrice died on 9 June 1290, and the incident depicted is one year later. The location of Florence is indicated by the statue of the city's patron saint, Santa Reparata; the figure of Dante is based on the supposed portrait by Giotto, discovered in Florence in 1840 (a copy of this had been sent to Rossetti's father in 1841). On the back of the chair and above the window is the Alighieri coat of arms. The central figure is meant to be Dante's fellow poet Guido Cavalcanti: he is shown with a pen and ink holder around his neck and he wears a costume derived from a fresco in the 14th-century Spanish Chapel in Santa Maria Novella, Florence. Rossetti found it in a book often used by the Pre-Raphaelites as a source for costume, Camille Bonnard's *Costumes Historiques* (Grieve 1973b, p. 15). The furniture and musical instruments are also intended to be in period.

12
The Girlhood of Mary Virgin
(S 40)
1848–9
signed and dated bottom left: DANTE GABRIELE ROSSETTI / P.R.B. 1849
oil on canvas, 83.2 x 65.4 cm
Tate. Bequeathed by Lady Jekyll 1937
figure 9

Rossetti's first painting depicts the Virgin Mary as a girl seated with her mother, St Anne, and embroidering a lily. He felt

this was 'more probable and at the same time less commonplace' than standard depictions of her reading a book at her mother's knee, for example by Murillo. The lily is tended by a child-angel, whilst Mary's father St Joachim prunes a vine. In the background is the Lake of Galilee. Rossetti described his picture as 'underived from any source... a symbol of female excellence, the Virgin being taken as its highest type. It was not her *childhood* but *Girlhood*' (F, I, pp. 75–6; II, p. 134).

Rossetti also wrote two sonnets to go with the painting. When the work was first shown, the first sonnet was printed in the exhibition catalogue and the second was on the frame, but both are now printed on gold paper attached to the frame. The first sonnet emphasizes the theme of the painting as the purity and virtue of the Virgin's upbringing, whilst also looking forward to the Annunciation, the subject of Rossetti's second great early painting; the second sonnet explains some of the symbols in the painting and also returns to the theme of purity.

cat. 10

cat. 11

cat. 12

I

This is that blessed Mary, pre-elect
God's Virgin. Gone is a great while, and she
Was young in Nazareth of Galilee.
Her kin she cherished with devout respect:
Her gifts were simpleness of intellect
And supreme patience. From her mother's knee
Faithful and hopeful; wise in charity;
Strong in grave peace; in duty circumspect.
So held she through her girlhood; as it were
An angel-watered lily, that near God
Grows, and is quiet. Till one dawn, at home,
She woke in her white bed, and had no fear
At all, — yet wept till sunshine, and felt awed;
Because the fulness of the time was come.

II

These are the symbols. On that cloth of red
I' the centre, is the Tripoint, — perfect each
Except the second of its points, to teach
That Christ is not yet born. The books (whose head
Is golden Charity, as Paul hath said)
Those virtues are wherein the soul is rich:
Therefore on them the lily standeth, which
Is Innocence, being interpreted.
The seven-thorned briar and the palm seven-leaved
Are her great sorrows and her great reward.
Until the time be full, the Holy One
Abides without. She soon shall have achieved
Her perfect purity: yea, God the Lord
Shall soon vouchsafe His Son to be her Son.

Rossetti used an abundance of symbolic language to convey his meaning. The lily is a symbol of purity; the vine alludes to the Truth; the dove to the Holy Spirit; the lamp is a symbol of Piety; the rose is associated with the Virgin; the books, each a different colour, represent the three theological virtues and three of the four cardinal virtues (Justice being omitted): gold for Charity, blue for Faith, green for Hope, buff for Prudence, white for Temperance and brown for Fortitude. The picture also includes references to the future Passion of Christ — the red cloth, representing Christ's robe, is draped on a stone altar with the trellis above forming a cross, referring to the Crucifixion; in the foreground, the palm leaves and thorns represent the seven joys and seven sorrows of the Virgin. Faintly visible on the red cloth is a finely drawn triangle outlined in gold with an alpha and omega at the apex and a gold flame at the right-hand point; this is the Tripoint of the second sonnet and its left point is omitted because Christ is not yet born. The omission of Justice from the virtues may also be explained for the same reason as, according to St Ambrose, Justice was brought by Christ (Heffner 1985).

Two further levels of meaning would have been more apparent at the time of the first exhibition of the painting in 1849. The first is its connection with the contemporary Tractarian movement, which introduced greater ritual and dignity into Anglican church architecture, decoration and worship, through the use of symbolism, colour, the revival of church music and the use of embroidered vestments and decorative objects. The symbolism in the painting and the inclusion of embroidery, the stone altar, the lamp and other objects used in church ritual, such as the organ on the extreme right, refer to contemporary High Anglican practice, to which Rossetti's mother and his sisters subscribed. (His mother modelled for St Anne, whilst the Virgin was taken from his sister Christina.) Many contemporaries were hostile to Tractarianism, considering its features as covert examples of Roman Catholicism, especially when associated with excessive veneration of the Virgin Mary.

The second level of meaning arises from the archaic style of the painting, originally more marked than it is now, perhaps recalling the devotional images of the German Nazarene school. When first exhibited, the painting had an arched top and a different frame; the gilding on the haloes, the star on the angel's head, the lamp and the Virgin's hair was more pronounced, and some of the colours were originally lighter, for example Rossetti later repainted the angel's wings, originally white, to red. Rossetti and the Pre-Raphaelites intended this archaic style to emulate the holiness and purity of the early Italian period before Raphael, in a deliberate challenge to the accepted academic conventions of drawing, shading, colour and composition (Grieve 1973b, pp. 3–11).

Shown at the 'Free Exhibition' in London in 1849, one month before the opening of the Royal Academy Summer exhibition, this was the first publicly exhibited painting to bear the initials P.R.B.

13

Ecce Ancilla Domini!

(s 44)

1849–50

signed and dated bottom left:

DGR / March 1850

oil on canvas, 72.4 x 41.9 cm

Tate. Purchased 1886

figure 10

The subject of Rossetti's second painting, shown at the National Institution in London in 1850, is the Annunciation: the Angel Gabriel appears before the Virgin Mary to tell her that she is with child, and that her child is the Son of God. The title *Ecce Ancilla Domini* is Latin for 'Behold the handmaid of the Lord', the words spoken by Mary to the Angel Gabriel (Luke 1:38). Several models sat for this painting, including Rossetti's sister Christina for the Virgin and his brother William Michael for the angel.

Rossetti includes the traditional attributes of this subject, the lily for purity and the dove for the Holy Spirit, but otherwise rejects the conventional iconography of a winged Angel bringing the news to Mary kneeling in prayer. Instead of the sweetness and gracefulness usually associated with this subject, Rossetti couches it in disturbing and unfamiliar terms. The Angel Gabriel has no wings or conventional robes, but hovers above the floor with flames at his feet, his gown parted at one side to reveal his naked flank. A burst of radiant light emanating from his body casts harsh shadows. He holds a lily stem with three flowers, one still in bud, which he points at Mary's womb, making the lily a symbol of both the Trinity and the Virgin Birth. Mary is dishevelled after waking from sleep and shrinks back on the bed, staring fixedly at the lily stem with a mixture of fear and compulsion. Above her the lamp (associated with piety) is still lit, and in front of her is the embroidery stand with the red cloth that she was working with a lily in *The Girlhood of Mary Virgin* (cat. 12).

This echo of the earlier painting emphasizes that there is less illustrative detail and less elaboration of symbolism than in the earlier picture. *Ecce Ancilla Domini!* is stark and concentrated, expressing its meaning through the dramatic relationship of the two figures and the simplicity of the colour symbolism. The painting is divided into two areas by the almost vertical line down the centre; on one side is the Angel and on the other side Mary, as if in zones representing heaven and earth, with only the dove and the lily stem bridging the two sides. The picture is largely restricted to primary colours – blue for the Virgin (the heavens and the cloth at the head of the bed), red for Christ's Passion (the embroidery) and yellow or gold for holiness (the flames and the haloes). The colour scheme is dominated by white; this was an essential part of the idea from the start, for when Rossetti was planning it, his brother wrote that 'The picture…will be almost entirely white' (Fredeman 1975, p. 29). The primary colours, the fresco-like whiteness, the linear and vertical character of the design and the shallow space emulate the purity of archaic art, a purity that had its modern equivalent in the piety of Rossetti's subject (Grieve 1973b, pp. 12–24).

cat. 13

The early Pre-Raphaelite circle

The Pre-Raphaelites drew many portraits of each other, their families and friends. They could not often afford professional models and so they sat for characters in each other's paintings, but they also made portrait drawings as tokens of love and friendship; for example, after one of the Brothers had emigrated to Australia, the others drew their portraits to send out to him (cats. 16, 17; Ormond 1967).

By 1853, the original Brotherhood had disintegrated as a coherent group, but other artists entered the Pre-Raphaelite circle. The nature of the Pre-Raphaelite circle also changed from the early period. As the artists matured, the Brotherhood ceased to be a purely male society, and women – sisters, girlfriends, wives – became part of the group. Rossetti virtually stopped exhibiting in public after 1850; he formed his own network of likeminded friends, artists and patrons.

14
Christina Rossetti
(s 425)
c. 1848–50
pencil on paper, 15 x 11.5 cm
private collection

Rossetti's younger sister had already embarked on her career as a poet with a privately printed booklet of *Verses* in 1847. The drawing may have been made in connection with *The Girlhood of Mary Virgin* (cat. 12), for which she posed for the figure of Mary.

15
Thomas Woolner
(s 539)
dated lower right beneath mount: July / 52
pencil on paper, 15.5 x 14.6 cm
National Portrait Gallery, London

The sculptor and Pre-Raphaelite brother Thomas Woolner sailed from Plymouth on 24 July 1852 along with two other artists, Bernhard Smith and Edward Bateman, to seek their fortune in the Australian goldfields. This drawing must have been done very shortly before their departure. Australia was not a success for Woolner, and he returned to Britain in October 1854.

cat. 14

cat. 15

cat. 16

16

William Michael Rossetti
signed and inscribed bottom right:
D G Rossetti / to / Thomas Woolner /
Edward Bateman / Bernhard Smith;
dated bottom left: April 12 / 53
pencil on paper, 29 x 21 cm
National Portrait Gallery, London

17

William Holman Hunt
(s 341)
inscribed beneath the mount in another
hand: '12th April 1853. D.G. Rossetti
to Thomas Woolner, Edward Bateman,
Bernhard Smith'
pencil on paper, 27.4 x 20.5 cm
Birmingham Museums & Art Gallery.
Presented by subscribers

On 12 April 1853, eight months after Woolner
had left for Australia, William Michael and
Dante Gabriel gathered in Millais's studio
with the other three surviving Brothers,
Hunt, Millais and Stephens, and their friend
the sculptor Alexander Munro. They drew
portraits of each other and sent them to their
fellow artists in Australia, hence the dedi-
catory inscriptions.

William Michael Rossetti, Dante Gabriel's
younger brother, was only twenty-four when
this portrait was made, but he was already
prematurely bald. Though not himself an
artist, he had been a member of the original
Pre-Raphaelite Brotherhood. He worked as
a clerk in the Excise Office but was also
beginning to write art and literary criticism.

After receiving the portraits, Woolner
replied to William Michael from Australia
in September 1853, 'Your brother's drawing
of you is a very great boon to me: it looks as
calmly upon me as your own face was wont,
and as I contemplate it my own soul in some
unknown way holds communion with yours'
(Woolner 1917, p. 62).

The portrait of Hunt was drawn in Millais's
studio on the same occasion. Whilst Rossetti
was making this sketch of Hunt, Hunt was
himself drawing Rossetti in coloured chalks
(Manchester City Galleries).

18

Ford Madox Brown
(s 269)
signed and dated bottom right:
DGR (monogram) / Nov. / 52
pencil on paper, 17.1 x 11.4 cm
National Portrait Gallery, London

Brown first met Rossetti in 1848 after the
latter, admiring the older artist's work, wrote
asking Brown to give him painting lessons.
They became close friends. At the time this
drawing was made, Brown was working on
The Last of England (Birmingham Museums
& Art Gallery), the painting inspired by the
recent departure of Woolner for Australia.
Brown was impecunious and depressed,
considering emigration himself. His tense
and dishevelled appearance in Rossetti's
drawing may reflect Brown's mood of despair
at trying to make a living in Britain: he
described himself as 'intensely miserable very
hard up & a little mad' (Brown 1981, p. 78).

19

Emma Madox Brown
(s 272)
signed and dated bottom:
DGR (monogram) 1st May / 53
ink on paper, 12.5 x 10 cm
Birmingham Museums & Art Gallery.
Presented by subscribers

Brown's second wife Emma had 'a pink
complexion, regular features and a fine
abundance of beautiful yellow hair, the
tint of harvest corn' (W.M. Rossetti 1906,
I, p. 137). She has a wary expression in this
portrait, drawn by Rossetti by candlelight
shortly after the marriage, which took place
in secret on 5 April 1853, Rossetti being one
of only two friends present. Emma was the
illiterate daughter of a country bricklayer.
Brown had met her about 1848; she bore
his child Catherine in 1850, but they did
not marry until 1853.

20

Robert Browning
(s 275)
dated top left: October; top right: 1855
pencil, chalks, watercolour and bodycolour
on paper, 12 x 10.8 cm
Syndics of the Fitzwilliam Museum,
Cambridge

'His head is most stunning, and even hand-
some in the common sense of the term,'
wrote Rossetti of Browning after their first
meeting, in August 1851 (F, I, p. 181).
Browning's poetry was one of Rossetti's

cat. 17

cat. 18

cat. 19

youthful enthusiasms and a deep influence on his work. Rossetti started this watercolour during one of Browning's visits to London in 1855. Browning left for Paris before it was finished, but Rossetti, travelling to Paris to meet Elizabeth Siddal, completed it there.

Portraits of Elizabeth Siddal

Siddal entered the Pre-Raphaelite circle as a model about 1849–50. The daughter of a cutler, she worked in dressmaking and millinery; like Emma Madox Brown (cat. 19) she came from a lower social class than that of the Pre-Raphaelite painters. She sat for several artists of the Pre-Raphaelite circle, but in the early 1850s she developed a close relationship with Rossetti and became his principal obsession as model, muse, pupil and eventually wife, until her tragic death in 1862. During the 1850s, she posed for characters in Rossetti's paintings and may have been the inspiration for some of his poetry, but especially in the early and mid 1850s she was the subject of an intense series of portrait drawings. These show her in everyday dress, but nearly always passive and withdrawn; only occasionally does she appear in some activity, such as painting at her easel, reading or cutting a pattern.

Shy and reserved, kept by Rossetti away from polite society, she was frequently ill, and several of the drawings show her at Hastings, where she was sent by doctors for a change of air. Rossetti had various pet names for her, including Lizzie, the Sid, the Dove, Gug and Guggums, and drew her obsessively, as Brown noted on 7 October 1854: 'Called on Dante Rossetti saw Miss Siddall looking thinner & more deathlike & more beautiful & more ragged than ever, a real artist, a woman without parralel [sic] for many a long year. Gabriel…Drawing wonderful & lovely "Guggums" one after an other each

one a fresh charm each one stamped with immortality' (Brown 1981, p. 101).

In the mid to late fifties Siddal was plagued by ill health, and Rossetti must have contemplated breaking off the relationship. But after much hesitation he married her in 1860. The following year she gave birth to a stillborn child and in 1862 she died tragically from an overdose of laudanum. She had probably been suffering from post-natal depression, but it is not clear whether her death was an accident or suicide.

21

Elizabeth Siddal kneeling, playing a double pipe
(s 459; Surtees 1991, no. 3)
dated bottom right: 1852
pencil on paper, 19.6 x 13.6 cm
Visitors of the Ashmolean Museum, Oxford. Bequeathed by John N. Bryson 1977

This may be a study for an angel musician. A companion drawing (Ashmolean Museum, Oxford, s 460; Surtees 1991, no. 4) shows her with a stringed instrument.

22

Rossetti sitting to Elizabeth Siddal
(s 440)
dated bottom right: Sept 1853
brown ink on paper, 12.9 x 17.5 cm
Birmingham Museums & Art Gallery. Presented by subscribers

Elizabeth Siddal's reputation as an artist has been obscured by her role as Rossetti's muse,

cat. 20

cat. 21

cat. 22

cat. 23

cat. 24

cat. 25

cat. 26

cat. 27

cat. 28

cat. 29

cat. 30

cat. 31

fig. 92
Head of Elizabeth Siddal
reclining on a pillow
1850s
Syndics of the Fitzwilliam Museum,
Cambridge
cat. 37

model, mistress and wife. Rossetti gave her informal lessons, and her talent as an artist was eventually recognized by Ruskin, who gave her financial support. Here she is seen in Rossetti's studio at 14 Chatham Place, Blackfriars, drawing his portrait by lamplight; no drawing of him by her survives. The impression of immediacy and speed given by this sketch, done on writing paper with the ink in part shaded with the finger, belies the skill with which Rossetti has caught the intensity of their relationship.

23
Elizabeth Siddal asleep
(S 468; Surtees 1991, no. 13)
c. 1854
pencil on paper, 19.1 x 12.7 cm
private collection

24
Elizabeth Siddal standing at a window
(S 464; Surtees 1991, no. 15)
dated top left: Hastings May 1854
ink on paper, 22.2 x 9.7 cm
Victoria & Albert Museum, London
figure 83

25
Elizabeth Siddal reading
(S 465; Surtees 1991, no. 17)
dated bottom beneath chair:
Hastings / June 2. 1854
pencil with some ink on paper,
29.2 x 23.8 cm
Syndics of the Fitzwilliam Museum,
Cambridge

26
Elizabeth Siddal seated in an armchair
(S 495; Surtees 1991, no. 19)
1854
pencil on paper, 18.4 x 11.8 cm
The British Museum, London

27
Elizabeth Siddal seated by a window
(S 466; Surtees 1991, no. 20)
dated bottom left: Hastings June 1854
pencil and ink on paper, 23.3 x 17.8 cm
Syndics of the Fitzwilliam Museum,
Cambridge

28
**Head of Elizabeth Siddal full face,
looking down**
(S 472; Surtees 1991, no. 26)
signed and dated bottom left: DGR
(monogram) / Feb.6 / 1855
brown and black ink and wash on paper,
12.8 x 11.2 cm
Visitors of the Ashmolean Museum, Oxford
figure 20

29
**Head of Elizabeth Siddal,
looking down to the right**
(S 499; Surtees 1991, no. 27)
c. 1855
pencil on paper, 12.1 x 11.4 cm
Victoria & Albert Museum, London

30
Study of Elizabeth Siddal as Rachel
(S 74 A; Surtees 1991, no. 28)
c. 1855
pencil on paper, 32 x 16.6 cm
Birmingham Museums & Art Gallery.
Presented by subscribers

Posing on a card table with the flap raised, she is modelling for the figure of Rachel seated by a stone basin, looking at her reflection in a stream, in *Dante's Vision of Rachel and Leah* (cat. 45).

31
Study of Elizabeth Siddal as Delia
(S 62 D; Surtees 1991, no. 8)
c. 1855
pencil on paper, 41 x 32.2 cm
Birmingham Museums & Art Gallery.
Presented by subscribers
figure 56

In 1851 Rossetti began a watercolour, *The Return of Tibullus to Delia*, inspired by a famous elegy by the Roman poet Tibullus, in which the writer asks his mistress Delia to await his return chastely, spinning to while away the hours. The watercolour shows Tibullus entering to find Delia seated with her eyes closed, listlessly passing a strand of hair between her lips in an erotic gesture, and holding a shuttle in her other hand. The earliest study of Siddal in this role is dated 1851. The watercolour (private collection, S 62) was not completed until 1853, but this drawing is slightly later in date and probably relates to an intended replica.

cat. 32

cat. 33

cat. 34

32

Elizabeth Siddal painting at an easel
(s 488; Surtees 1991, no. 34)
1850s
pencil on paper, 25 x 20.3 cm
private collection

33

Elizabeth Siddal seated in a basket chair
(s 489; Surtees 1991, no. 42)
signed bottom right: DGR (monogram)
1850s
ink and brown wash on paper, 19.1 x 12.7 cm
private collection

34

Elizabeth Siddal cutting with scissors
(s 498; Surtees 1991, no. 44)
1850s
pencil on paper, 18.8 x 15.3 cm
The British Museum, London

35

**Elizabeth Siddal seated,
resting her head on one arm**
(s 487; Surtees 1991, no. 47)
1850s
pencil on paper, 16.2 x 10.5 cm
private collection

36

Elizabeth Siddal half-length
(s 476; Surtees 1991, no. 58)
1850s
pencil and brown and black ink on paper,
25.4 x 18.7 cm
private collection

37

**Head of Elizabeth Siddal
reclining on a pillow**
(s 477; Surtees 1991, no. 60)
1850s
pencil on paper, 26 x 25.4 cm
Syndics of the Fitzwilliam Museum,
Cambridge
figure 92

38

Study of Elizabeth Siddal for *Beata Beatrix*
(s 168 B)
probably 1850s
pencil on paper, 15 x 11.9 cm
William Morris Gallery
(London Borough of Waltham Forest)
exhibited at Liverpool only

Though the finished painting (cat. 98)
dates from 1863–70, this study must have
been made before 1862, the date of Elizabeth
Siddal's death.

cat. 35

cat. 36

cat. 37

Dante

The Florentine poet Dante Alighieri (1265–1321) was the national poet of the Rossettis, as Italians; he was their family poet (five Rossettis published literary works related to Dante); and he was Dante Gabriel Rossetti's personal poet, his namesake and intellectual mentor (as Dante had made Virgil his mentor in the *Divine Comedy*). From childhood Rossetti would have heard Dante's work discussed, along with contemporary politics, by the Italian political exiles who congregated around his father, Gabriele Rossetti, revered equally as a patriot and Dante scholar (indeed, the elder Rossetti interpreted the *Divine Comedy* as a political allegory relevant to the contemporary struggle for Italian liberation). If, as a boy, Rossetti was a more avid reader of modern 'Romantic' literature (the historical novels of Walter Scott, Goethe's *Faust*, the poems of Poe and the tales of E.T.A. Hoffmann), his affinity for Dante was manifest by 1848, when he announced the completion of his translation of Dante's *Vita Nuova* (F, I, p. 76; the translation was first published in 1861, cats. 90, 156). At the same time he was already planning a series of pictorial designs to accompany the translation. The *Vita Nuova* project can therefore be seen as the intellectual and artistic foundation of Rossetti's career both as poet and as painter. Perhaps it was in recognition of this that, soon after completing the translation, he altered his own name to identify himself with Dante. Although he had been christened 'Gabriel Charles Dante Rossetti', he chose from early 1849 to sign himself 'Dante Gabriel Rossetti'. Unsurprisingly, both his poetry and his painting demonstrate an intimate knowledge of Dante's *Divine Comedy*, the three-part vision of Hell, Purgatory and Paradise, epic in length and literary importance, on which his father had written extensively (see Milbank 1998, pp. 118–23). But the crucial text for Rossetti always remained the *Vita Nuova* (The New Life), the earlier and shorter work, in prose interspersed with verse, that tells the story of Dante's love for Beatrice on earth. Most of the Dante subjects in Rossetti's visual work derive from the *Vita Nuova* (see also cats. 11, 98, 143–4, 147). Moreover his Dante pictures tend to be more faithful to their textual source than Rossetti's other works based on literary texts (such as the Tennyson illustrations, cats. 76–83). But the *Vita Nuova* was much more important to Rossetti than a mere source of subjects. Its way of transforming autobiography into art, as well as its explorations of questions of artistic meaning and interpretation, inform all of Rossetti's work in both painting and poetry.

cat. 38

cat. 39

39

Beatrice meeting Dante at a marriage feast, denies him her salutation
(s 50 R I)
1855
watercolour on paper, 34.3 x 41.9 cm
Visitors of the Ashmolean Museum, Oxford

This is a close copy of a composition of 1851 (private collection, s 50), the first work in which Elizabeth Siddal serves as the model for Beatrice. The carriage of the figure's head, with upturned chin and a slight drawing back, is characteristic of many of the drawings of Siddal from the next few years. It is also appropriate to the subject from the *Vita Nuova*: Beatrice, disapproving of Dante's excessive (or perhaps indelicate) attentions to another woman (whom he has pretended to favour in order to conceal his purer love for Beatrice), declines to greet him when they meet at a marriage feast. This was one of the thirteen subjects from the *Vita Nuova* that Rossetti had envisaged for pictorial treatment as early as 1848 (F, I, p. 76). The watercolour illustrates the passage with the exactness that characterizes Rossetti's representations of subjects from Dante: '... I began to feel a faintness and a throbbing at my left side, which soon took possession of my whole body. Whereupon I remember that I covertly leaned my back unto a painting that ran round the walls of that house; and being fearful lest my trembling should be discerned of them, I lifted mine eyes to look on those ladies, and then first perceived among them the excellent Beatrice. And when

I perceived her, all my senses were overpowered by the great lordship that Love obtained, finding himself so near unto that most gracious being, until nothing but the spirits of sight remained to me....' (D.G. Rossetti 1911, p. 320). Dante then writes a sonnet about this episode, which continues the emphasis on the sense of sight, and on eye contact between Dante and Beatrice; this also forms the central incident of the watercolour (the bride and groom are thus relegated to the top left corner). The pale-toned fresco painting against which Dante leans represents haloed angels in attitudes that seem to refer to hearing and speech, the faculties Dante has lost as the sight of Beatrice rivets his gaze. This emphasis on the sense of sight is common to all of Rossetti's representations of Beatrice. It is an expression of ideal or spiritual love, since it preserves physical distance between the lovers yet can be overwhelming in emotional power, in this case robbing Dante of his other senses.

40

Giotto painting the portrait of Dante
(s 54)
signed and dated lower left:
DGR (monogram) Sept 1852
watercolour over pencil on paper,
36.8 x 47 cm
Collection Lord Lloyd-Webber
exhibited at Amsterdam only
figure 16

This complex subject can be interpreted on several different levels, just as Dante's own

works have traditionally been seen to contain multiple kinds of meaning. On the literal level, the picture represents a historical event: Giotto is painting Dante's portrait in the Bargello Chapel in Florence. The historicity of this incident (recorded in Vasari's *Lives of the Artists*) had apparently been confirmed by the discovery of such a portrait in that location in 1840 (see cat. 41). On a second level, the picture conveys a moral about the fame of artists and poets, with reference to a famous passage in canto XI of Dante's *Purgatorio*: 'In painting Cimabue thought to hold the field and now Giotto has the cry, so that the other's fame is dim; so has the one Guido taken from the other the glory of our tongue, and he, perhaps, is born that shall chase the one and the other from the nest' (Sinclair 1971, II, p. 147). Rossetti shows Cimabue peering over Giotto's shoulder, and Guido Cavalcanti to the left of Dante, holding a book by the older poet Guido Guinicelli, whose fame he has eclipsed. The implication of the *Purgatorio* passage would seem to be that the fame of Dante will supersede Cavalcanti's in turn, which might imply that Rossetti, by analogy, aspires to succeed Giotto. However, the context is a warning against pride (the sin punished on the first terrace of the mountain of Purgatory, where Dante hears these lines). The moral of Rossetti's picture may, then, be that the artist should work, not for worldly fame, but for the glory of art itself. Thus Giotto immortalizes the features of his great poet-contemporary, and Rossetti's picture keeps alive the memory of the early

cat. 40

cat. 41

Renaissance painters and poets. Rossetti devoted himself to reviving the fame not only of Dante, but also of Cavalcanti and Guinicelli, both of whom are among the poets he translated and published in his volume of 1861 (see cats. 90, 156).

The drawing also suggests further levels of meaning. The presence, alongside Dante, of Cavalcanti, Giotto and Cimabue refers to the idea of friendship, as well as to the sisterhood of the arts of painting and poetry. Moreover, Dante is shown looking at his beloved, Beatrice, who passes in a procession in the church below; as always in Rossetti's work, Dante's idealized love for Beatrice is represented by the act of looking (see cats. 39, 43, 147). Thus the picture, as Rossetti himself summed it up in a letter to his own close artist-friend Thomas Woolner, includes 'all the influence of Dante's youth – Art, Friendship and Love – with a real incident embodying them' (F, I, p. 224).

41
Dante in meditation holding a pomegranate
c. 1852
signed upper right: DGR (monogram)
ink and pencil on paper, 22.9 x 20 cm
Yale Center for British Art, New Haven, Paul Mellon Fund

This study for cat. 40 is presumably based on the watercolour copy, made by the English artist Seymour Kirkup for Rossetti's father, of the portrait uncovered in the Bargello Chapel in 1840 (see Milbank 1998, pp. 2–4);

it shows Dante from his left side, the viewpoint from which Giotto observes him in cat. 40. As in the Bargello portrait, Dante holds a pomegranate, prefiguring his later journey to Hell (by analogy with the story of Proserpina, who ate a pomegranate while in the underworld; see cat. 155). Because Proserpina returned to earth every year, the pomegranate was used in Christian symbolism to denote immortality. Perhaps its inclusion suggests that Dante's fame will, after all, be lasting, despite the warning of the *Purgatorio* (see cat. 40).

42
The first anniversary of the death of Beatrice
(S 58)
signed and dated bottom right:
DGR (monogram) / 1853
watercolour on paper, 42 x 61 cm
Visitors of the Ashmolean Museum, Oxford. Bequeathed by Mrs Thomas Combe 1894
exhibited at Liverpool only
figure 15

This is a watercolour version of the subject Rossetti had treated in 1849, his most thoroughgoing essay in the drawing style of the Pre-Raphaelite Brotherhood (cat. 11); the subject was one of thirteen from the *Vita Nuova* that Rossetti was already contemplating late in 1848 (F, I, 76). The watercolour retains many of the elements of the earlier drawing: the *vanitas* symbols, the religious image, the window-ledge that serves as a desk, the open door at the rear. However,

these are reorganized into a new composition, no longer in the strictest Pre-Raphaelite style: the figures and the spaces they occupy are volumetric rather than angular. The interior setting is at least as elaborate as that of the earlier drawing, but the inscriptions and heraldry that had helped to elaborate the subject matter have vanished. The complex background space, with a staircase that leads nowhere in particular, a spherical cistern with basin, towel and brush borrowed from a print by Dürer (Christian 1973, pp. 58–9), and vases of flowers, serves no obvious narrative function, but hints at the complicated designs of the watercolours of the later 1850s (cats. 86–7). The oval mirror in the corner marks the first appearance of an accessory that would become ubiquitous in Rossetti's work of the 1860s (and in his Chelsea house, where the abundance of mirrors was remarked by visitors).

43
The Meeting of Dante and Beatrice in Paradise
(S 116 D)
c. 1853–4
signed bottom left: DGR
watercolour, bodycolour and ink on paper, 29.2 x 25.2 cm
Syndics of the Fitzwilliam Museum, Cambridge
figure 14

This watercolour develops the right-hand scene of an earlier double composition, in pen-and-ink, representing parallel subjects

cat. 42

cat. 43

from the *Vita Nuova* and the *Divine Comedy*: the meeting between Dante and Beatrice in Florence, while Beatrice was still alive, and their meeting in Eden after her death (fig. 5). This is the second meeting, set in the Garden of Eden, or the Earthly Paradise, at the summit of the mountain of Purgatory. The pen-and-ink design includes an inscription quoting canto XXX of the *Purgatorio* (also printed on the frame of cat. 43), Beatrice's poignant assurance to Dante: 'Guardami ben; ben son, ben son Beatrice' ('Look at me well; I am, I am indeed Beatrice', Sinclair 1971, II, p. 397). As in Rossetti's other representations of Dante and Beatrice, the subject centres on an act of looking. Indeed Rossetti has conflated Beatrice's first appearance in canto XXX with the later scene, in cantos XXXI–XXXII, when she finally lifts her veil, and Dante is overwhelmed by the sight of her. This recalls the similar event, at the marriage feast in the *Vita Nuova* (cat. 39). Again Dante's other senses leave him, but now the experience is more profound; his sight is dazzled for a time, as though he had looked at the sun. The two attendants, playing psalteries of strange shape, perhaps represent both Beatrice's handmaids and psychopomp musicians, angels who escort the soul to Heaven (Powell 1993, p. 18).

44
Paolo and Francesca da Rimini
(S 75 R I)
signed and dated lower left of centre scene: DGR (monogram) / 1862; inscribed top of centre scene: O lasso!; bottom of left scene: Quanti dolci pensier Quanto disio; bottom of right scene: Menò costoro al doloroso passo!
watercolour on paper, 31.7 x 60.3 cm
Trustees of the Cecil Higgins Art Gallery, Bedford
figure 18

This ingenious tripartite composition places the poets Dante and Virgil in the centre against a gold background. The subject is not the story of Paolo and Francesca *per se*, but rather Dante's encounter with the lovers, and his pity for their tragic story, in canto V of the *Inferno*. Thus the inscription, which weaves through all three compartments, records Dante's exclamation: 'Alas, how many sweet thoughts, how great desire, brought them to the woeful pass!' (Sinclair 1971, I, p. 79). The left compartment offers a flashback to the 'sweet thoughts' and 'great desire': the adulterous lovers are moved to embrace as they read the story of Lancelot and Guenevere in a large illuminated book. On the right is the 'woeful pass' to which they are doomed for all eternity; they whirl in the relentless wind of the Second Circle of Hell, reserved for the lustful. The flames are Rossetti's invention, and suggest simultaneously the ardours of love and the torments of hell (although Dante

does not mention fires, Rossetti makes the flames blow diagonally in the wind that characterizes Dante's Second Circle). This is a larger copy, with slight variations, of a design first made in 1855 (Tate, S 75), as one of the *Divine Comedy* subjects commissioned by Ruskin (see cat. 45).

45
Dante's Vision of Rachel and Leah
(S 74)
1855
watercolour on paper, 35.2 x 31.4 cm
Tate. Bequeathed by Beresford Rimington Heaton 1940
figure 17

This watercolour represents the scene Dante sees in a dream, in canto XXVII of the *Purgatorio*, as he is about to enter the Garden of Eden (see cat. 43); Dante himself is glimpsed, observing the scene from the left background. Rachel and Leah, from the story of Jacob in Genesis, can be taken as allegories of the contemplative and active life: Rachel, on the left, contemplates her own reflection in the pool of water, while Leah, on the right, is actively engaged in gathering flowers to adorn herself. The two women also prefigure the pairing of Beatrice and Matilda in the following cantos. Ruskin, who commissioned this watercolour in 1855 along with the parallel subject, *The Vision of Matilda Gathering Flowers* (untraced), emphasized the doubled pairing in a letter to his protégée, Ellen Heaton, who acquired the watercolour from him. Ruskin was encour-

cat. 44

cat. 45

aging Rossetti at this period to attempt more elevated subjects, with religious or spiritual rather than romantic implications. Rossetti did not, however, respond to Ruskin's suggestions for further subjects from the *Purgatorio*.

A drawing of Elizabeth Siddal (cat. 30) appears to be a study for this watercolour.

46
Dantis Amor
(S 117 A)
c. 1860
inscribed upper left, around sun: QUI EST PER OMNIA SAECULA BENEDICTUS; lower right, around moon: QUELLA BEATA BEATRICE CHE MIRA/CONTINUAMENTE NELLA FACCIA/DI COLUI; on central diagonal line: L'AMOR CHE MUOVE IL SOLE E L'ALTRE STELLE; on sundial: 1290
brown ink on paper, 25 x 24.1 cm
Birmingham Museums & Art Gallery.
Presented by subscribers

The title *Dantis Amor*, or 'Dante's Love', summarizes the complex set of ideas brought together in this closely knit design, unusual for Rossetti in its non-naturalistic presentation, uniting symbolic pictorial elements with verbal texts. The quotation, from the end of the *Vita Nuova*, begins at bottom right, encircling the crescent moon, and continues at top left, where it surrounds the sun: 'that blessed Beatrice who now gazeth continually on His countenance *qui est per omnia saecula benedictus*' ('Who is blessed throughout all ages', D.G. Rossetti 1911, p. 346). This idea

is expressed visually in the drawing: the head of Beatrice, in the crescent moon, gazes upwards at the head of Christ in the sun (the same idea is represented in a different way in Rossetti's later *Beata Beatrix*, cat. 98). The allegorical figure of Love, in the centre, is also drawn from the *Vita Nuova*, in which Love appears to Dante in dreams (see cat. 147); the figure carries a sundial inscribed with the date of Beatrice's death, 1290, and pointing to the number associated with her (nine). Thus Beatrice's death is the visual pivot to the design, just as it is the conceptual pivot around which the *Vita Nuova* is organized. However, this emblematic summary of the *Vita Nuova* is also linked ingeniously to the *Divine Comedy*, the last line of which is inscribed on the diagonal dividing line: 'the Love that moves the sun and the other stars' (Sinclair 1971, III, p. 485). This quotation, too, is translated into visual terms, in the two areas of the background that contain the rays of the sun (in Christ's section) and the stars (in Beatrice's). As a whole, then, the design presents the two phases of Dante's love for Beatrice, earthly in the *Vita Nuova* and heavenly in the *Divine Comedy*, in cosmic unity.

Rossetti had envisaged elements of this composition as early as 1848, when he designed an 'emblematical frontispiece' for his translation of the *Vita Nuova* (F, I, p. 76). The figure of Love with the sundial reappeared between the two pen-and-ink compositions of 1849–50, representing the meetings of Dante and Beatrice on earth and in heaven (fig. 5; see cat. 43); in this context

it marks Beatrice's death, which separates the two meetings. In 1859 Rossetti repeated the two compositions of the meetings, and expanded the figure of Love into a third composition, *Dantis Amor* (fig. 93), on three panels painted in oils for a cabinet at Red House, built for William and Jane Morris in the early years of their marriage. The drawing *Dantis Amor* presents the fullest elaboration of the ideas explored in all of these works (and, with variations, in the later *Beata Beatrix*, cat. 98).

cat. 46

fig. 93
Dantis Amor
1860
Tate. Presented by F. Treharne James 1920

Love and Morality

One of the aims of the Pre-Raphaelites was to express important ideas in their art, and Rossetti remained true to this ideal. Between 1848 and the late 1850s his work was preoccupied with questions of love and morality. His chosen subjects often depict moments of strong emotion, or confrontations between innocence and debauchery. He was also fascinated with pairs and doubles, and with depicting artists at work. Most of his subjects were set in the past, but he attempted one major oil painting about contemporary morality, *Found* (cat. 57). Apart from this work, which was never completed, he painted no oils during this period, though many of his drawings represent ideas for oil paintings that were never executed. Rossetti seems to have found the medium of oils difficult and time-consuming; but equally, the painstaking and minute technique he used for many of his drawings must have required great patience and control. Rossetti's drawings and watercolours exhibit a variety of techniques, often original and experimental, and involving patching, scraping out and repainting. The results were highly expressive.

47
The Laboratory
(s 41)
1849
watercolour over ink on paper,
19.7 x 24.8 cm
Birmingham Museums & Art Gallery.
Presented by subscribers

Rossetti's first work in watercolour (over an ink drawing) illustrates Browning's poem of the same title, set in the 18th century. The scene takes place in a dark, intimate and over-crowded interior. The heroine visits an alchemist to obtain a phial of poison to kill her rival. With a virulent expression, she rises in her seat and clenches her fist in pent-up fury, as she gives up all her jewels and offers her mouth to the man to 'kiss if he will' in payment.

48
The Duenna
(s 675)
c. 1850–2
ink on paper, 18.1 x 12.3 cm
Syndics of the Fitzwilliam Museum,
Cambridge

This may be an illustration to Sheridan's comic opera *The Duenna* (1775). It shows a couple in 18th-century dress, the woman with a fan, and behind them, standing watchfully in the shadows, is the Duenna of the title. It is not clear whether the couple are engaged in amorous discourse, though the fan is often used as a symbol of flirtation or feminine luxury.

cat. 47

cat. 48

49
Love's Mirror
(s 668)
c. 1849–50
ink and wash on paper, 19.3 x 17.5 cm
Birmingham Museums & Art Gallery.
Presented by subscribers

A female artist in medieval dress is painting
her self-portrait using a mirror; her hand is
guided by a man who gazes intently into the
mirror at the woman's reflection. No one's
eyes meet, and a curious tension is created
by the reflected, painted and real faces of the
couple, like the *doppelgänger* images that so
fascinated Rossetti. The mirror reflects the
image of the two lovers, whereas the painting
shows only the self-portrait. The drawing is
partly autobiographical, as the woman is a
portrait of Elizabeth Siddal. Though not
dated, it is close in style to cat. 50, dated
1850, and may even date from the previous
year (Wildman 1995, p. 102). If this is correct, then this is Rossetti's earliest portrayal
of her; he may already have considered her
as his pupil as well as his model, though the
artist is a likeness of the sculptor Thomas
Woolner. The scene takes place in an artist's
studio: at the back are two maids, one of
whom plays with a cat. The drawing has an
alternative title, *A Parable of Love*, but if there
is a textual source it is unknown.

50
To caper nimbly in a lady's chamber
To the lascivious pleasing of a lute
(s 47)
signed and dated bottom left: Dante Rossetti
/ 1850; inscribed with title below
pencil and ink on paper, 21 x 17.1 cm
Birmingham Museums & Art Gallery.
Presented by subscribers

51
Borgia
(s 48)
1851 / 1854 / 1858–9
signed and dated bottom right: DGR 1851
(monogram added 1860)
watercolour on paper, 23.2 x 24.8 cm
Tullie House Museum and Art Gallery,
Carlisle
figure 23

In these two variants of the same subject, a
boy and a girl dance to the music of a *femme
fatale* playing the lute; the latter is flanked by
lecherous old men whilst an ape, traditionally symbolic of human vice, looks on.

The earlier drawing (cat. 50) was originally
described by William Michael Rossetti simply
as 'Music, with a dance of children' (Fredeman 1975, p. 84), but for Rossetti music was
often associated with sensual love. The title,
'To caper nimbly in a lady's chamber ...' perhaps
added after the drawing was complete, is
from Shakespeare's *Richard III* Act I, scene I.
As so often with Rossetti, the quotation is
only obliquely related to the subject. It sets
the mood but is not a literal source.

The following year Rossetti started a second
version of the same composition (cat. 51),
and later still he substantially reworked
it with scraping, patching and repainting
(Boyce 1980, pp. 7, 12, 25–6). He changed
the subject and the title, adopting sumptuous
colour and luxurious Renaissance costume
to develop the mood of sensuality and vice.
Whilst the first version seems to condemn
carnal love, the effect of the reworking seems
to celebrate it: this anticipates Rossetti's
paintings of the 1860s on the theme of
female beauty and sensuality. The woman
playing the lute now represents the notoriously wicked Lucrezia Borgia. The old man
on the right with his arm around her is Pope
Alexander VI. He waves the feather fan that
rested on the sofa in the drawing. On the left
her brother Cesare Borgia smells a rose in
her hair and beats in time to the music with
a knife on a wineglass. Lucrezia's gown,
with big puffed sleeves and decorated all over
with bows, was taken from a late 15th-century
Italian dress illustrated in Bonnard's *Costumes
Historiques* (Grieve 1978, p. 53).

cat. 49

cat. 50

cat. 51

52

Hesterna Rosa

(s 57)

signed and dated bottom left: Dante Rossetti 1853; inscribed below: Composed – 1850 – drawn, and given to his P.R. Brother Frederic G. Stephens – 1853

ink on paper, 19 x 23.5 cm

Tate. Bequeathed by H.F. Stephens 1932

The drawing is on a similar theme to the previous two items, a condemnation of carnal love, but here Rossetti points the moral through a typical use of contrasting pairs. In a lighted tent at night is a scene of debauchery with two gamblers throwing dice accompanied by two women. One woman wraps her arms around her lover; to her right is an ape, symbol of lechery. The other woman is having her hand kissed by her partner but turns away in shame from the scene of depravity; she gazes towards an innocent girl playing a lute. She is the 'yesterday's rose' of the title. The contrasting attitudes of the two women are exemplified in the two verses written below the drawing, Elena's song from Sir Henry Taylor's play in the style of an Elizabethan drama, *Philip van Artevelde* (1834):

Quoth tongue of neither maid nor wife,
To heart of neither wife nor maid:
'Lead we not here a jolly life
Betwixt the shine and shade?'

Quoth heart of neither maid nor wife
To tongue of neither wife nor maid:
'Thou wag'st, but I am worn with strife,
And feel like flowers that fade.'

53

Boatmen and Siren

(s 63)

c. 1853

inscribed bottom right: Lo marinaio oblia, / che passa per tal via

brown ink on paper, 11 x 18.4 cm

Manchester City Galleries

A man in a boat tries desperately to restrain his companion from being lured to death by the intense gaze of the siren, whose hair streams out in the wind as her boat speeds by. The inscription is from a *canzone* by the Italian Renaissance poet Jacopo da Lentino, which Rossetti translated in *The Early Italian Poets* (published 1861; cats. 90, 156):

I am broken, as a ship
    Perishing of the song
Sweet, sweet and long, the songs the sirens know.
    The mariner forgets,
    Voyaging in those straits,
And dies assuredly.

(D.G. Rossetti 1911, p. 445)

54

Fra Angelico painting

(s 694)

undated; probably mid to late 1850s

brown ink and wash on paper, 17.8 x 11.1 cm

Birmingham Museums & Art Gallery. Presented by subscribers

55

Giorgione painting

(s 695)

undated; probably mid to late 1850s

brown ink and wash on paper, 11 x 17.6 cm

Birmingham Museums & Art Gallery. Presented by subscribers

Rossetti made a number of drawings featuring artists at work, as he believed that they possessed special powers. In one drawing (cat. 54), Fra Angelico kneels at an easel to paint the Virgin and Child whilst a monk leaning on the easel reads to him from a prayer book or Bible. Beyond are a crucifix and a bottle-glass window. In another drawing (cat. 55), Giorgione paints a seated girl with long hair and dress in the Venetian style, as three well-dressed men look on, two white and one, at the right, black. The two drawings seem to embody a contrast between sacred and secular art; this is reflected in Rossetti's use of shape, the tall narrow format being preferred for religious subjects, as in *Ecce Ancilla Domini!* (cat. 13; Grieve 1973b, p. 23). Fra Angelico was, for the Pre-Raphaelites as for many contemporary writers on art, the prototype of the spiritual painter (Dietrich 2000, p. 66). Giorgione was a

cat. 52

cat. 53

cat. 54

more personal enthusiasm of Rossetti: he admired Giorgione's *Concert Champêtre* in the Louvre and wrote a sonnet about it, conveying its atmosphere of listless sensuousness (published in *The Germ*) (F, I, p. 114; D.G. Rossetti 1911, p. 188).

56
Study for *Found*
(s 64 B)
signed and dated bottom left: DGR (monogram) 1853; inscribed along lower edge: I remember thee: the kindness of thy youth, the love of thy betrothal (Jeremiah 2:2); and on the gravestone, top left: There is m[ore] joy am[ong] the ange[l]s in hea[ven] one sinn[e]r that (cf. Luke 15:7)
black and brown ink and wash with white heightening on paper, 20.5 x 18.2 cm
The British Museum, London
figure 94

57
Found
(s 64)
1854–5 / 1859–81
oil on canvas, 91.4 x 80 cm
Delaware Art Museum, Samuel and Mary R. Bancroft Memorial, 1935
figure 13

Rossetti's only attempt at a modern life moral subject represents a 'fallen woman', an urban prostitute confronted by a former suitor, a reminder of her earlier, more innocent life in the country. It gave the artist a great deal of trouble on account of his difficulties with perspective, drawing and technique, and he never finished it.

He described it in 1855: 'The picture represents a London street at dawn, with the lamps still lighted along a bridge which forms the distant background. A drover has left his cart standing in the middle of the road (in which, i.e. cart, stands baa-ing a calf tied on its way to market) and has run a little way after a girl who has passed him, wandering in the streets. He has just come up with her and she, recognizing him, has sunk under her shame upon her knees, against the wall of a raised churchyard in the foreground, while he stands holding her hands as he seized them, half in bewilderment and half guarding her from doing herself a hurt. These are the chief things in the picture, which is to be called "Found", and for which my sister Maria has found me a most lovely motto from Jeremiah....The calf, a white one – will be a beautiful and suggestive part of the thing...' (F, II, p. 13).

The ink drawing of 1853 (cat. 56) shows Rossetti's most complete realization of his idea, including some symbolic details not in the oil, for example the contrast between the black of the girl's shawl and the white of the man's smock; the two birds carrying straw from the cart to make a nest; the figures on the bridge including a sleeping vagrant and a policeman; the discarded rose in the gutter; and the gravestone above the girl with an incomplete inscription on the theme of forgiveness. The girl's plight is paralleled in that of the calf, an innocent animal trapped and on its way to be sold. The motto, with the word espousal changed to betrothal (which Rossetti thought a more accurate translation from the Hebrew), is written along the bottom of the drawing of 1853: *I remember thee; the kindness of thy youth, the love of thy betrothal.* Yet the picture remains ambiguous. Is the prostitute rejecting salvation or is she accepting it; or is she repentant but unable to escape her fate, like the calf? Rossetti started painting the subject in oils in the autumn of 1854, probably the unfinished version now in Carlisle (s 64 M). Ford Madox Brown recorded him 'getting on slowly with his calf he paints it in all like Albert Durer hair by hair & seems incapable of any breadth...From want of habit I see nature bothers him' (Brown 1981, p. 106). After he met Fanny Cornforth (see fig. 12) in the late 1850s Rossetti changed the head of the woman to portray her; the rosebuds scattered over her dress replace the rose in the gutter seen in the drawing. This oil version was probably started after November 1859, when it was commissioned by the Newcastle patron James Leathart. Rossetti later enlarged the canvas, and worked on it intermittently, but without enthusiasm, often laying it aside for other things. His assistants Henry Treffry Dunn and Frederic Shields helped him with parts of it, and he himself worked on it as late as 1881. It was still incomplete at his death, after which further work may have been done by Dunn and Burne-Jones.

When Rossetti had begun the painting in the early 1850s moral subjects in modern dress and contemporary settings were current

cat. 55

cat. 56

cat. 57

within the Pre-Raphaelite circle. Rossetti's views on the moral content of pictures changed radically in the late 1850s, and in the final analysis Rossetti was 'thoroughly indisposed to ameliorate anybody's condition by means of pictures' (Stephens 1894, p. 3). Nevertheless the subject was important to him, otherwise he would not have persisted with the painting so long. His early poem 'Jenny' concerns a young man's visit to a prostitute; he often painted women who had sinned and repented, such as Gretchen, the Magdalene and Guenevere, and he wrote a sonnet for *Found* in 1881 (Grieve 1976, pp. 1–17).

58
Writing on the sand

(S 111)
signed and dated bottom right:
DGR (monogram) / 1859
watercolour on paper, 26.3 x 24.1 cm
The British Museum, London
figure 19

A man and a woman holding hands walk along a windy beach. Their clothes and hair flutter in the wind; the man draws a rough outline of her face in the sand with his stick. The subject may have autobiographical meaning, for it was painted at the time when Rossetti was examining his relationship with Elizabeth Siddal, unable to decide whether or not to marry her: there is a drawing of the same subject with Elizabeth Siddal's face (c. 1858, private collection, S 111 A). The contrast of the billowing crinoline, revealing

a glimpse of ankle, with the figures of the naked bathers in the distance may be intended as a joke; the subject has something in common with contemporary cartoons of seaside subjects by John Leech and others.

The watercolour was made for the actress Ruth Herbert, one of Rossetti's favourite models, and the features of the lady are probably hers; the man is a portrait of Richard Holmes, later Librarian of Windsor Castle. For the background, Rossetti, impatient with the effort of painting a real landscape, borrowed two sketches of Babbacombe Bay, Dorset, from his friend the artist George Price Boyce (Boyce 1980, p. 24). A Boyce watercolour of Babbacombe Bay is in the Astley Cheetham Art Gallery, Stalybridge, though it does not correspond to the background in the Rossetti.

59
Study for *Bonifazio's Mistress*

(S 121 B)
c. 1856
ink on paper, 19.4 x 17.1 cm
Birmingham Museums & Art Gallery.
Presented by subscribers

'It is a subject from an old story of mine — a woman dying while her lover is painting her portrait,' wrote Rossetti (F, II, p. 322). The story 'St Agnes of Intercession' was written for the fifth number of *The Germ*, which folded after four issues (D.G. Rossetti 1911, pp. 557–70). It is a strange tale about a contemporary artist and his alter ego, an early Italian painter. The modern artist, haunted

by an old portrait he had seen in a book, went to Italy to find it. It turned out to be a Renaissance portrait of a woman dressed up in her finery and jewels, dying whilst being painted: she had the face of the woman the artist loved. A self-portrait of the early Italian painter likewise bore his own features. This is another version of the story of the *doppelgänger*, seen also in *How They Met Themselves* (cat. 89). The woman has fallen back in her chair dead, supported by her attendants, whilst the painter has dropped his palette and kneels before her, trying to revive her. An etching of the same subject by Millais was intended to accompany Rossetti's story in *The Germ* (repr. Fredeman 1975, fig. 8). This is a study for a watercolour in a private collection (1860, S 21).

60
Cassandra

(S 127)
signed and dated lower right:
DGR (monogram) 1861
ink on paper, 33 x 46.4 cm
The British Museum, London

This elaborate pen-and-ink drawing represents the Trojan hero Hector departing for the battle in which he will be slain. Of all Rossetti's subjects this has the surest claims to high status in the High Art tradition: it represents the crucial turning-point in the greatest war of classical antiquity. Rossetti, however, treats the subject not as a history painting in the classical tradition, but rather in the manner of his medievalizing

cat. 58

cat. 59

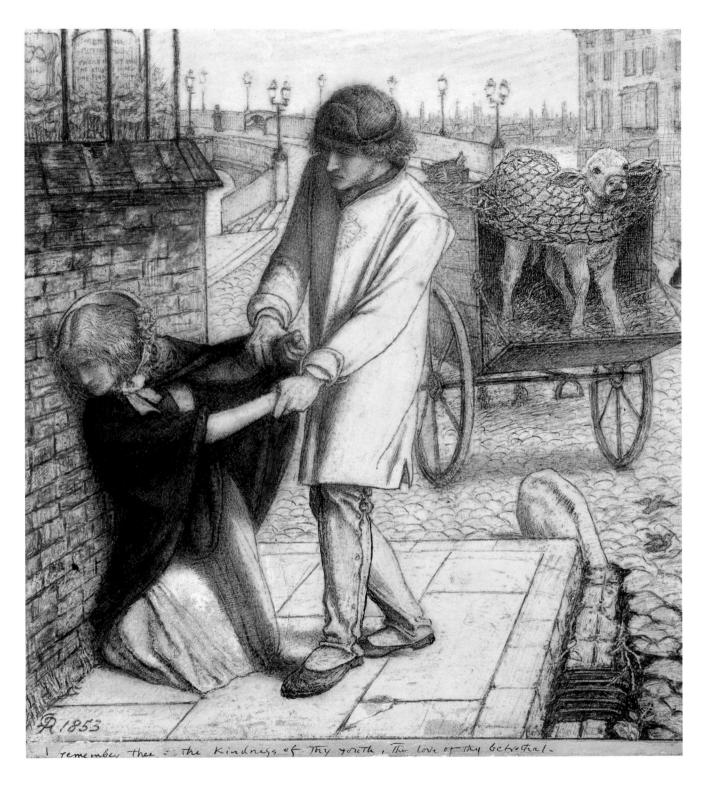

I remember thee: the Kindness of thy youth, The love of thy betrothal.

fig. 94
Study for *Found*
1853
The British Museum, London
cat. 56

work of the late 1850s. Indeed, the subject is a version of the most frequent theme, knights departing for battle, found in drawings by Burne-Jones and Siddal as well as Rossetti; it is one of the earliest explorations of the medievalizing approach to classical subject matter that would become prominent in the group's work in the 1860s. The cast of characters and style are closely related to William Morris's unfinished poem *Scenes from the Fall of Troy* (begun 1857), and to medieval and Renaissance retellings of the story of Troy, in particular Chaucer's *Troilus and Criseide* and Shakespeare's *Troilus and Cressida*.

The principal classical source, Homer's *Iliad*, is invoked in several of the episodes. On the left, Hector's wife Andromache appears with their baby, Astyanax, behind Hector, alluding to one of the most famous incidents in the *Iliad*: Hector's farewell to his wife and child, when his plumed helmet frightens the child (Book VI). Paris and Helen (see cat. 99) are seen towards the right dallying on a couch, as in an episode from Book III. However, the central incident, Cassandra prophesying doom for the Trojan cause, is not found in Homer, and the overall organization of the drawing, a compilation of separate episodes from the Trojan War, is more reminiscent of Morris's *Scenes* than of the unified action of the ancient epic. The central characters, who include Priam and Hecuba behind Helen's head, are fitted ingeniously into a compositional design framed by the warriors exhorting one another to battle. Despite the classical sub-

ject, the intricacy of the design and the dramatic edge-cropping are typical of the medievalizing illustrations and watercolours of the late 1850s (for example cats. 79–80, 86–7).

cat. 60

Religious subjects

Rossetti regarded the Virgin Mary as the highest ideal of female virtue. Following on from his early oils, he conceived a number of other subjects about her, stressing her purity. He was also fascinated by the contrasting image of Mary Magdalene, the repentant sinner. Though he began with the traditional figures from the Bible, his interpretations and his imagery were always personal and deeply felt. In technique, Rossetti's drawings and watercolours were equally personal and original, conveying intense effects even on a small scale.

Though most of his work was not publicly exhibited, he undertook one major public commission, the altarpiece for the recently restored Llandaff Cathedral, Cardiff, *The Seed of David* (cat. 64). This was on a much larger scale than he was used to, and the nature of the commission dictated a more conventional technique. Even so, a large-scale altarpiece in itself was unusual for the period; the other religious paintings of the Pre-Raphaelites, such as those by Holman Hunt, were exhibition pictures, not made to be shown in churches.

61

The Passover in the Holy Family
(s 78)
1854–5
watercolour on paper, 40.6 x 43.2 cm
Tate. Presented by Charles Ricketts
in memory of Henry Michael Field 1916
figure 27

Rossetti imagines Jesus and his family preparing for the feast of the Passover, 'a subject which must have actually occurred during every year of the life led by the Holy Family' (F, II, p. 73). The ritual was prescribed in Exodus 12:1–13. Every household was to slaughter a lamb and to mark the doorposts and lintels of their houses with its blood as a sign that the Lord would pass over and not visit the plague on the Israelites. The lamb was to be roasted and eaten with bitter herbs and unleavened bread, and the ritual meal was to be eaten in haste, with shoes on the feet ready for quick departure. Rossetti shows Zachariah marking the doorposts and lintel of the hut with the lamb's blood, from a bowl held by Jesus, standing in the centre. John kneels to fasten Jesus's sandal, and Mary stoops to gather bitter herbs. In the unfinished section, top left, Joseph holds the lamb whilst Elizabeth lights the fire to roast it. Within the house the table is laid with bread and wine. The subject stresses the continuity between the Jewish and Christian religions, making a typological link between Christ's sacrifice and that of the Passover lamb.

cat. 61

cat. 62

The watercolour was commissioned by Ruskin, who complained that Rossetti kept altering it, for example changing Jesus's robe from white to red. Ruskin eventually took it from Rossetti before it was ready, and thus it remains unfinished, some parts being more detailed than others. The models were Elizabeth Siddal for the Virgin, a family servant named Williams for Zachariah and a schoolboy for Jesus.

62
The Annunciation
(s 69)
1855, retouched 1858
watercolour on paper, 35.6 x 24.1 cm
private collection
figure 30

As in *Ecce Ancilla Domini!* (cat. 13) Rossetti has devised a deliberately unconventional version of the subject, in this case showing the Virgin Mary out of doors, washing clothes in a stream, startled by the appearance of the Angel Gabriel, brightly lit in the trees, his wings folded in front of him. The white lilies traditionally associated with the subject and representing purity are here shown growing in the stream with purple irises, and the use of green is especially vivid. Though surrounded by a later frame, the wood-grained mount is original and is inscribed along the top: *My Beloved is mine and I am his: he feedeth among the lilies*, and at the bottom: *hail, thou that art highly favoured: blessed art thou among women* (the first is Song of Solomon 6:3, the second is Luke 1:28).

63
The Seed of David
(s 105 b)
1855–7
watercolour on paper, triptych, centre :
40.6 x 29.2 cm; wings: 27.9 x 13.3 cm
Tate. Purchased 1924

64
The Seed of David
(s 105)
1858–64
oil on canvas, triptych, centre:
230 x 150 cm; wings: 185.5 x 62 cm
Llandaff Cathedral, Cardiff
figure 26

65
Study of Jane Morris for the Virgin in *The Seed of David*
(s 105 d)
1861
signed and dated bottom right:
DGR (monogram) / Sept. 1861
pencil on paper, 27 x 25.7 cm
The Society of Antiquaries of London (Kelmscott Manor)
exhibited at Liverpool only

66
Study of William Morris for David as King in *The Seed of David*
(s 105 j)
c. 1861
pencil on paper, 24.5 x 22.3 cm
Birmingham Museums & Art Gallery.
Presented by subscribers

In 1856 Rossetti received the commission to paint a large-scale altarpiece for Llandaff Cathedral, Cardiff, through the architect J.P. Seddon, who was working on the interior. Rossetti proposed a triptych, originally with a central *Nativity* flanked by *King David* and *Paul,* representing worship, song and sermon, the three major functions of a cathedral. This was considered too Roman Catholic, and the subject was altered to more democratic imagery, described by Rossetti as 'intended to show Christ sprung from high and low in the person of David, who was both Shepherd and King, and worshipped by high and low – a King and a Shepherd – at his nativity' (D & W, II, p. 508). The title *The Seed of David* alludes to David being the ancestor of Christ.

In the central panel of *The Adoration* a kneeling angel accompanies the Shepherd and the King in the stable. Mary holds out the Christ Child's hand for the Shepherd to kiss, and his foot for the King, 'so showing the superiority of poverty over riches in the eyes of Christ; while one lays his crook, the other his crown, at the Saviour's feet.' Angels look on from the rear and play musical instruments above. The left-hand wing, *David as Shepherd*, shows him as a youth aiming his sling at Goliath. On the right-hand wing the richly dressed *David as King*, seated on a peacock throne, plays on the harp.

The watercolour design for the triptych is in a more angular, earlier style; its central section was first painted in 1855 as a *Nativity* for Ruskin, and later adapted to form the model for the altarpiece, with the side scenes

cat. 63

cat. 64

added (Marsh 1999b, p. 608). In the earlier version, the Virgin and Child are facing in the opposite direction, the angel is standing and Joseph has a more prominent position. The Virgin in the watercolour is of the Elizabeth Siddal type; Ruth Herbert was the original model for the Virgin in the oil, but in 1861 the face of Jane Morris was substituted, and William Morris, then aged twenty-seven, sat for David as King. The more rounded, fully modelled style of the final work was influenced by Rossetti's growing enthusiasm for Venetian art, encouraged by Ruskin, who wished to purge Rossetti's work of its quaintness and minuteness.

William Michael Rossetti considered the real subject as 'the equality in the eyes of God of all sorts and conditions of men from the monarch to the peasant' (W.M. Rossetti 1884). This relates to the cathedral's aim of bringing all classes together for worship (Marsh 1999b, p. 609).

67
Study for *Mary Magdalene*
at the door of Simon the Pharisee
(s 109 c)
c. 1853
brown ink on paper, 23.4 x 18.4 cm
Birmingham Museums & Art Gallery.
Presented by subscribers

68
**Mary Magdalene at the door
of Simon the Pharisee**
(s 109)
1858–9
ink on paper (mounted on linen),
52.7 x 45.7 cm
Syndics of the Fitzwilliam Museum,
Cambridge
figure 32

Mary Magdalene, on her way to a wedding, turns to Christ and renounces the material world of sensual love, repenting of her sins. She enters the house of Simon the Pharisee, where Christ is at table. Subsequent to the moment of spiritual awakening depicted by Rossetti, Mary anointed Christ's feet with oil, proving her love, and was rewarded with forgiveness of her sins. The subject can be interpreted as a Biblical equivalent to *Found* (cat. 57); the confrontation between secular and spiritual, guilt and forgiveness, enacted in *Found* by the prostitute and her innocent suitor here becomes Mary Magdalene's repentance of sin at the sight of Christ.

Rossetti first mentioned the subject in 1853, when he was working on *Found* (F, I, p. 271), and the smaller drawing (cat. 67) may date from this period. More broadly executed than the larger work, it shows Mary Magdalene going up a stair towards Christ; an old woman tries to stop her, and two lovers look on. Rossetti returned to the subject in 1858–9, working it up into the powerful large drawing (cat. 68), crowded with figures and minutely finished in a style

showing his study of Dürer. The direction has been reversed, and the pair of lovers has become an elaborate wedding procession with musicians, garlands of flowers and richly patterned silk fabrics. Ruth Herbert was the model for the magnificently sensual figure of Mary Magdalene, casting out roses from her luxuriant hair; the Magdalene is traditionally depicted with long, flowing hair, both for its erotic associations and because she used it to wipe the feet of Christ. The richly dressed figures in the centre were described by Rossetti as Mary's lover and a woman, both 'laughingly trying to turn her back' (see s, p. 62). Burne-Jones modelled for Christ, whose stark profile appears in the window, a representation more symbolic than realistic; Simon the Pharisee and his servant are seen in the shadowy interior preparing the meal.

The theme is amplified by details such as the beggar girl who has been given food from the feast; the fawn (drawn from nature) representing the soul longing for God (Psalm 42); and the sunflower, perpetually turning towards the sun, a traditional symbol of longing (Grieve 1978, pp. 43–5).

cat. 65

cat. 66

cat. 67

69
Mary Nazarene
(s 87)
c. 1855
watercolour on paper, 34.3 x 19.7 cm
Tate. Purchased 1911
figure 28

Mary is shown tending a lily, symbolic of
purity, and a rose, the flower particularly
associated with her. The dove of the Holy
Spirit hovers over the flowers. This is one
of the scenes in the life of Mary planned
by Rossetti after painting her girlhood
(cat. 12): the title alludes to her living at
Nazareth. Rossetti at first intended it as
part of a triptych, never realized. The central panel was to show the Holy Family eating
the Passover meal. On one side would have
been this scene of the young Mary and on
the other *Mary in the House of St John*, showing
her as an old woman after the Crucifixion.
Mary is dressed unusually in green, perhaps
symbolic of spring and youth (Grieve 1973b,
p. 17; Grieve 1978, pp. 32–3).

70
**Mary Magdalene leaving
the house of feasting**
(s 88)
signed and dated bottom right:
DGR (monogram) / 1857
watercolour on paper, 35.6 x 20.6 cm
Tate. Purchased 1911
figure 29

Mary Magdalene is leaving the revellers,
holding her traditional attribute, the jar of
ointment, which she used to anoint Christ's
feet. Her own feet are bare and her hair
is long and loosely flowing, as is traditional
in representations of the Magdalene. Christ
is shown as a minute figure kneeling in the
distance. Though related in subject to cat.
68, this is a simpler version of the theme of
the Magdalene's repentance. The subject was
probably made as a pendant to *Mary Nazarene*
(cat. 69; Grieve 1978, pp. 42–3), contrasting the purity of the Virgin with the penitent
Magdalene. Rossetti has also employed colour
symbolism, giving the Magdalene a red robe,
for passion. The simplified geometrical
form of the steps, the well and buildings in
the background appears to be based on the
study of medieval manuscript illumination,
though Rossetti has shown the steps covered
in moss.

cat. 68

cat. 69

cat. 70

Romantic Medievalism

Rossetti's childhood reading of Sir Walter Scott's novels and medieval ballads nurtured a fascination with the Middle Ages. Medieval subjects appeared in his work from the early 1850s, and his interest developed through his reading of the legend of King Arthur and through his friendship with Ruskin, who encouraged him to study medieval art, especially illuminated manuscripts. After 1856, when he met the young William Morris and Burne-Jones, also enthusiasts for the Middle Ages, Rossetti's interest became more intense, and in a group of works of c. 1857 he created a highly original and imaginative vision of the Middle Ages. This vision was seen in the Oxford Union murals (1857), which faded almost as soon as they were painted; and it received a wider circulation through Rossetti's book illustrations, particularly those for Moxon's edition of Tennyson, published 1857.

The high point of Rossetti's medieval phase is a group of watercolours mostly from 1857. They exhibit intensely glowing colour and playfully inventive details of costume, furniture and heraldic devices. Their shallow spaces and rectilinear compositions emphasize flatness and surface pattern. They do not attempt to recreate or reproduce the reality of medieval life, but to evoke a world of the imagination. Their rejection of realism or narrative in favour of mood and suggestion make these pioneering works, leading towards the formal abstraction of the Aesthetic Movement.

71
Carlisle Wall
(s 60)
signed and dated right:
DGR (monogram)
Carlisle 1853
watercolour on paper, 24.1 x 16.8 cm
Tate. Bequeathed by Miss E.K. Virtue Tebbs 1949 (on loan to Ashmolean Museum, Oxford)
figure 95

Also called *The Lovers*, this richly coloured picture of a passionate embrace on the windswept battlements of an ancient castle wall was inspired by Rossetti's enthusiasm for the medieval Border Ballads, from his reading of such collections as *Reliques of Ancient English Poetry* (1765) by Thomas Percy and Sir Walter Scott's *Minstrelsy of the Scottish Border* (1802–3). Rossetti painted it after a visit to Carlisle in late June 1853, whilst on a visit to his friend William Bell Scott, who was Master of the School of Design in Newcastle. The overall red tonality suggests that the title may be derived from the motto 'The sun shines red on Carlisle Wall' (Sharp 1882, p. 150).

72
The Ballad of Fair Annie
(s 68)
c. 1855
brown and black ink over chalk on paper, 14.6 x 16.5 cm
private collection

cat. 71

cat. 72

fig. 95
Carlisle Wall
1853
Tate.
Bequeathed by Miss E.K. Virtue Tebbs 1949
(on loan to Ashmolean Museum, Oxford)
cat. 71

The ballad *Fair Annie*, published by Sir Walter Scott in *Minstrelsy of the Scottish Border* (1802, II, p. 102), tells the story of two sisters, one wealthy and one poor. The poor sister is the mistress of Lord Thomas, by whom she has had seven children; but he is engaged to marry the rich sister. After long separation the two sisters meet: the rich one gives her dowry to the poor sister, who finally marries Lord Thomas. Rossetti depicts the dramatic moment when the two sisters meet, in a confined, cottage-like interior with a child sleeping in a recess over a bunk bed. The dress of the sisters reveals their contrasting fortunes, and the geometrical arrangement of the rectangular spaces and built-in furniture is strikingly original, articulating the composition whilst avoiding deep recession. The drawing was made for a book of Scottish ballads to be edited by William Allingham, for which Rossetti and Elizabeth Siddal were to make illustrations; it was never published (F, I, pp. 342, 354).

73
Arthur's Tomb
(S 73)
1854–5
signed and inscribed bottom right:
DGR (monogram) / 1854 Arthur's Tomb
watercolour on paper, 23.3 x 37.4 cm
The British Museum, London
figure 25

After King Arthur's death and the dissolution of the Round Table, his widow, Queen Guenevere, became a nun at Almesbury

(present day Malmesbury). Her former illicit lover, Sir Launcelot, came to see her and demanded that she kiss him, but she repudiated him. Rossetti took the incident from Sir Thomas Malory's *Morte d'Arthur* (XXI, chapters 9–10) but conflated it with the description of Arthur's tomb (XXI, chapter 7). The inclusion of the tomb, which was at Glastonbury, emphasizes the guilt of both parties.

Rossetti depicts the dramatic moment of confrontation between the two. The angular, doll-like gestures, characteristic of Rossetti's style at this time, are effective in conveying the highly charged emotions, the brazen persistence of Launcelot and the ambiguous refusal of Guinevere. Arthur's effigy lies stiffly on the tomb, on the sides of which are depicted earlier episodes in the story: Arthur and Guenevere in the act of knighting the kneeling Launcelot, and a dove showing the Holy Grail to the knights of the round table. The red of Launcelot's gown is symbolic of passion; the apple tree on the right and the snake and apple lower left are associated with temptation and original sin.

The composition carries echoes of Titian's *Sacred and Profane Love* and the woodcut of the tomb of Adonis in the famous Renaissance book, the *Hypnerotomachia Poliphili* (Bentley 1976). This was Rossetti's first Arthurian subject: he dated it 1854, but it was not finished until 1855 (F, II, p. 64). Already at this date Rossetti had developed a highly original use of watercolour, minutely hatched and stippled, sometimes

mixed with gum, to convey the glowing colour of his vision of the medieval world.

74
The Maids of Elfen-Mere
(S 67)
1854
ink on paper, 12.7 x 8.3 cm
Yale Center for British Art, New Haven, Paul Mellon Fund

75
The Maids of Elfen-Mere
The Music Master, A love story, with two series of Day and Night Songs by William Allingham, published by Routledge, 1855, illustration facing p. 202
wood engraving by Dalziel brothers after Rossetti's design, 12.6 x 7.6 cm
The British Library, London

This drawing was made to illustrate William Allingham's poem, which was itself based on an old German tale. It tells of the supernatural appearance of three women dressed in white, who sang and spun each night but vanished on the stroke of eleven. One night the pastor's son, desperate for them to stay longer, put back the village clock. The maids came once more but never returned, leaving only bloodstains in the lake; the son died of a broken heart.

Besides illustrating an episode in the poem, Rossetti evokes its intense and haunting mood through the contrast between dark and light and the rhythmic movements of the maids. They are like the three Fates

cat. 73

cat. 74

dominating the man, who looks away from them in a way that suggests they are supernatural images of his imagination. The figures are enlarged so that they almost burst out of the confined space, in contrast to the minute view of the town and clock tower, glimpsed through the tiny windows at the rear.

Because the drawing was made for engraving, the maids are reversed and drawn as though left-handed. However, Rossetti's drawing differs in other respects from the published illustration – in the drawing the man is in a different position, his face in shadow, and he wears a more explicitly medieval dress with embroidered sleeves. In the engraving, the man looks out of the picture; his troubled expression and simplified clothing produce a more concentrated and contemporary image, in which the real and supernatural worlds are more clearly separated.

This was Rossetti's first published illustration, and he had a great deal of trouble with it, first failing to reverse it for the woodblock, and then complaining that the Dalziel brothers, who were responsible for cutting the design on the wood, had ruined it in the process. Nevertheless, the engraving was highly praised: Burne-Jones considered it 'the most beautiful drawing for an illustration I have ever seen' (Reid 1928, pp. 30–5; Lasner 1990, pp. 177–8, 193–4).

Drawings for Moxon's edition of Tennyson

Rossetti was approached by the publisher Edward Moxon in January 1855 to contribute to an illustrated edition of Tennyson's poems; Millais, Hunt and many others also provided illustrations, though not Elizabeth Siddal, whom Mrs Tennyson had wished to be included. It was finally published in May 1857 with five wood-block engravings after drawings by Rossetti, though he was not happy with the way his drawings had been cut on the wood.

Rossetti did not illustrate literally the passages from the poems he chose, but evoked the spirit of the poetry, only sometimes using details mentioned in the text and often inventing his own images: in his own words, he wanted to 'allegorize on one's own hook on the subject of the poem, without killing...a distinct idea of the poet's' (F, II, p. 7). In these illustrations and the related drawings, he created a highly original vision of the Middle Ages, including delicately drawn details derived from his knowledge of manuscript illumination and Flemish painting, quirky inventions of his own and daring contrasts of scale between close-up and distance.

76
The Lady of Shalott
Illustration from *Poems* by Alfred Tennyson, published by Edward Moxon, 1857, p. 75
wood engraving by Dalziel brothers after Rossetti's design, 9.4 x 8 cm
Stephen Calloway

Suggested by the closing lines of the poem, describing the Lady's body floating in the barge down the river past the 'lighted palace'. Richly clad, Sir Launcelot leans over the Lady's body, lit by flickering candles and a torch held by an unseen figure above. The starry sky, the swans, the tiny figures of courtiers and the daring close-up of the principal figures add to the mood of solemnity and mystery.

The composition may have been suggested by a medieval manuscript illumination from a 14th-century *Lancelot du Lac* in the British Museum (Faxon 1989, p. 93).

77
Mariana in the South
(s 86)
c. 1856–7
ink on paper, 9.8 x 8.3 cm
Birmingham Museums & Art Gallery.
Presented by subscribers

cat. 75

cat. 76

cat. 77

78

Mariana in the South

Illustration from *Poems* by Alfred Tennyson, published by Edward Moxon, 1857, p. 82 wood engraving by Dalziel brothers after Rossetti's design, 9.5 x 8.1 cm

Stephen Calloway

The lonely Mariana, whose fate is 'To live forgotten and love forlorn', kneels before a crucifix, kissing Christ's feet with 'melancholy eyes divine'. She clasps to her 'old letters, breathing of her worth', written to her by the lover who never comes. Rossetti has captured the mournful and claustrophobic spirit of the poem, though he has substituted a crucifix for the image of 'Our Lady' mentioned in the poem, and the mirror reflects Mariana's back view not 'the clear perfection of her face'.

79

St Cecilia

(s 83)

c. 1856–7

signed bottom right: DGR (monogram)

brown ink on paper, 9.8 x 8 cm

Birmingham Museums & Art Gallery.

Presented by subscribers

80

St Cecilia

Illustration from *Poems* by Alfred Tennyson, published by Edward Moxon, 1857, p. 113 wood engraving by Dalziel brothers after Rossetti's design, 9.2 x 7.8 cm

Stephen Calloway

Rossetti took as his starting point lines from the poem 'The Palace of Art':

> Or in a clear-wall'd city on the sea,
>   Near gilded organ-pipes, her hair
> Wound with white roses, slept St. Cecily;
>   An angel look'd at her.

In a small compass Rossetti has created a detailed, intricate vision of the distant medieval city, harbour and wall mentioned by the poet; but in the foreground he introduced a soldier improbably munching an apple, juxtaposed with the figure of St Cecilia at the organ, swooning ecstatically in the embrace of the angel. A dove flies out, as if freed from prison. The exact significance of these details is not known, but the general effect is one of a medieval fantasy world, quaint and enigmatic, mixing the sensual with the spiritual: in the drawing the angel looks at St Cecilia, as in the poem, but the engraving shows him kissing her, the sensuality emphasized by the long, flowing hair of both figures.

81

King Arthur and the weeping queens

(s 84)

c. 1856–7

signed bottom right: DGR (monogram)

brown ink on paper, 8.2 x 9.5 cm

Birmingham Museums & Art Gallery.

Presented by subscribers

82

King Arthur and the weeping queens

Poems by Alfred Tennyson, published by Edward Moxon, 1857, illustration on p. 119 wood engraving by Dalziel brothers after Rossetti's design, 7.9 x 9.4 cm

Stephen Calloway

Based on Tennyson's lines from 'The Palace of Art' about the death of Arthur 'watch'd by weeping queens'. Each of the ten queens tending the body of Arthur wears a crown of different design, and the ship moored in the background has a patterned sail and a fluttering pennant. The design may have been suggested by a medieval manuscript illumination from a 14th-century *Lancelot du Lac* in the British Museum (Faxon 1989, p. 93). The queen to right of centre resembles Christina Rossetti.

83

Sir Galahad

Poems by Alfred Tennyson, published by Edward Moxon, 1857, illustration on p. 305 wood engraving by Dalziel brothers after Rossetti's design, 9.4 x 8 cm

Stephen Calloway

84

Sir Galahad at the ruined chapel

(s 115) 1859

signed bottom centre: DGR (monogram)

watercolour and bodycolour on paper, 29.1 x 34.5 cm

Birmingham Museums & Art Gallery

figure 36

cat. 78

cat. 79

cat. 80

Then by some secret shrine I ride;
  I hear a voice, but none are there;
The stalls are void, the doors are wide,
  The tapers burning fair.
Fair gleams the snowy altar-cloth,
  The silver vessels sparkle clean,
The shrill bell rings, the censer swings,
  And solemn chants resound between.

Inspired by the lines describing Sir Galahad's discovery of a mysterious shrine on his quest for the Holy Grail, the watercolour is a later version, in expanded format, of the engraving. Both use the ingenious invention of a concealed choir of angels for the hidden voices in the poem. In the watercolour the angels resemble Elizabeth Siddal. On the altar in the engraving is a chalice and basket of bread, but the vessels have been changed in the watercolour, possibly to avoid confusion with the Holy Grail itself.

85
St Catherine
(s 89)
1857
signed and dated bottom right:
DGR (monogram) / 57
oil on canvas, 34.3 x 24.1 cm
Tate. Bequeathed by Mrs Emily Toms in memory of her father, Joseph Kershaw, 1931
figure 34

A humorously treated scene in the workshop of an improbably overdressed medieval artist, who is painting a model posing as St Catherine with her traditional attributes, the spiked wheel and the palm of martyrdom. 'I mean the lady to be a person of wealth, probably the donor of the picture in hand to some church, and wishing that the figure of the saint should be her own portrait. The period is not nearly early enough for this vanity to be out of place, I think. The pupils behind are all engaged in a rapid act of painting on a martyrdom of St. Sebastian' (F, II, p. 191). It was originally commissioned by Ruskin, who later rejected it, calling it an 'absurdity' (see S, p. 50). Rossetti accorded great importance to depicting artists at work, and this is one of several paintings showing the creative act. It is the only oil he painted between 1850 (*Ecce Ancilla Domini!*, cat. 13) and 1859 (*Bocca Baciata*, cat. 94)

86
The Blue Closet
(s 90)
signed and dated bottom right DGR (monogram) / 1857
watercolour on paper, 34.3 x 24.8 cm
Tate. Purchased with assistance through the National Art Collections Fund from Sir Arthur Du Cros Bt and Sir Otto Beit 1916
figure 35

One of a group of medieval subjects all done around 1857, *The Blue Closet* derives its title from the blue and white tiles that line the interior, where four women in fanciful medieval dress make music, singing and playing an imaginary instrument, an inventive combination of keyboard, plucked strings and bells. As is often seen in Rossetti's work, the figures are in contrasting pairs, each almost mirroring the other, with alternating colours.

Various suggestions have been put forward as to the source and meaning of this work (Parris 1984, p. 280, cat. 219). The composition may have been inspired by medieval paintings of angels making music, such as the panel by Orcagna (Christ Church, Oxford). The sprigs of holly suggest Christmas or perhaps the time of year the work was painted. The sun and moon device is used elsewhere by Rossetti to denote the passage of time. The solemn expressions of the ladies making mournful music may connect the watercolour to the death of Arthur or the illustration of *King Arthur and the weeping queens* (cat. 82). William Morris, who bought this watercolour and others in the group, wrote a poem inspired by the painting, in which he linked the orange lily growing in the foreground with death, but Rossetti denied that the poem, which was written after the work was painted, had anything to do with his own ideas about the watercolour (S, p. 50, n. 4).

Whatever its personal meaning for the artist, *The Blue Closet* evokes the same medieval fantasy world seen in other similar works by the artist. The archaic treatment, with flat chequered background, heraldic colour and decorative inventiveness come from Rossetti's familiarity with medieval illuminated manuscripts. F.G. Stephens, whose writings about Rossetti were often

cat. 81

cat. 82

cat. 83

based on conversations with the artist, later described *The Blue Closet* as 'intended to symbolise the association of colour with music' (Stephens 1894, pp. 41–2). Whether this was Rossetti's explicit intention or not, the watercolour together with others in the same group mark the beginnings of the Aesthetic Movement in its rejection of narrative in favour of suggestion and mood, and in its emphasis on decorative values.

87

The Tune of Seven Towers
(s 92)
signed and dated bottom right:
DGR (monogram) / 1857
watercolour on paper, 31.4 x 36.5 cm
Tate. Purchased with assistance through the National Art Collections Fund from Sir Arthur Du Cros Bt and Sir Otto Beit 1916
figure 31

Dating from the same year as the previous item, and also bought from Rossetti by William Morris, this work displays similar features – decorative fantasy, heraldry, patterning, rich colour, elaborate medieval dress, shallow space and 'built-in' furniture. A woman sits in a strange oak chair with a canopy above containing a bell. She is playing a stringed instrument on her lap whilst a fancifully attired man in another canopied chair listens intently. Behind her a maid also listens.

No specific source has been identified for the subject but it may be partly autobio-graphical, relating to the artist's preoccupation at this period with whether or not to marry the ailing Elizabeth Siddal (Parris 1984, p. 281, cat. 220). The woman resembles Siddal and wears a scallop shell, associated with pilgrimage, perhaps alluding to Siddal's travels for her health. A dove, often used to indicate Siddal, flies in a recess on the right. Marriage is suggested by the maid on the left placing a branch of orange tree on the bed. The title of the work refers to the heraldic device of seven towers on the canopy above the man, and also to the seven towers on the pennant hanging at the left from the daringly placed diagonal pole. The pennant also includes the sun, moon, lily and rose, symbols of male and female, purity and passion. The heavy oak chairs reflect the 'intensely medieval' furniture that Morris was experimenting with at this time, including a medieval chair 'with a box overhead in which Gabriel suggested owls might be kept with advantage' (Burne-Jones 1904, I, p. 177).

88

Hamlet and Ophelia
(s 108)
c. 1858–9
signed bottom right: DGR (monogram)
ink on paper, 30.8 x 26.1 cm
The British Museum, London
figure 21

In choosing to draw Act III, scene 1 from Shakespeare's play, Rossetti depicted another highly charged confrontation between male and female protagonists. Hamlet, full of self-doubt, shocks Ophelia by denying his love for her and urges her to enter a nunnery. In a Christ-like pose, he perches on the carved wooden stalls whilst Ophelia leans back in an attitude of exhaustion. Rossetti's description explains many of the quirky details: 'I mean [Hamlet] to be ramping about on the stalls of the little oratory turning out of the main hall, to which Ophelia has retired with the devotional book which her father gives her to read. He throws his arms wildly along the sill of the screen and frays the roses to pieces as he talks, hardly knowing what he says. She still holds out to him the letters and jewels which she wishes to return, but has done speaking and lets him rave on. In the woodwork are symbols of rash introspection – the Tree of Knowledge, and the man who touched the Ark and died. The outer court is full of intricate stairs and passages and leads to the ramparts where the ghost walks at night' (see S, p. 61). Rossetti first conceived the subject in 1854, but by the time it was realized in this drawing of about 1858–9 he had developed a finely drawn, elaborately detailed style. The symbols of Hamlet's rash introspection include self-devouring serpents on the arms of the seats; the inscription carved on the seat by the Tree of Knowledge reads 'ERITIS SICUT DEUS SCIENTES BONUM ET MALUM' (you will be like God, knowing good and evil) and below, on the tipped-up misericord, is a representation of Uzzah, who dared to touch the Ark of the Covenant and was smitten by God (2 Samuel 6:6).

cat. 84

cat. 85

cat. 86

89

How They Met Themselves
(s 118)
signed and dated bottom right:
DGR (monogram) / 1851 / 1860
ink and wash on paper, 27.3 x 21.6 cm
Syndics of the Fitzwilliam Museum,
Cambridge
figure 33

In a dark wood, a pair of lovers in medieval
dress are suddenly confronted by their
doubles. The lovers are shocked; the woman
faints and the man draws his sword at the
sight of the ghosts, on the left, outlined in
a pale halo of light and glowering implacably
at their earthly counterparts. Rossetti called
it 'the Bogie'; it depicts the German legend
of the *doppelgänger*, which had fascinated
him since he was a boy. His original drawing
of 1851 was either lost or destroyed, and this
version was made in 1860 in the artist's
dense, Düreresque style.

90

The Rose Garden
*The Early Italian Poets from Ciullo
d'Alcamo to Dante Alighieri...*translated by D.G.
Rossetti, published by Smith, Elder and Co.,
1861
title page and frontispiece
relief print, 18.5 x 23.5 cm
Stephen Calloway

Two lovers in medieval dress kiss in a garden.
Swinburne posed for the man embracing a
female model, as he put it, 'in the most fer-

vent and abandoned style.... Everyone who
knows me already salutes the likeness with
a yell of recognition' (see s, p. 78). Rossetti
made the design to be etched on copper,
but disliked the plate and is said to have
destroyed it, though a few impressions
exist. He reused the composition for an oil,
Love's Greeting (1861, Isabella Stewart Gardner
Museum, Boston, s 126), and a watercolour,
Roman de la Rose (1864, Tate, s 126 R I).
This is an extremely rare copy of the book
with the cancelled frontispiece; most books
have a plain title page. There is also a copy
of the book at Princeton containing drawings
by Rossetti for some of the poems, suggesting that he planned the book to be illustrated (Surtees 1972, pp. 230–1).

91

The First Madness of Ophelia
(s 169)
signed and dated bottom left:
DGR (monogram) April 1864
watercolour on paper, 39.4 x 29.2 cm
Gallery Oldham, Charles Lees collection
figure 22

From Act IV, scene 5 of Shakespeare's
play, showing Ophelia mad with grief from
Hamlet's rejection of her and from her
father's death. The title *The First Madness
of Ophelia* suggests the first time she is seen
as mad, with the King, Queen and Horatio
looking on. But Ophelia's appearance, gar-
landed with flowers, and the tender gesture
of the man on the left, suggest that Rossetti
may have had in mind the later part of the

scene when, in the presence of her shocked
brother Laertes, she recites the names of
the plants – rosemary for remembrance,
pansies for thoughts, fennel, columbine,
rue, daisies and violets.

Rossetti employs the elaborate costume,
the jewel-like colour and the delight in
pattern seen in the medieval watercolours
of 1857, but with a simpler approach to
composition and space, laying the emphasis
on the emotional tension between the characters. Significantly, Ophelia is given the
features of Elizabeth Siddal.

cat. 90

cat. 87

cat. 88

cat. 89

Oxford Union Murals

In 1857, Rossetti came to Oxford to visit his friend Benjamin Woodward, architect of the new Debating Hall of the Oxford Union Society, and offered to decorate the upper part of the interior with mural paintings of scenes from Malory's *Morte d'Arthur*. He recruited six artist friends to help him, William Morris, Edward Burne-Jones, Arthur Hughes, Valentine Cameron Prinsep, J. Hungerford Pollen and John Roddam Spencer Stanhope. There were ten bays, each of which was pierced by two circular six-foil windows, which made for difficulties of design and viewing. Rossetti chose two bays for his own paintings, and made two designs, *Sir Launcelot's Vision of the Sanc Grael* and *The Attainment of the Sanc Grael*, though only the first was painted on the wall. A third subject, *Sir Launcelot in the Queen's Chamber,* may have also been intended for the Hall, which is now used as a Library. Despite the considerable contemporary debate about mural technique, which accompanied the technical failures of the murals in the Palace of Westminster, Rossetti and his friends naively painted the Oxford murals in distemper upon new brick walls, prepared only with a coat of whitewash. When newly painted, the colours were described as 'so brilliant as to make the walls look like the margin of a highly illuminated manuscript' (Patmore 1857, p. 584). But the paintings deteriorated almost immediately, because the technique was not resistant to damp, and despite several attempts at restoration they are now only dimly visible.

92
Study for *Sir Launcelot's Vision of the Sanc Grael*
(S 93 G)
1857
ink and pencil on paper, 22.5 x 13.6 cm
Syndics of the Fitzwilliam Museum, Cambridge

This is a study for the only mural painted by Rossetti on to the wall (cf. fig. 96), described by the artist as 'Sir Launcelot prevented by his sin from entering the chapel of the Sangrael. He has fallen asleep before the shrine full of angels, & between him & it, rises in his dream the image of Queen Guenevere, the cause of it all. She stands gazing at him with her arms extended in the branches of an apple tree' (F, II, p. 225). This study shows the left-hand portion of the mural, with the 'shrine full of angels': in front of the altar lit by three candles kneels the Angel of the San Grael holding the Bread and Chalice (the Grail itself is not shown). Above her hovers the Dove with a censer in its beak, and a group of winged angels' heads. All the angels look like Elizabeth Siddal. The semicircular cut-out indicates the position of one of the windows.

93
Sir Launcelot in the Queen's Chamber
(S 95)
signed and dated bottom right:
DGR (monogram) Oxford / 1857
ink on paper, 26.5 x 35.2 cm
Birmingham Museums & Art Gallery.
Presented by subscribers
exhibited at Liverpool only
figure 24

The original title, inscribed on the gold frame, now lost, is a direct quotation from Malory's *Morte d'Arthur* (XX, chapter 3): *How Sir Launcelot was espied in the Queen's Chamber, and how Sir Agravaine and Sir Mordred came with twelve knights to slay him.* Whilst her husband King Arthur was out hunting, Launcelot illicitly visited Guenevere in her chamber. Rossetti shows her fainting, her crown hanging above the bed whilst her maids cower in the background; Launcelot threatens the knights with his sword. Despite having only a sword but no armour, Launcelot defeated the knights, but Guenevere was condemned to be burned at the stake for treason. She was dramatically rescued by Launcelot, and the conflict between him and Arthur led to the dissolution of the Round Table.

Despite the absence of spaces for the two windows, the drawing may be connected with the Oxford Union scheme, and was probably done in response to Ruskin's offer to cancel a debt if Rossetti were to do another Union mural (see S, p. 54). The claustrophobic space combined with intricate detail empha-size the intensity of feeling, whilst Guenevere's

cat. 91

cat. 92

cat. 93

provocatively half-closed eyes and parted
lips are similar to the series of portraits of
beautiful women that Rossetti was beginning
at this time. The model for Guenevere was
Jane Burden, who had recently entered the
Pre-Raphaelite circle.

fig. 96
**Sir Launcelot's Vision
of the Sanc Grael**
1857
unfinished study
Visitors of the Ashmolean Museum, Oxford

Beauties of the 1860s

The subjects of Rossetti's pictures of single female figures may seem to be mere pretexts for the endless repetition of the same artistic idea, the celebration of the physical beauty of woman. In many cases Rossetti is known to have painted the picture first and added the title later (or even changed it subsequently; see cats. 100, 154). The sound and rhythm of the female names are clearly a crucial factor in the choice of titles. Moreover, the same few models are called upon to impersonate a variety of historical, literary or mythological women in turn. All of these factors may seem to suggest that the particular subject matter — the stories of the particular women named in the titles — is of secondary importance. Yet Rossetti was a poet, a translator of poems (particularly of poems in the medieval courtly love tradition), and exceptionally widely read in classical, medieval and modern literature. He is hardly likely, then, to have been insensitive to the allusions and resonances of the female figures named in the titles. The procedures of courtly love poetry, which often involve a direct address from the poet to the woman he loves, can also be seen to inform the visual presentation of the Rossettian female figure. Moreover, in medieval love poetry amorous or erotic content can be interpreted symbolically, as in Dante, to refer also to religious, political or other ideas; in Rossetti's work, too, the literal reference to female beauty or to love may be accompanied by other layers of potential meaning.

The gorgeous accessories in the pictures of the 1860s, again, have often been seen as merely decorative adjuncts to the female figures — indeed Rossetti himself referred to them as 'bricabrac' (W.M. Rossetti 1889, p. 69). After Elizabeth Siddal's death in 1862, Rossetti moved to Tudor House in Cheyne Walk, next to the Thames in Chelsea, then somewhat removed from central London. Over the next few years he filled its many large rooms with multifarious collections of objects — Chippendale furniture, antiquarian books, blue-and-white ceramics, metalwork and lacquer-work, textiles and jewellery from around the world (cats. 172–4); his collecting mania even extended to animals, including peacocks, marmots, parrots and a wombat (Marsh 1999a, p. 267). The studio assistant who joined him in 1867, Henry Treffry Dunn, later recalled the bizarre assortment of musical instruments — 'Mandolins, lutes, dulcimers, barbarous-looking things of Chinese fashion which I could imagine would be a great trial of patience to hear played upon' — and above all the mirrors: 'Mirrors and looking-glasses of all shapes, sizes and design lined the walls. Whichever way I looked I saw myself gazing at myself' (Dunn 1984, pp. 18–19, 14). Countless objects from the Tudor House collections made their way into the pictures, as if Rossetti's collecting mania were simply overflowing from his life into his art. Yet this was also the period of the formation and early years of William Morris's firm of decorators, and Rossetti was acutely sensitive to the design qualities of objects; there is a strong aesthetic consistency to the types of objects included in the pictures. Moreover, his letters, and the poems he wrote to accompany the pictures, show that he was often alert to the symbolic meanings of the objects he represented.

How far should we go, then, in interpreting either the subjects or the accessory objects in Rossetti's pictures of the 1860s? Certainly there is a decisive shift away from Pre-Raphaelite procedure, in which every detail could serve a precise narrative or symbolic function (see, for example, cat. 12). On the other hand, Rossetti was never a formalist; he did not regard his paintings as abstract patterns of shape and colour. His works of the 1860s encourage the viewer no longer to decipher specific symbols as in Pre-Raphaelite days, but rather to muse more freely on the possible connotations of the images – or, in Rossetti's own phrase, to 'allegorize on one's own hook' (F, II, p. 7).

94

Bocca Baciata

(S 114)

signed bottom left: DGR (monogram); inscribed on reverse: Bocca baciata non perde ventura, anzi rinnova come fa la luna, 'Boccaccio' (not in Rossetti's hand) and 'painted by D G Rossetti 1859' (in George Price Boyce's hand)

oil on panel, 32.2 x 27 cm

Museum of Fine Arts, Boston. Gift of James Lawrence 1980.261

figure 39

This painting was designed as a bust-length portrait of the model, after the manner of 16th-century Venetian paintings of voluptuous women, often identified as courtesans (figs. 40, 54; see pp. 56, 58, 72 above). The subject matter seems to have been devised only after the picture was painted; nonetheless, it announces Rossetti's new concerns of the 1860s. Alatiel, in a tale from *The Decameron* by the 14th-century author Giovanni Boccaccio, is the most beautiful woman in the world, and the most sensual: she gives and receives sexual joy with eight men before marrying a ninth and living happily ever after (her name is an anagram of 'La Lieta', 'the happy one'; *Decameron*, Second Day, Seventh Story). Rossetti's picture need not be taken as an illustration, but the title quotes the final line of the tale, which is inscribed on the reverse of the panel and may be translated: 'The mouth that has been kissed does not lose its fortune, rather it renews itself just as the moon does.' Many

cat. 94

writers have linked the implication of promiscuity in the quotation to the model represented in the picture, Fanny Cornforth, a woman with whom both Rossetti and the watercolour artist who commissioned the painting, George Price Boyce, had close (and possibly sexual) relationships (see cats. 112–13). Thus the visual reference to the Venetian 16th-century 'courtesan' pictures, the literary reference to the 14th-century tale from the *Decameron*, and the private meanings that the representation of the modern model may have had for Rossetti and Boyce combine to suggest not a single narrative or historical subject, but rather a many-layered exploration of female sensuality.

The accessories may be interpreted symbolically: the rose is a standard symbol of love, the marigolds may denote grief, the apple may refer to temptation (via the apple of the Garden of Eden). The art historian Sarah Phelps Smith links these symbols together, to propose that the painting presents the figure as a temptress (hence the apple) who offers grief (the marigold) in return for the kiss of the title (Phelps Smith 1978, p. 84; it should be noted that this interpretation is inconsistent with the *Decameron* tale, which presents sexual love as unequivocally happy).

95
Regina Cordium
(S 120 B)
signed and dated upper left: DGR (monogram) / 1860 (in heart-shaped device); inscribed upper right: The Queen of Hearts red chalk tracing on paper, 20.6 x 19.2 cm Birmingham Museums & Art Gallery. Presented by subscribers

The Latin title *Regina Cordium* is translated as 'The Queen of Hearts' in the upper right corner; this is a tribute to the sitter, Elizabeth Siddal, at the time of her marriage to Rossetti. The tracing is related to an oil painting of 1860 (fig. 37). The abbreviated treatment suggests a reference to the playing-card character, the Queen of Hearts, perhaps with the implication that love may be like a game of chance. However, the Latin title also recalls the phrase 'Regina Caeli', or 'Queen of Heaven'; the double reference to earthly and heavenly love would be characteristic of Rossetti.

96
Fair Rosamund
(S 128)
signed and dated on parapet, lower right: D.G.R. 1861
oil on canvas, 52.1 x 41.9 cm
National Museums and Galleries of Wales, Cardiff
figure 38

This painting represents Rosamund Clifford, the mistress of the 12th-century English King Henry II, in the maze he built to conceal her dwelling; the red cord indicates the path through the maze, followed by the King to visit his mistress, and more ominously by his wife, Queen Eleanor of Aquitaine, who eventually discovered Rosamund's hiding-place and murdered her. As in other paintings of this period, the story emphasizes illicit love. It was a story much favoured by artists and writers of Rossetti's circle, who would have known it from a variety of sources, such as Michael Drayton's *Englands Heroicall Epistles* (1597), Thomas Percy's *Reliques of Ancient English Poetry* (1765), or Tennyson's 'Dream of Fair Women' (1832). The rose symbolism, implicit in Rosamund's name ('rosa mundi', rose of the world) and ubiquitous in medieval love poetry, is repeated throughout the picture (see p. 52 above). The parapet is ornamented with a heart-and-crown motif, which refers to the King's love for Rosamund and perhaps to her sovereignty in love (as opposed to Eleanor's political sovereignty). Other roundels on the parapet show birds

cat. 95

cat. 96

and roses, perhaps alluding to Rosamond's captivity in the maze (the bird motif is similar to that on the small blue-and-white vase in the foreground of *Woman combing her hair*, cat. 102). The coral beads may have been those Rossetti borrowed in summer 1861 from Georgiana Burne-Jones (F, II, p. 383; see cat. 115).

97
Girl at a lattice
(S 152)
signed and dated bottom left:
DGR (monogram) 1862
oil on canvas, 30.5 x 27 cm
Syndics of the Fitzwilliam Museum,
Cambridge
figure 42

This study of a model is unusual in Rossetti's work, for it was never given an allusive title. The model was a servant in Ford Madox Brown's household, yet the picture is not merely a scene of everyday life, for the figure is given an elaborate coral necklace reminiscent of the one in *Fair Rosamund* (cat. 96), and she is positioned behind a parapet as in many of Rossetti's 'Venetian' pictures. It has been suggested that the subject recalls the episode in the *Vita Nuova* in which a lady looks with pity at Dante, after Beatrice's death, from a window; this picture was made shortly after the death of Elizabeth Siddal. But the allusion, if it is one, is by way of poignant contrast; the figure, a mere girl, does not make eye contact and cannot offer much consolation. Perhaps, then, the title is

important after all: this is not Dante's Lady of the Window (whom Rossetti later represented; see cats. 143–4), but only a girl at a lattice window.

98
Beata Beatrix
(S 168)
c. 1863–70, perhaps executed on top of an earlier beginning
signed bottom left: DGR (monogram)
oil on canvas, 86.4 x 66 cm
Tate. Presented by Georgiana, Baroness Mount-Temple in memory of her husband, Francis, Baron Mount-Temple 1889
figure 57

The picture has a double subject: the principal figure represents both Dante's Beatrice and Elizabeth Siddal. The title, *Beata Beatrix* (or 'blessed Beatrice'), refers to the end of the *Vita Nuova*, also quoted in *Dantis Amor* (cat. 46). Thus the picture links Siddal (the person literally represented in the picture) to Beatrice in heaven, after her death. The symbolism of the picture also conflates the two stories of Siddal's and Beatrice's deaths, and Dante's and Rossetti's loves. The dove bears a white poppy, symbol of sleep or death and the source of laudanum (Siddal had died of an overdose). The dove can be a symbol either of love (it is associated with Venus, the goddess of love) or of the Holy Spirit (see cat. 13); it is red, the colour of love, but its halo suggests that it is also a messenger from heaven. Rossetti associated the dove with Siddal, as Dante associated

the number nine with Beatrice; the sundial on the parapet points to the number nine. Behind the parapet, Dante (on the right) is dimly seen before a well (perhaps symbolizing rebirth) and a thicket of trees (perhaps representing the dark forest in which Dante finds himself at the beginning of the *Divine Comedy*); he looks towards Love, dressed in red and holding a flame in his hand. In the background is a bridge, usually identified as the Ponte Vecchio of Dante's Florence; surely it also recalls the bridges of London.

It should be noted that the picture is perfectly comprehensible as a representation of Beatrice and does not depend on recognition of the features of the artist's dead wife (indeed Rossetti, for obvious reasons, stresses the Dantesque subject and not the likeness to Siddal in his letters to the picture's purchasers; see S, pp. 93–4). Moreover, elements of the composition go back to Rossetti's earliest ideas for making designs from Dante's *Vita Nuova*, before he met Siddal (see cat. 46). By the time of the memorial exhibitions of Rossetti's works, the winter after his death, the identity of the portrait was, however, public knowledge.

For a more extensive discussion of this picture see pp. 80-6.

cat. 97

cat. 98

99

Helen of Troy

(s 163)

signed and dated bottom left: DGR
(monogram) / 1863; inscribed on reverse:
Helen of Troy ἐλέναυς, ἔλανδρος,
ἐλέπτολις (destroyer of ships, destroyer
of men, destroyer of cities). Painted by
D.G. Rossetti. 1863.

oil on panel, 32.8 x 27.7 cm

Hamburger Kunsthalle

figure 43

The subject of Helen of Troy brings together
important ideas from this period of Rossetti's
work: she was the most beautiful woman in
the world, the adulterous lover of the Trojan
prince Paris, and a crucial figure in the
Western poetic tradition. She appears in
many of the texts favoured by Rossetti and
his circle, from Homer's *Iliad* and numerous
other classical sources through Dante's *Inferno*
(canto v) and Boccaccio's *De mulieribus claris*
('Concerning Famous Women'), to Goethe's
Faust, Poe's 'To Helen' and Tennyson's 'A
Dream of Fair Women'. The Greek inscription on the reverse is from the *Agamemnon* of
Aeschylus and describes Helen as 'destroyer
of ships, destroyer of men, destroyer of
cities' (each of the three Greek words begins
with the syllable 'hel', repeating the first syllable of Helen's name). In the painting,
Helen points to a pendant showing a fire-
brand, the symbol of her Trojan lover Paris;
his mother, when pregnant, had dreamed
that she would give birth to a torch that
would set fire to her palace. It was, of course,

Paris's abduction of Helen from her husband
Menelaus that led to the Trojan War and
the burning of Troy, seen in the background
of the painting. Helen's gesture may indicate
that she is justifying her actions by appealing
to her love for Paris, or that she is revelling
in her own destructive power. The fire also
glitters in Helen's right eye; the ancient
dramatist Euripides used images of flames
or burning to describe the dangerous allure
of Helen's eyes. The red and gold of Helen's
hair and robe also repeat the colours of
the raging fire. The model was Annie Miller
(see cat. 114).

100

Fazio's Mistress (Aurelia)

(s 164)

signed and dated bottom left:
DGR (monogram) / 1863

oil on panel, 43.2 x 36.8 cm

Tate. Purchased with assistance through
the National Art Collections Fund from
Sir Arthur Du Cros Bt and Sir Otto Beit
1916

figure 51

The original title refers to a poem by Dante's
contemporary Fazio degli Uberti, which
Rossetti had translated and included in
his volume of 1861, *The Early Italian Poets*
(see cats. 90, 156). The picture might even
be called a second translation, this time into
visual form. The poem describes the poet's
act of looking at his beloved, in the present
tense, as if she is appearing before his very
eyes (as indeed she does in the painting).

Each stanza begins with a reference to one of
her physical beauties:

I look at the crisp golden-threaded hair
Whereof, to thrall my heart, Love twists a net
…
I look at the amorous beautiful mouth
…
I look at her white easy neck, so well
From shoulders and from bosom lifted out
…
I look at the large arms, so lithe and round,—
At the hands, which are white and rosy too,—
At the long fingers, clasped and woven through,
Bright with the ring which one of them doth wear.

(D.G. Rossetti 1911, pp. 488–9)

The painting dwells on the same physical
features, including the single ring. It combines this with the Titianesque motif of a
woman dressing her hair before a mirror;
the woman's action, plaiting her hair, sets
up a parallel between Titian's *Woman with
a mirror* (fig. 40) and Fazio's description
of the hair, 'Whereof … Love twists a net'.

In 1869, however, Rossetti asked the picture's owner, George Rae, to change the
title to *Aurelia*. This was at the height of discussion about 'art for art's sake', and Rossetti
may have wished to play down any hint that the
picture was an illustration of a pre-existing
literary source, rather than an independent
work of art in its own right. The new title
may be read as a name for the figure or as a
reference to her golden hair — in either case
something in the picture itself, not in an

cat. 99

cat. 100

extraneous source. However, it may also relate to a story, 'Aurélia', by the French writer Gérard de Nerval, published in 1855 and itself related to Rossetti's story of 1849–50, 'Hand and Soul'; both stories, moreover, respond to Dante's *Vita Nuova* (McGann 2000, p. 19). Thus the change of title actually expanded the picture's literary associations beyond the original reference to Fazio degli Uberti, at the same time binding the picture's allusiveness more closely to its visual appearance. In his letter to Rae, Rossetti also called attention to the numerous accessories: 'the thing is much too full of queer details to embody the poem quoted.' Again the suggestion is that the picture means more, visually, than a simple illustration of the poem, although Rossetti gives the patron a casual explanation: 'it was done at a time when I had a mania for buying bricabrac' (W.M. Rossetti 1889, p. 69). The accessories are typical of the diverse collections Rossetti amassed in the 1860s at Tudor House. The house was full of mirrors, no doubt including the one depicted here.

101
Morning Music
(S 170)
signed and dated bottom right:
DGR (monogram) / 1864; inscribed lower left: MORNING MUSIC
watercolour and bodycolour on paper, 30.5 x 27.3 cm
Syndics of the Fitzwilliam Museum, Cambridge
figure 50

This watercolour combines different pleasures of the senses: hair-dressing, music-making and beautiful visual objects. The comb, blue-and-white vase, egg-shaped metalwork container and knotted cords are similar but not identical to objects in *Woman combing her hair* (cat. 102; yet another gold spherical container appears on the mantelpiece in Henry Treffry Dunn's watercolour of Rossetti's sitting room, cat. 172). They also have the same function in the picture, indicating the luxury of the woman's toilette. Since Rossetti evidently continued to imitate objects quite literally, in Pre-Raphaelite fashion (see cat. 104), the diversity of individual objects in his pictures may suggest how extensive his collections were.

102
Woman combing her hair
(S 174)
signed and dated bottom left:
DGR (monogram) 1864
watercolour on paper, 34.3 x 31.1 cm
private collection
exhibited at Liverpool only
figure 49

103
Woman combing her hair
(S 174 A)
signed and dated lower left:
DGR (monogram) / 1864
pencil on paper, 38.5 x 37 cm
Birmingham Museums & Art Gallery.
Presented by subscribers
exhibited at Amsterdam only

These drawings (cats. 102-3) belong to the group of toilette scenes that also includes *Fazio's Mistress* (cat. 100), *Morning Music* (cat. 101) and *Lady Lilith* (cat. 107). Unlike the others, they were not given a literary title and seem to catch the model (Fanny Cornforth) in a spontaneous moment. Nonetheless, the composition is carefully planned; the pencil drawing appears to be a preparatory study. The accessories are similar to those in the other pictures, but not the same: each time Rossetti has designed a fresh composition. The circular background mirror in the watercolour makes a direct reference to the identically positioned mirror in Titian's *Woman with a mirror* (see fig. 40), the painting that echoes through all of Rossetti's toilette scenes. But Titian's mirror has become Rossetti's: circular mirrors were prominent in the décor at Tudor House (cats. 172–4), and this one reflects what appears to be one of the house's tall sash windows (fig. 89).

104
Venus Verticordia
(S 173)
c. 1863–8
signed bottom left: DGR (monogram)
oil on canvas, 83.8 x 71.2 cm
Russell-Cotes Art Gallery and Museum, Bournemouth
figure 53

The title, 'Venus, turner of hearts', derives from Latin literature, where it designates Venus's role in turning women's hearts

cat. 101

cat. 102

cat. 103

towards virtue and chastity (Valerius Maximus, VIII.15.12; Ovid, *Fasti* IV.160). However, Rossetti at first took it in the opposite sense, to mean turning men's hearts away from fidelity. This is evident in his sonnet for the picture:

She hath the apple in her hand for thee,
   Yet almost in her heart would hold it back;
   She muses, with her eyes upon the track
Of that which in thy spirit they can see.
Haply, 'Behold, he is at peace,' saith she;
   'Alas! The apple for his lips,— the dart
   That follows its brief sweetness to his heart,—
The wandering of his feet perpetually!'

A little space her glance is still and coy;
   But if she give the fruit that works her spell,
Those eyes shall flame as for her Phrygian boy.
   Then shall her bird's strained throat the woe foretell,
   And her far seas moan as a single shell,
And through her dark grove strike the light of Troy.

(D.G. Rossetti 1911, p. 210)

When Rossetti printed the sonnet in his *Poems* of 1870, he omitted the surname 'Verticordia' to call it simply 'Venus', having been advised of the error by his brother (D & W, II, p. 727). In later editions, however, he returned to the title 'Venus Verticordia', which can be seen as a creative misinterpretation of the Latin epithet.

The sonnet links the accessories in the picture to the events leading up to the Trojan War: Paris, the Trojan or 'Phrygian boy', awarded the golden apple to Venus in a con-test among three goddesses, in return for which Venus promised him the most beautiful woman in the world – in other words, Helen (see cat. 99). As a result of the contest, Paris turned his heart away from the nymph Oenone (the subject of a poem by Tennyson), and Helen turned hers away from her Greek husband Menelaus, thus causing the Trojan war. The bird, mentioned in the sonnet, is seen at top right, singing its prophecy of doom. The dart is usually associated with Cupid, Venus's son, and it inspires love as it wounds; here it points to Venus's own heart beneath her exposed breast. It may, however, also allude to the arrow that killed Paris in the Trojan War.

Rossetti's picture and sonnet can be said to generalize the story of Paris, and to implicate the viewer: Venus holds the apple 'for thee', that is, perhaps, for the spectator she addresses in the picture. The butterflies, traditional symbols for the human soul, may suggest the souls of those enthralled by love and beauty. The halo behind the head startlingly equates Venus to a Christian saint, recalling the potentially blasphemous comparison between Venus and the Virgin Mary in Swinburne's 'Hymn to Proserpine' of the early 1860s. In a letter of 1864 to Ford Madox Brown Rossetti asked: 'What do you think of putting a nimbus behind my Venus's head? I believe the Greeks used to do it' (D & W, II, p. 519). This sounds like self-justification, but in fact the Greek historian Pausanias records a famous statue of Venus with an apple and a sphere around her head (Pater 1895, p. 248). This distinctly obscure reference demonstrates the extent of Rossetti's learning.

In 1864, Rossetti went to enormous trouble to acquire real roses and honeysuckle to paint, rejecting examples that were not perfectly full-blown (and borrowing money from his brother to cover the expense; see D & W, II, pp. 516–19). This is a reminder of Rossetti's continuing commitment to painting from nature, even in imagined subjects such as this one. Ruskin, however, found the naturalism of the flowers overly blatant (see above, pp. 76-8). The roses behind the figure are symbols of Venus and of love (see cats. 94, 96); the honeysuckle can be seen as a more earthy sexual symbol. The flowers powerfully reinforce the sensuality of the nude upper body, almost the sole example of a nude in Rossetti's work. However, in the later 1860s a number of English artists began to experiment with the nude figure (Smith 1996, pp. 99–161). Rossetti's painting, designed as early as 1863, was among the first in this remarkable Victorian revival of the nude.

The original model was an unusually tall woman who served as a cook, but around 1867 Rossetti repainted the head from Alexa Wilding, a model he often used for more 'spiritual' figures (see cat. 107). Although Rossetti's friends regretted the substitution (W.M. Rossetti 1889, p. 45), the combination of Wilding's 'classical' features with the nude breast — like the juxtaposition of the halo with the pulpy, sensual flowers — presents a characteristically Rossettian blend

cat. 104

of earthiness and spirituality, suited to the conception of the ancient goddess of love.

105
The Blue Bower
(s 178)
signed and dated bottom right:
DGR (monogram) / 1865
oil on canvas, 84 x 70.9 cm
The Trustees of the Barber Institute
of Fine Arts, The University of Birmingham
figure 47

The title recalls that of *The Blue Closet* (cat. 86); the word 'bower', denoting the private apartment of a medieval woman, was a favourite of Rossetti's in his poetry (compare *The Bower Meadow*, cat. 148). The medievalizing associations of the title are combined, however, with the Titianesque red hair, close-up composition and vivid colour of Rossetti's 'Venetian' mode, and moreover with hints of the Far East: the instrument has been identified as a Japanese *koto* (Spencer-Longhurst 2000, pp. 11–12), and the fanciful tiles behind the figure bear the prunus blossom motif of Chinese blue-and-white pots (see p. 234). The heart-shaped pendant of the necklace is based on a piece of costume jewellery later owned by Jane Morris (cat. 177); no doubt the other jewels were also based on objects from Rossetti's collections. Thus the picture is a kind of compendium of the interests in decorative art of Rossetti and his circle at this date. By the same token, it is resolutely non-historicist, juxtaposing beautiful

objects regardless of their origins; it does not represent any particular place or time, but rather a 'bower' of the imagination in which the sensuous pleasures of sight, sound and texture are combined with the erotic address of the figure. The passion flowers and convolvulus behind the figure can be read as symbols of passion and the 'bonds of love' respectively (Phelps Smith 1978, pp. 99–100); the blue cornflowers on the foreground ledge are perhaps associated with the name of the sitter, Fanny Cornforth.

106
The Beloved
(s 182)
signed and dated bottom left:
DGR (monogram) / 1865–66
oil on canvas, 82.5 x 76.2 cm
Tate. Purchased with assistance through the National Art Collections Fund from Sir Arthur Du Cros Bt and Sir Otto Beit 1916
figure 52

The painting was designed as a representation of Dante's Beatrice, but Rossetti found the colouring of the professional model he used, Marie Ford, too 'bright' for that subject (s, p. 105; Rossetti's mental idea of Beatrice was perhaps irrevocably associated with the pale complexion of Elizabeth Siddal). He therefore substituted a new subject, the Bride of the Song of Solomon, the Old Testament book in which religious and erotic imagery are fused. Yet, as Alastair Grieve has noted (Parris 1984, p. 210), this too may

relate to Dante, for when Beatrice finally appears in the *Divine Comedy*, towards the end of the *Purgatorio*, her attendants sing lines from the Song of Solomon: 'Veni, sponsa, de Libano' ('Come with me from Lebanon, my spouse', Song of Solomon 4:8). Thus the final picture may preserve a trace of the original reference to Beatrice within the new context of the Biblical lines inscribed on the frame:

My Beloved is mine and I am his. (Song of Solomon, 2:16). Let him kiss me with the kisses of his mouth: for thy love is better than wine. (Solomon 1:2). She shall be brought unto the King in raiment of needlework: the virgins her companions that follow her shall be brought unto thee (Psalms 45:14).

The quotation might imply that the 'Beloved' of the title is not the depicted woman but rather the male figure before whom she appears, just as Beatrice appears to Dante in the parallel episode from the *Purgatorio* (see cat. 43). This reiterates the constant feature of Rossetti's compositions of this period, the sense of direct address from the depicted figure to the picture's viewer.

The composition with multiple figures is highly unusual in Rossetti's work of this period, and he takes the suggestion of the Biblical subject to introduce a variety of racial types. The figure to the right was modelled by Kiomi Gray, a gipsy woman brought into the Rossetti circle by the artist Frederick

cat. 105

cat. 106

Sandys (Marsh 1999a, p. 319). Ford Madox Brown's grandson thought that another of the figures was Jewish (Hueffer 1902, p. 65); this may be the right rear figure, said to have been modelled by a Mrs Eaton, who often sat for Jewish subjects by artists in Rossetti's circle (Marsh 1999a, p. 291). As Jan Marsh has noted, the black child in the foreground can be seen as a reference to contemporary concern about slavery in the American South (the picture was painted at the time of the American Civil War; see Marsh 1996, pp. 115–23). Several scholars have also proposed a relationship to the black figure in Manet's *Olympia*, which Rossetti had presumably seen when he visited Manet's studio late in 1864. However, the primary allusion is surely to the famous passage in the Song of Solomon, 'I am black, but comely' (1:5). The array of racial types can be interpreted as a hierarchy, presenting the 'bright' Caucasian features of the central figure as most beautiful, with the other figures subordinated. Alternatively, the picture can be read as a celebration of ethnic diversity following the cue of the Song of Solomon itself; the close-knit composition encourages the spectator to catch the eyes of each of the figures in turn. The accessories, too, represent a plurality of origins: the sumptuous hair ornament of the central figure has been identified as Chinese featherwork (Bury 1976, p. 101), the green robe as a Japanese kimono, which Rossetti borrowed from his friend George Price Boyce along with the jewel on the black child's head (Boyce 1980, p. 42). The pendant around

the child's neck is North African (Bury 1976, p. 101). The spiralling pearl ornament on the hair of the right rear figure was a particular favourite of Rossetti's, found in a number of other pictures (for example, cats. 109, 141, 148).

107
Lady Lilith
(s 205)
signed and dated on background table:
D.G. Rossetti 1868
oil on canvas, 97.8 x 85.1 cm
Delaware Art Museum, Samuel
and Mary R. Bancroft Memorial, 1935
figure 44

The subject and meaning of this picture seem to have evolved gradually. It may have been designed as early as 1864 simply as a toilette scene. Probably in 1866, Rossetti began to associate the picture with the distinctly obscure subject of Lilith, in Talmudic tradition the original wife of Adam before the creation of Eve. He asked his brother to copy out one of the rare literary references to Lilith, four lines from Goethe's *Faust* that emphasize the enthralling magic of her hair. Rossetti elaborates this motif in his own sonnet, at first entitled, like the picture, 'Lady Lilith':

Of Adam's first wife, Lilith, it is told
  (The witch he loved before the gift of Eve,)
  That, ere the snake's, her sweet tongue could deceive,
And her enchanted hair was the first gold.
And still she sits, young while the earth is old,
  And, subtly of herself contemplative,
  Draws men to watch the bright web she can weave,
Till heart and body and life are in its hold.

The rose and poppy are her flowers; for where
  Is he not found, O Lilith, whom shed scent
And soft-shed kisses and soft sleep shall snare?
  Lo! as that youth's eyes burned at thine, so went
  Thy spell through him, and left his straight neck bent
And round his heart one strangling golden hair.

(D.G. Rossetti 1911, p. 100)

By 1868 the painting *Lady Lilith*, together with its sonnet, had taken on further meaning as an oppositional counterpart to *Sibylla Palmifera* and its sonnet (see cat. 108; the two pictures were related to each other only after both were well underway, perhaps as a result of writing the sonnets). Swinburne published both sonnets in his review of current art in 1868, together with an extended discussion of the two pictures. Later the sonnets were renamed 'Body's Beauty' and 'Soul's Beauty' respectively, but the idea of the contrast is already present in Swinburne's article, which describes the pictures as 'types of sensual beauty and spiritual, the siren and the sibyl' (Swinburne 1868, p. 46). In one sense the pictures and sonnets represent opposite aspects of beauty, but they are also subtly linked. Both kinds of

cat. 107

beauty have the power to 'draw' those who contemplate them, and the rose and poppy of Lilith's sonnet are also the flowers of *Sibylla Palmifera*. If Lilith is the 'witch', it is she who wears virginal white, while her alter ego has the red robe of passionate love. Thus Rossetti undermines the conventional Victorian pairing of good and bad woman, virgin and whore, which the two pictures seem at first to reinforce. In the early 1870s the features of Fanny Cornforth, the original model, were replaced with those of Alexa Wilding, the model for *Sibylla Palmifera*: as they now appear, the two paintings represent the same woman.

The meanings of *Lady Lilith*, then, became increasingly complex as Rossetti worked on it. However, the additional layers of meaning did not supersede the first conception, for Rossetti continued to insist that the painting represented 'a *Modern Lilith* combing out her abundant golden hair' (D & W, II, p. 850). This has led some scholars to interpret the painting in relation to Victorian debates about the role of women in modern society (see for example Allen 1984). Although the picture has generally been interpreted as expressing a Victorian male fear of female emancipation, it can also be taken as a celebration of women's independence. Indeed, a correspondent of Rossetti's noted jokingly that the legendary Lilith, who refused to submit to Adam's dominion, 'was evidently the first strong-minded woman and the original advocate of women's rights' (W.M. Rossetti 1903, p. 484). Rossetti's Lilith is both the most ancient of women

(she even predates the first woman, Eve) and the most modern, 'young while the earth is old'. She is thus a crucial precedent for Walter Pater's famous description of Leonardo's *Mona Lisa* (1869): 'She is older than the rocks among which she sits' and also 'the symbol of the modern idea' of humanity (Pater 1980, p. 99).

108
Sibylla Palmifera
(s 193)
1865–70
oil on canvas, 98.4 x 85 cm
National Museums Liverpool
(Lady Lever Art Gallery, Port Sunlight)
figure 45

When the picture was devised, towards the end of 1865, the title was simply *Palmifera* ('palm-bearing'). In letters to the picture's purchaser, George Rae, Rossetti explains the connotations of the word variously. At first, the figure bears the palm 'to mark the leading place which I intend her to hold among my beauties'. Later Rossetti suggests that the picture (with its sonnet) embodies the idea of '*Beauty the Palm-giver, i.e.*, the *Principle of Beauty*, which draws all high-toned men to itself'; this implies that the figure (or the picture) offers the palm to the viewer who is able to partake of the experience of beauty (W.M. Rossetti 1889, pp. 55–6). Thus the motif of the palm alludes to an important aspect of 'art for art's sake': the close correspondence between the beautiful object of contemplation and the viewer's

subjective experience of beauty. At the same time it responds to the appearance of the sitter, Alexa Wilding, whose beauty was considered specially pure or classical, as opposed to the earthier beauty of Fanny Cornforth or the more exotic beauty of Jane Morris.

By May 1866 Rossetti had written a sonnet to accompany the picture; later the sonnet was known as 'Soul's Beauty' and juxtaposed with the sonnet, 'Body's Beauty', that accompanied *Lady Lilith* (cat. 107). Yet the sonnet does not present spiritual beauty as purified or purged of human passions, as in some interpretations of the notion of 'art for art's sake':

Under the arch of Life, where love and death,
   Terror and mystery, guard her shrine, I saw
   Beauty enthroned; and though her gaze struck awe,
I drew it in as simply as my breath.
Hers are the eyes which, over and beneath,
   The sky and sea bend on thee,—which can draw,
   By sea or sky or woman, to one law,
The allotted bondman of her palm and wreath.

This is that Lady Beauty, in whose praise
   Thy voice and hand shake still,—long known to thee
     By flying hair and fluttering hem,—the beat
     Following her daily of thy heart and feet,
   How passionately and irretrievably,
In what fond flight, how many ways and days!

(D.G. Rossetti 1911, p. 100)

cat. 108

The dualities of the sonnet – love and death, terror and mystery – correspond to the imagery of the two sides of the picture. To the left are the roses of love and a blind-fold Cupid ('love is blind') above a burning flame; to the right are poppies and a skull, symbols of death, above a censer which emits a wisp of smoke, and two butterflies, symbols of the human soul (see cat. 104). The semi-circular niche behind the figure's head has carvings of a serpent or monster on the left and a sphinx on the right – perhaps to represent 'terror' and 'mystery' respectively (the mythological Sphinx asked a riddle of her victims). By 1867 Rossetti was using the title *Sibylla Palmifera*, which adds to the original connotations of the word 'palmifera' those of the Sibyl, in classical mythology a woman gifted with secret knowledge of the future. Perhaps this also imports an association with the seated figures of the Sibyls on Michelangelo's ceiling of the Sistine Chapel. The inscrutable or expressionless beauty given to Wilding's features is not, then, a bland or neutral counterpoise to the heady sensuality of *Lady Lilith*. Rather it indicates the mysterious or unfathomable fascination of the beautiful, with its overtones of love, death and fate.

109
A Christmas Carol
(s 195)
signed and dated bottom left: DGR / 1867
oil on canvas, 46.4 x 39.4 cm
Executors of the late Lord Leverhulme
figure 48

Like *The Blue Bower* (cat. 105), this picture presents a music-making subject with exotic accessories and medievalizing overtones. The Christmas carol is of medieval origin, and an inscription on the frame reads: 'Here a maid, well-apparelled, sings a song of Christ's birth with the tune of Bululalow: "Jesus Christus hodie natus est de Virgine" ' ('Today Jesus Christ is born of the Virgin'). The heart-shaped ornament on the back-drop behind the figure represents the Virgin and Child, perhaps as a visual equivalent for the carol. The two-stringed instrument is similar, if not identical, to the one seen in *The first anniversary of the death of Beatrice* of 1853 (cat. 42). The figure wears the spiral hair ornament seen in many of Rossetti's works (cats. 106, 141, 148), a necklace similar to that in *Morning Music* (cat. 101), and what Henry Treffry Dunn described as 'a resplendent eastern dress' (Dunn 1984, p. 32). Historical consistency was not important to Rossetti at this date; rather, the accessories seem to have been chosen to create an appropriately sumptuous setting for the Christmas subject.

cat. 109

110

**Buy from us with a golden curl
Golden head by golden head**

Goblin Market and other poems by Christina
Rossetti, published by Macmillan and Co.,
1862, frontispiece and title page
engraving on paper, 17.5 x 22.5 cm
frontispiece engraved by Morris, Marshall,
Faulkner & Co.; title page engraved by
W.J. Linton, both after designs by Rossetti
The British Library, London

'Goblin Market', the principal poem in
Christina Rossetti's first volume (which
appeared in 1862, eight years before her
brother published his own *Poems*, cat. 161),
can be interpreted as a fairy tale, a moral
fable, or a religious parable. The sisters,
Laura and Lizzie, draw water at a brook
where goblins entice them to buy luscious
fruits. Laura succumbs; after enjoying
the fruits she pines away, but Lizzie outwits
the goblins and saves her sister. For his sister's
volume Rossetti made two of his rare illustrations (as well as designing the binding,
cat. 157). The first shows Laura paying for
the fruit with one of her own golden curls
while Lizzie rushes away; the illustration
adumbrates Rossetti's pictures of women
dressing their hair (cats. 100, 102-3, 107).
It also echoes *Found* (since the reproduction
process reverses the image, Rossetti would
have drawn the figure facing left as in *Found*,
cat. 57); this likens Laura's bargain with the
goblins to prostitution. The second illustration shows Laura and Lizzie asleep in one
another's arms, the night after Laura's fall

from grace, with the goblins gleefully dancing
in a roundel. Rossetti thus concentrates on
the more sensual earlier events of the poem,
and ignores the moralizing conclusion.

111

**You should have wept her yesterday
The long hours go and come and go**

The Prince's Progress and other poems by Christina
Rossetti, published by Macmillan and Co.,
1866, frontispiece and title page
engraving on paper, 17.7 x 21.8 cm
engraved by W.J. Linton after Rossetti's
design
private collection

Rossetti encouraged his sister to expand
a sixty-line lyric of mourning into a full-
length narrative to serve as the title poem
for her second volume of 1866 (again
he also designed the binding, cat. 160).
His frontispiece illustrates a line from the
original dirge, in which the Prince is chas-
tised for his selfish neglect of his Bride,
who has died during his long absence
(the episode may have struck a chord with
Rossetti, remorseful about his own neglect
of Elizabeth Siddal). The title page illustration shows the Bride looking in vain for
the Prince's arrival.

cat. 110 a

cat. 110 b

cat. 111 a

Later Pre-Raphaelite Circle

After the early 1850s the members of the Pre-Raphaelite Brotherhood gradually drew apart from one another, and the charismatic Rossetti began to gather a new circle around himself. In 1856 he met Edward Burne-Jones and William Morris, still undergraduates at Oxford University; with Rossetti's encouragement both embarked on artistic careers, Burne-Jones as painter, Morris as designer and poet. The alliance produced a new social and artistic grouping, often called the 'second generation' of Pre-Raphaelitism. Rossetti himself was the crucial link between the earlier phase of the Pre-Raphaelite Brotherhood and this later grouping, in which women played an increasingly prominent part, as artists, models, wives or lovers.

Three important events consolidated the collaborations in the new group. The project to provide the Oxford Union with mural decorations, in 1857 (cats. 92–3, fig. 96), brought the aspiring poet Algernon Charles Swinburne (then an Oxford undergraduate) and the young Jane Burden (later Jane Morris) into close contact with Rossetti, Morris and Burne-Jones. In 1861 the founding of Morris, Marshall, Faulkner & Co. gave a new focus for artistic collaboration in a variety of applied art media (see cats. 163–71). Finally, Rossetti's move to Tudor House provided a new social centre for the group. Rossetti's role in these developments went far beyond his contributions as an artist and as a designer for the Morris firm. His unshakeable and generous confidence in the talents of his friends, as well as his inspirational leadership in the innovative artistic practices that grew up in the social circles around him, made possible the remarkable artistic flowering, encompassing the fine and applied arts as well as poetry, that Oscar Wilde was later to call the 'English Renaissance of Art'.

112
Fanny Cornforth and G.P. Boyce
c. 1858
ink on paper, 21.5 x 31.1 cm
Tullie House Museum and Art Gallery,
Carlisle
figure 97

This drawing, undocumented until 1973, has been identified as a double portrait of Rossetti's model Fanny Cornforth and the watercolour artist George Price Boyce. The setting may be either the rooms at 14 Chatham Place, Blackfriars Bridge, which Rossetti occupied from 1852 to 1862 (Surtees 1973), or Boyce's studio in Buckingham Street, off the Strand (Marsh 1999a, p. 203). The profile portrait, behind the figures, evidently represents Ruth Herbert, an actress whose beauty was much admired in Rossetti's circle (she was the model for cat. 68). Boyce's diary for 1858, the probable date of the drawing, records frequent contact with Rossetti and the latter's use of both Herbert and Cornforth as models (Boyce 1980, pp. 24–5). From about this date Cornforth became a close friend of both Rossetti and Boyce, and she has been said to have been the mistress of both men; the triangular relationship has become famous through Rossetti's *Bocca Baciata*, originally commissioned by Boyce as a portrait of Cornforth (cat. 94). Although the slender female figure in modern dress scarcely suggests the heady eroticism of *Bocca Baciata*, the intimacy of the pose is a touch improper for this date, and (with the

cat. 111 b

The long hours go and come and go

cat. 112

portrait of Herbert) perhaps hints at the 'Bohemian' studio life of Rossetti's circle.

113
Fanny Cornforth
(S 286)
c. 1860
brown ink and wash on paper,
22.4 x 21.1 cm
Visitors of the Ashmolean Museum, Oxford.
Bequeathed by John N. Bryson 1977
figure 59

Recent research on the sitter questions her traditional reputation as a Cockney prostitute; she was born Sarah Cox in Steyning, West Sussex, and there is no evidence that she ever worked as a prostitute (Drewery, Moore and Whittick 2001). Nor is it known whether, or at which periods, her relationship with Rossetti was sexual. She was, however, one of his closest friends from the late 1850s to the end of his life, and visitors frequently encountered her at Tudor House from the time of Rossetti's move there in 1862. This drawing shows her at an earlier date, about 1860, and presents a quieter view of her than that seen in the many paintings for which she served as model (cats. 57, 94, 96, 100, 102–3, 105).

114
Annie Miller
(S 354)
signed bottom right: DGR (monogram); dated bottom left: 1860; inscribed upper left: Annie Miller in 1860, upper right: Aetat. XXI
ink on paper, 25.5 x 24.2 cm
The L.S. Lowry Estate
figure 58

Annie Miller entered the Pre-Raphaelite circle as the model for William Holman Hunt's *The Awakening Conscience* of 1854 (fig. 11). For a time, Hunt contemplated marrying her and gave her financial support. However, Miller annoyed Hunt by continuing to sit for, and socialize with, other artists, Rossetti in particular. This drawing dates from the period after her break with Hunt, when both Rossetti and George Price Boyce helped her by employing her as a model (she was the model for cat. 99).

115
Georgiana Burne-Jones
(S 276)
c. 1860
pencil on paper, 26.7 x 32.6 cm
private collection
exhibited at Liverpool only

Georgiana Macdonald married Edward Burne-Jones in 1860. Although she was unusually small and slender, as the drawing suggests, her strength of character was much respected, and she was well liked, particularly

by Rossetti himself (F, II, pp. 301, 306). Her biography of her husband, published in two volumes in 1904, is both a valuable source of information and a fine work of literature in its own right.

116
Algernon Charles Swinburne
(S 523)
signed and dated upper right: DGR (monogram) / 1861
pencil, chalks, watercolour and bodycolour on paper, 18.1 x 15.9 cm
Syndics of the Fitzwilliam Museum, Cambridge
figure 55

This drawing captures the eccentric flair of the redheaded young poet Algernon Charles Swinburne (1837–1909). Swinburne's erudition in obscure areas of classical, medieval, Elizabethan and modern literature complemented Rossetti's knowledge of Dante and the early Italian poets; these interests crucially informed the poetry and visual art of the Rossetti circle in the 1860s. At the time this watercolour was painted, Swinburne had published a volume containing two verse dramas, *The Queen-Mother* and *Rosamond* (see cat. 96); his volume of 1866, *Poems and Ballads*, proved controversial and was threatened with prosecution for obscenity and blasphemy.

cat. 113

cat. 114

cat. 115

fig. 97
Fanny Cornforth and G.P. Boyce
c. 1858
Tullie House Museum and Art Gallery,
Carlisle
cat. 112

117
Self-portrait
(s 438)
signed and dated lower right:
DGR (monogram) / Oct. 1861
pencil on paper, 28.5 x 23.1 cm
Birmingham Museums & Art Gallery.
Presented by subscribers

Rossetti rarely drew his self-portrait and
never painted himself. This drawing dates
from 1861, during his brief marriage to
Elizabeth Siddal, and shows him still youth-
fully slender in the face (later he would put
on weight), but with beard and thinning
hair.

118
Maria Zambaco
(s 542)
signed and dated upper right:
DGR (monogram) / 1870
coloured chalks on paper, 45.3 x 34.9 cm
private collection

The sitter is most famous as the lover (and
model) of Burne-Jones in the later 1860s,
although Burne-Jones remained committed
to his marriage to Georgiana (cat. 115).
Zambaco, born Maria Cassavetti and related
to the Ionides family, important patrons
of the Rossetti circle, was also a talented
sculptor.

119
Alexa Wilding
(s 564)
signed and dated bottom left:
DGR (monogram) / 1873
coloured chalks on paper, 53.3 x 38 cm
private collection

Alexa Wilding was one of Rossetti's most
frequent models from 1865 onwards, and
the two became loyal friends (Rossetti gave
Wilding generous financial support, in
addition to paying her a retainer fee for
modelling regularly, and Wilding reportedly
travelled in grief to lay a wreath on Rossetti's
grave; see Dunn 1984, pp. 45–6). Yet their
relationship never developed the intensity of
Rossetti's relationships with other frequent
models (Siddal, Cornforth, Jane Morris);
indeed, his letters show that he found Wilding
boring. Perhaps, though, it was precisely
this lack of emotional engagement that made
Wilding a suitable model for ideal or classi-
cizing figures, such as *Sibylla Palmifera* (cat.
108), *Roman Widow* (cat. 149), and *The Blessed
Damozel* (cat. 152; Wilding also modelled for
cats. 147–8). When Rossetti repainted *Venus
Verticordia* (cat. 104) and *Lady Lilith* (cat. 107),
he substituted Wilding's features for those
of the original models, perhaps to mute
the pictures' eroticism. This drawing, in
the coloured chalk medium Rossetti cultivated from the end of the 1860s, conveys
both the elegance and the impassiveness
that Rossetti observed in Wilding's beautiful
features.

120
**Christina Rossetti
and Frances Lavinia Rossetti**
(s 433)
1877
coloured chalks on paper, 42.5 x 48.3 cm
National Portrait Gallery, London

This compelling double portrait was made
in the autumn of 1877 at Herne Bay on
the Kent coast, where Rossetti, attended by
his mother and sister, was convalescing from
an operation. His letters record his relief
at being able to resume work, and he valued
this drawing highly; it can be seen in Henry
Treffry Dunn's watercolour of Rossetti's
sitting room (cat. 172). The composition
captures not only the resemblance between
mother and daughter but their close relationship; Christina, who never married, was
her mother's constant companion until
the latter's death in 1886.

cat. 116

cat. 117

cat. 118

121
Christina Rossetti
(s 431)

signed and dated upper right:
DGR (monogram)/ 1877
coloured chalks on paper, 38.7 x 29.8 cm
private collection, courtesy of Peter Nahum
At The Leicester Galleries, London

Like cat. 120, this was among the drawings
made at Herne Bay in 1877. By this date
Christina had published a substantial body
of poetry, including the volumes *Goblin
Market and other poems* (1862, cats. 110, 157),
The Prince's Progress and other poems (1866,
cats. 111, 160), and *Sing-Song, a nursery rhyme
book* (1872). Her correspondence with her
brother shows that the two constantly helped
and advised one another on their poetic
work (indeed the entire Rossetti family collaborated on their extensive literary output
throughout their lives).

Portraits of Jane Burden Morris

Jane Burden (1839–1914) was the daughter
of an Oxford stable worker; when she first
met Rossetti and his friends she was just
seventeen, poor and with little education,
and her unusual appearance was strikingly
at odds with any conventional notion of
feminine prettiness. Yet from the first she
inspired respect or even awe. Immediately
she was cast in the role of an Arthurian
Queen, in works by Rossetti related to
the Oxford Union project (cat. 93) and
in William Morris's only oil painting (*Queen
Guenevere* or *La Belle Iseult*, 1858, Tate), and
descriptions of her constantly emphasized
her loftiness or unapproachability. This may
reflect the social ideals of the group, prepared
to disregard her working-class background;
it is also a response to her commanding
presence. On hearing of her engagement
to Morris, whom she married in 1859,
Swinburne declared that 'The idea of his
marrying her is insane. To kiss her feet is
the utmost man should dream of doing'
(Lang 1959, I, p. 18). A similar reverence
is evident in Rossetti's later letters to Jane,
as well as in his paintings of her.

Rossetti made drawings of Jane Burden
before her marriage (cats. 122–3), and
she was the model for the figure of Mary
in his altarpiece for Llandaff Cathedral
(cats. 64–5). However, their relationship,
both personal and artistic, entered a new
phase after 1865, when the Morrises moved
to central London (in the early years of

their marriage they had lived in a house
designed for them by the architect Philip
Webb, Red House in Bexleyheath, Kent).
The new phase began with a group of haunt-
ingly beautiful drawings (including cat. 124),
followed by a formal portrait in oils
(cat. 125). It may have been the sittings
for the portrait that stimulated ideas for
the remarkable sequence of subject pictures
for which Jane modelled from 1868 onwards
(cats. 139–147, 153–155). Together, Rossetti
and Jane Morris created the compelling
image of female beauty that seemed to critics
to epitomize Rossetti's art when the paintings finally appeared in public in the memorial exhibitions held after his death. If these
paintings helped to make Jane Morris one
of the most famous women of her generation,
Rossetti's own posthumous fame, from
the time of the memorial exhibitions to
the present day, owes as much to Jane's distinctive appearance and manner. As Rossetti
wrote to Jane in 1877, 'Pictures from common models folk will not buy from me'
(B & T, p. 47). The power of his art de-
pended not merely on his own skill, but
crucially on the appearance of the model.

The intimacy that developed between
Rossetti and Jane Morris during the modelling sessions was profound and mutual.
We shall never know whether the two were
physical lovers; however this may have been,
their correspondence demonstrates that
their personal relationship was inseparable
from their artistic collaboration. William
Morris, whose egalitarian social ideals
included a belief that marriage should be

cat. 119

cat. 120

cat. 121

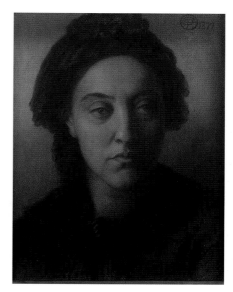

a matter of personal choice and not of legal constraint, allowed Rossetti and Jane to spend long periods together, in William's absence, at Kelmscott Manor in Oxfordshire, where Rossetti and William held a joint tenancy from 1871 to 1874. At Kelmscott the personal intimacy between Rossetti and Jane Morris flourished; so did the paintings for which Jane modelled. Later in the 1870s the contact between Jane and Rossetti gradually dwindled, as both were often ill; Rossetti's increasing addiction to drugs prescribed for insomnia placed a strain on the relationship, as it did on Rossetti's other friendships. However, they continued to correspond frequently, in particular about the pictures on which Rossetti was still at work. Although he increasingly relied on earlier drawings rather than fresh sittings, the last works he made before his death still represented Jane Morris (cats. 154–5).

122

Jane Burden

(s 363)

inscribed top left: J.B. Aetat XVII; bottom right: D.G.R. Oxoniae primo delt. Oct. 1857

pencil on paper, 47.6 x 33 cm

The Society of Antiquaries of London (Kelmscott Manor)

exhibited at Liverpool only

123

Jane Burden

(s 364)

signed and dated upper right:

DGR (monogram) Oxford 1858

ink, pencil and wash with white highlights on paper, 44 x 33 cm

National Gallery of Ireland, Dublin

Rossetti's earliest drawings of Jane Burden, before her marriage, already display the characteristic features of his later images of her: the abundant wavy hair, full lips, soulful expression, and the inclination of the head and neck. The Latin inscriptions on the earlier drawing allude to the learned environment at Oxford University; a Latin inscription also appears on Rossetti's later portrait, cat. 125.

124

Jane Morris

(s 367)

signed and dated right:

DGR (monogram) / 1865

black chalk on paper, 31.5 x 34.5 cm

private collection

figure 65

Jane Morris later remembered that Rossetti's best drawings of her dated from 1865, when she began to sit regularly to him (Marsh 1999a, p. 310). This drawing bears out that estimate, for it is one of the most beautiful Rossetti ever made. Most of Rossetti's earlier drawings had been in pencil or pen-and-ink; here, though, he adopts a new medium,

black chalk. The softer, more nuanced textures of the chalk medium give the head a special expressive tenderness, yet there is no loss of precision in the modelling of the features or in the delineation of the abundant waves of hair.

125

Jane Morris (The Blue Silk Dress)

(s 372)

inscribed on top edge: JANE MORRIS AD 1868 DG Rossetti pinxit. Conjuge clara poetâ, et praeclarissima vultu, Denique picturâ clara sit illa meâ!

oil on canvas, 110.5 x 90.2 cm

The Society of Antiquaries of London (Kelmscott Manor)

exhibited at Liverpool only

figure 63

This portrait marks the resumption of Jane Morris's modelling for Rossetti. Although not executed until 1868, it may have been planned as early as 1865, when Rossetti made at least half a dozen studies of Jane (for example cat. 124) and commissioned a series of photographs of her (cats. 131–8). The Latin inscription recalls the earliest of Rossetti's drawings of Jane (cat. 122) and the learned Oxford environment in which they first met; it also adds to the connotations of the image, making it more than a simple portrait. It can be translated: 'Famous for her poet husband, and most famous for her face, finally let her be famous for my picture!' The inscription adapts a common poetic motif, in which the

cat. 122

cat. 123

cat. 124

poet claims credit for making famous the person addressed in verse; the threefold phrasing acknowledges William Morris but gives the last word to Rossetti's painting. Nonetheless, the superlative of the middle phrase is crucial: it is for her own beauty that the sitter is 'most famous'. Letters from Rossetti to Jane Morris indicate that she made the sumptuous blue silk dress herself (the dress reappears in *Mariana*, cat. 141) and that she was involved in the choice of the pose (B & T, pp. 2–4). Portraiture was not a favoured category for Rossetti, who ordinarily preferred to invent literary or imaginative subjects for his pictures of single figures. However, the striking success of this portrait – evidently the one that so impressed Henry James (see pp. 92-3 above) – perhaps led Rossetti and Jane Morris to embark on the remarkable series of subject pictures that followed it.

126
Jane Morris lying on a sofa
(s 381)
dated right: Aug. 12 1870
pencil on paper, 24.1 x 45.1 cm
The Society of Antiquaries of London
(Kelmscott Manor)
exhibited at Liverpool only

127
Jane Morris reclining
(s 387)
c. 1870
pencil on paper, 25.4 x 23.8 cm
National Museums Liverpool (the Walker)

128
Jane Morris asleep on a sofa
(s 389)
c. 1870
pen and brown ink and ink wash on paper,
23.1 x 18.5 cm
Birmingham Museums & Art Gallery.
Bequeathed by James Richardson Holliday

Jane Morris suffered throughout her life from debilitating back pain and was often too ill to sit up or stand; visitors to the Morris house frequently encountered her, as in these drawings, reclining on a sofa (as Henry James did in 1869, James 1974, p. 94). Rossetti made at least fifteen drawings of Jane on a sofa, the large majority of which date from 1870. Most are in pencil or pen-and-ink, rather than the more elaborate coloured chalks he used for more formally posed drawings of the same period (for example cats. 139–40, 142–3).

129
Water Willow
(s 226)
signed and dated bottom left:
DGR (monogram) / Kelmscott 1871
oil on canvas, 33 x 26.7 cm
Delaware Art Museum, Samuel
and Mary R. Bancroft Memorial, 1935

This exquisite small painting documents the first period Rossetti and Jane Morris spent together at Kelmscott Manor; Rossetti made it, as he told correspondents, 'to fit a beautiful old frame I have' (D & W, III, p. 967).

The river background and the willow branches are typical of the countryside around Kelmscott, where Rossetti and Jane took long walks; the Manor is visible in the distance at upper left, Kelmscott church at upper right. This is a rare example in Rossetti's work of a landscape setting; the subdued grays and greens of the background are carefully harmonized in both colour and mood with the wistful figure, whose eyes appear greener than usual.

130
Jane Morris in Icelandic Dress
(s 399)
c. 1873
pencil on paper, 29.8 x 26.7 cm
Syndics of the Fitzwilliam Museum,
Cambridge

William Morris journeyed to Iceland in 1871 and 1873, to make researches for his translations of the Norse sagas; Rossetti and Jane Morris stayed together at Kelmscott, with the Morrises' two daughters, while William was away, apparently with his sanction (see cat. 129). Here Jane is seen in a characteristic reclining pose, wearing a decorated garment that William had brought back from Iceland.

131
John Robert Parsons
Photograph of Jane Morris
1865
albumen print, 21.3 x 16.8 (page 4 from album of photographs)
Victoria & Albert Museum, London
figure 67

cat. 125

cat. 126

cat. 127

132–138

Photographs of Jane Morris
albumen prints by Emery Walker
(1851–1933)
from the original photographs by Parsons
Birmingham Museums & Art Gallery

132
Jane Morris seated, full-length
20.2 x 12.5 cm
figure 90

133
Jane Morris seated, three-quarter-length
21.3 x 15.4 cm

134
Jane Morris reclining on a divan
16.6 x 19.3 cm

135
Jane Morris seated, half-length
18.5 x 15.1 cm

136
Jane Morris seated, leaning forward
16.2 x 14.9 cm
figure 99

137
Jane Morris seated on a divan,
three-quarter-length
20.1 x 15.5 cm

138
Jane Morris standing in a marquee
19.8 x 15.1 cm

In July 1865, Rossetti commissioned a series
of photographs of Jane Morris, posed in
a marquee in the garden at Tudor House
(Rossetti often had marquees erected for
outdoor parties). Perhaps the photographs
were meant to experiment with possible poses
for the portrait of Jane (cat. 125). Although
Rossetti also made many drawings of Jane,
as he had of Elizabeth Siddal (cats. 21–38),
the use of photography is a sign of the times;
portrait photography was becoming increasingly popular in the 1860s. In about 1865
Jane Morris had a more conventional portrait photograph taken, together with her
younger daughter, May (fig. 98, p. 203,
William Morris Gallery, London Borough
of Waltham Forest), in which she wears
a dress similar, if not identical, to the one
in the photographs commissioned by Rossetti,
but the difference is telling. Jane and May
appear before the conventional stage set
found in fashionable photographers' studios,
and the pose is a standard mother-and-child
composition. In the photographs commissioned by Rossetti, however, the poses are
more relaxed and inventive, and the figure
is seen from a variety of angles against vaguely
described backgrounds: these are art photographs, even though they were taken by
a photographer hired for the purpose.
The poses perhaps represent a collaboration
between Rossetti's ideas and Jane Morris's
way of carrying herself and moving.

The photographs can be related loosely
to later subject pictures; for example,
cat. 133 is reminiscent of *Mariana* (cat. 141),
cat. 135 of *La Pia* (cat. 140), cat. 136 of *Reverie*

(cat. 139), and cat. 138 of *Pandora* (cat. 145).
However, none of the poses exactly matches
either the oil portrait or any of the subject
pictures. Rossetti's letters to Jane suggest
that he continued to rely primarily on
drawings when she was unable to sit to him,
and he always preferred to work directly
from the living model. Thus the photographs are probably best regarded as experiments in pose, as well as mementoes of the
sitter, rather than as substitutes for preparatory drawings.

Parsons used the wet collodion process
to make his negatives, from which he made
albumen prints. His original photographs,
which had been cropped for framing, were
later unframed and bound into an album for
May Morris in 1933 (cat. 131; Parry 1996,
p. 28, cat. A.14). The album also includes
later silver gelatin prints of most of Parsons'
originals. The later prints in the album were
made by Emery Walker before 1930 but show
the images without cropping. The photographs now at Birmingham (cats. 132–8)
are also by Emery Walker and probably date
from c. 1890. There is a further set of prints
in a private collection. Walker's negatives are
in the St Bride's Printing Library, London.

cat. 128

cat. 129

cat. 130

cat. 131

cat. 132

cat. 133

cat. 134

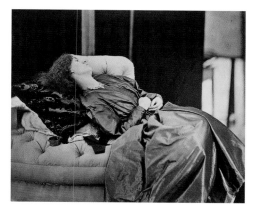

cat. 135

cat. 136

cat. 137

cat. 138

fig. 98

203

fig. 99
Jane Morris seated, leaning forward
albumen print by Emery Walker fom the
original photograph by John Robert Parsons
Birmingham Museums & Art Gallery
cat. 136

Late Work

In the years between 1868 and his death in 1882 Rossetti produced many of his largest and most powerful paintings, including *Dante's Dream* (cat. 147), the most ambitious work of his career, and the extraordinary sequence of pictures for which Jane Morris was the model and for which he is still most famous. In his final years he suffered increasingly from ill health, largely the result of a steadily increasing addiction to chloral hydrate, a new drug the destructive effects of which were poorly understood when it was prescribed to combat his chronic insomnia. Many writers have attributed the characteristics of his late style, particularly the mannered or exaggerated treatment of facial features and hands, to his addiction. But if there is some loss of delicacy or finesse in comparison to earlier works, that can also be attributed to the increasing monumentality of scale and conception in the late canvases; far from displaying the debility that might be expected of an artist in failing health, the pictures are highly finished, and the sense of the model's presence more intense than ever. Moreover the symbolic resonances of many of the late subjects, involving ideas of reverie and dreaming, of death and remembrance, add to their haunting power. Mannered as they may be, Rossetti's late works had the greatest impact on the Symbolist artists of the next generation, and they remain among the most memorable images in Western art.

139
Reverie
(s 206)
signed and dated upper left:
DGR (monogram)/ 1868
coloured chalks on paper, 81 x 71 cm
private collection
figure 79

In 1868, when he was at work on Jane Morris's portrait (cat. 125), Rossetti also began to design independent subjects with Jane as model. These were either literary subjects of the kind familiar in his earlier work (such as *La Pia de' Tolomei*, cat. 140) or a new kind of subject, in which the title describes an abstract idea. *Reverie* is the first of the latter type. The pose is the closest in Rossetti's work to one of the photographs of 1865 (cat. 136). It also refers to a traditional way of representing thoughtfulness or contemplation, with head on hand and elbow on knee, as in Dürer's famous engraving *Melancholia* (1514), or (later) Auguste Rodin's *The Thinker* (1880–1).

140
La Pia de' Tolomei
(s 207A)
signed and dated lower right:
DGR (monogram)/ 1868; inscribed on top edge: SIENA MI FÈ, DISFECEMI MAREMMA
coloured chalks on paper, 71.1 x 80.8 cm
private collection
figure 80

This finished drawing corresponds closely to

cat. 139

the painting of the same subject, begun in 1868 but resumed and finished only in 1881 (fig. 100). The subject is from canto V of the *Purgatorio*, in which Dante encounters La Pia, a Sienese woman who had died of malaria, or perhaps of poison, after being imprisoned by her husband in the unhealthy marshland of the Maremma; her name, which means pious or loyal, suggests that her imprisonment was wrongful. The line inscribed at the top of the drawing is uttered by La Pia, who begs Dante to remember her fate: 'Siena gave me birth, Maremma death' (Sinclair 1971, II, p. 75). The action of the figure's long fingers refers to the next lines, in which La Pia mentions the wedding ring that bound her to her cruel husband. The branch of foliage on the left, suggestively vague in the drawing, reads clearly in the later painting as ivy, symbolic of fidelity and thus an analogue of La Pia's name. Writers on Rossetti have often interpreted this composition, one of the first subject pictures designed by Rossetti with Jane Morris as model, as a reference to Jane's own unhappiness in her marriage to William Morris; thus the subject can be seen as parallel to those of other pictures that involve neglected or unwilling wives, such as *Mariana* (cat. 141) or *Proserpine* (cat. 155). If, in this case, Rossetti is implicitly casting himself in the role of Dante, he can have no hope of rescuing the wronged woman; he can, however, memorialize her fate in artistic form, as La Pia asks Dante to do. The subject thus involves the ideas of death and remembrance that would haunt Rossetti's later works.

141
Mariana
(s 213)
signed and dated bottom left:
DGR (monogram) 1870
oil on canvas, 109.2 x 90.5 cm
Aberdeen Art Gallery & Museums Collections
figure 64

So striking was Rossetti's portrait of Jane Morris (cat. 125) that one of his patrons, William Graham, tried to commission a replica, even though it was a portrait of someone unrelated to him (W.M. Rossetti 1903, pp. 327, 487). Unwilling to copy the portrait, Rossetti instead transformed the composition into a subject picture. By adding a page boy (modelled by Graham's own son), the figure turns into Mariana, from Shakespeare's *Measure for Measure*, deserted by her betrothed. This subject, like those of *La Pia* (cat. 140) and *Proserpine* (cat. 155), involves a woman neglected or unsatisfied by her husband (or, in this case, her fiancé), and thus seems specially suited to Rossetti's series of paintings of Jane Morris. However, the subject was not novel in Pre-Raphaelite circles – perhaps, indeed, the striking blue dress in Millais's *Mariana* of 1850–1 (Tate) helped to suggest the subject for Rossetti's own composition with a blue dress; Rossetti's Mariana, like Millais's, pauses wearily from her needlework, perhaps dreaming of the love denied to her. In fact Millais's *Mariana* is an illustration of one of Tennyson's two poems about the Shakespearean character, which Millais also

illustrated for the Moxon Tennyson of 1857; Rossetti himself provided the illustration for the other poem, 'Mariana in the South' (cats. 77–8). For the later oil painting, however, Rossetti went directly to Shakespeare. The scene is that of Act IV, scene I, in which Mariana is discovered in melancholy seclusion, listening to her page's song.

142
Silence
(s 214)
signed and dated bottom right:
DGR (monogram) / 1870
black and red chalk on paper, 104.5 x 76 cm
Brooklyn Museum of Art, New York.
Gift of Mr. Luke Vincent Lockwood 46.188
figure 77

This drawing, as usual with Rossetti's works, can be given either a biographical or a wider symbolic interpretation. According to contemporaries, Jane Morris was an unusually silent woman; indeed her reticence must have been a crucial source of the impression she projected of remoteness or unfathomability. Thus the drawing can be seen simply as a character study of the model. However, the abstract idea of silence also has connections to mysticism and Neoplatonic philosophy, to which Rossetti was increasingly attracted in his later years; evocations of silence and mystical inwardness would become important, along with Rossetti's influence, in the Symbolist art of the later 19th century (see pp. 120-4, fig. 76). Such ideas are adumbrated in the brief

cat. 140

cat. 141

cat. 142

fig. 100
La Pia de' Tolomei
1868-81
Spencer Museum of Art,
University of Kansas, Lawrence

legend Rossetti wrote to accompany the drawing when it was reproduced as an autotype in 1878: 'Silence holds in one hand a branch of peach, the symbol used by the ancients; its fruit being held to resemble the human heart and its leaf the human tongue. With the other hand she draws together the veil enclosing the shrine in which she sits' (B & T, p. 71). The drawing may appear unfinished, particularly in comparison with the intricately wrought surfaces of most of Rossetti's work, but the blank spaces correspond to the conception of the picture, representing what cannot be seen or heard: the idea of silence.

143
La Donna della Finestra
(s 255 A)
signed and dated upper right:
DGR (monogram)/ 1870; inscribed on scroll bottom centre: Color d'amore e di pietà sembiante
coloured chalks on paper, 84.8 x 72.1 cm
Bradford Art Gallery
figure 81

144
La Donna della Finestra (unfinished)
(s 255 R I)
1881
oil on canvas, 95.9 x 87 cm
Birmingham Museums & Art Gallery

The composition was designed in 1870 (cat. 143); as with other compositions modelled by Jane Morris, Rossetti repeated it several times in the remaining decade of his life, both in drawing media and in oils (cat. 144 and fig. 101). It can easily be given an autobiographical interpretation: it represents the 'Donna della Finestra' (or 'Lady of the Window') who looked compassionately at Dante from a window after the death of Beatrice, just as Jane Morris (the model for the Lady) can be said to have consoled Rossetti after the death of Elizabeth Siddal (the model for Beatrice in so many of Rossetti's pictures). Yet this was one of the thirteen subjects from the *Vita Nuova* that Rossetti first contemplated designing in 1848, long before he met either Elizabeth Siddal or Jane Morris (F, I, p. 76; see also cat. 97). Moreover, the subject itself constitutes a warning against limiting interpretation to the biographical level. The line quoted on the scroll at the bottom of the drawing is a quotation, not from the description of the event in the *Vita Nuova*, but rather from the sonnet in which Dante transforms life into art; in Rossetti's translation, it reads 'Love's pallor and the semblance of deep ruth' (with reference to the compassionate face of the Lady). In Dante scholarship, there was — and still is — continual debate about whether the events and characters of Dante's works can be seen as historical facts, belonging to Dante's own life, or whether they should be interpreted in symbolic or allegorical terms, or both. The Lady of the Window is an obvious focus for such debates: does she represent Dante's wife in real life, or is she an allegory of some abstract idea, such as Philosophy? According to William Michael Rossetti, his brother rejected the kind of allegorical interpretation that would make the Lady no more than a sign for a concept; but he also refused to limit the meaning of the incident to the literal level (W.M. Rossetti 1889, p. 108). Neither interpretation is adequate on its own. The Lady of the picture is *both* a real woman — Jane Morris, represented with Pre-Raphaelite fidelity to individual appearance — *and* a 'poetic suggestion' of further thoughts and emotions (in this case, particularly those of pity or compassion). Such ideas, explored throughout Rossetti's work in both painting and poetry, were of the greatest importance to the Symbolist art and literature of the later 19th century.

145
Pandora
(s 224)
signed and dated lower right:
DGR (monogram) / 1871; inscribed on casket: NESCITUR IGNESCITUR
oil on canvas, 128.3 x 76.2 cm
private collection, courtesy of Peter Nahum At The Leicester Galleries, London
figure 102

cat. 143

cat. 144

cat. 145

146

Pandora
(S 224 R I A)
signed and dated lower left:
DGR (monogram)/ 1878; inscribed
on casket: ULTIMA/ MANET/SPES
coloured chalks on paper, 100.8 x 66.7 cm
National Museums Liverpool
(Lady Lever Art Gallery, Port Sunlight)
figure 72

Pandora is one of various mythological
figures identified as the first woman; thus
she is a Greek analogue of the Biblical Eve
and the Talmudic Lilith (cat. 107). Jupiter
gives her a casket, which she is forbidden to
open. In some versions of the story it is her
husband who opens the casket, in others
(as in Rossetti's composition) it is Pandora
herself; either way, the casket lets forth all
the evils into the world, leaving inside, and
safe, only Hope. Like the story of Lilith, this
can be given either a misogynist or a feminist
interpretation: is Pandora a *femme fatale* who
ruins men by her disobedience? Or is she
a heroic woman who defies her husband
and the gods, to take control of her own
fate? In 1869, probably the date at which
he first designed the pictorial composition,
Rossetti wrote an accompanying sonnet, but
it leaves these questions open:

What of the end, Pandora? Was it thine,
  The deed that set these fiery pinions free?
  Ah! Wherefore did the Olympian consistory
In its own likeness make thee half divine?
Was it that Juno's brow might stand a sign
  For ever? And the mien of Pallas be
  A deadly thing? and that all men might see
In Venus' eyes the gaze of Proserpine?

What of the end? These beat their wings at will,
The ill-born things, the good things turned to ill,—
  Powers of the impassioned hours prohibited.
  Aye, clench the casket now! Whither they go
  Thou mayst not dare to think: nor canst thou know
If Hope still pent there be alive or dead.

(D.G. Rossetti 1911, p. 211)

On the casket in the oil version is the inscription 'Nescitur Ignescitur'. The Latin is obscure, but it can perhaps be translated, with
reference to hope: 'it is not known, but is
kindled'. This would correspond to the emphasis, in the last lines of the sonnet, on the
unfathomability of hope. The inscription on
the later drawing, 'Ultima Manet Spes' ('Hope
remains last'), is consistent with the autobio-
graphical interpretation favoured by some
writers, according to which Jane Morris as
Pandora holds out a last hope to Rossetti. The
winged creatures, swirling in the smoke that
rises from the casket, are remarkable inventions
in both versions, more sinister and brooding
in the earlier oil, which perhaps hints at
Rossetti's interest in spiritualism at about this
date, more stylized in the later drawing, anticip-
ating the decorative rhythms of Art Nouveau.

147

Dante's Dream
(S 81 R I)
1871
signed bottom right: D.G. Rossetti
oil on canvas, 216 x 312.4 cm
National Museums Liverpool (the Walker)
figure 61

Appropriately, Rossetti's largest and
most magnificent painting is also the most
elaborate of his subjects from Dante, conceived as early as 1848 (F, I, p. 76), painted
in watercolour in 1856 (fig. 60), and most
fully developed in this oil. It represents
the episode in the *Vita Nuova* when Dante
dreams of seeing Beatrice in death. In the
dream, love is an abstract concept or a feeling of Dante's, but in the poem he then
writes, he makes Love into an embodied
character (the legitimacy of this poetic
personification is then discussed at some
length, in one of the many passages in the
Vita Nuova that deal with literary theory).
Rossetti represents Love in embodied
form, as in the poem, imagining him
as both an angel and a Cupid, with wings
and an arrow; the scallop shell of a pilgrim
is on his shoulder. Poppies, the flower
of sleep or death, litter the floor; the white
veil is laden with may-blossom, perhaps
alluding to the season of Beatrice's death
(June 9); Love carries a branch of apple-
blossom, again a spring flower, and also
a symbol of unconsummated love, plucked
before it comes to fruit. In the oil, Jane
Morris is the model for Beatrice. When

cat. 146

cat. 147

fig. 101
La Donna della Finestra
1879
Fogg Art Museum,
Harvard University Art Museums.
Bequest of Grenville L. Winthrop

fig. 102
Pandora
1871
private collection, courtesy of Peter Nahum
At The Leicester Galleries, London
cat. 145

the picture was sold to the Walker Art Gallery, Rossetti retouched the figure to combine Jane Morris's features with the red colour of Elizabeth Siddal's hair. Thus Rossetti's grandest representation of Beatrice has elements of both his most important models; he experimented with this conflation of Jane Morris and Elizabeth Siddal in other works at the very end of his life (see cat. 155). For a more extensive discussion of this picture see pp. 86-91.

148
The Bower Meadow
(s 229)
signed and dated bottom left:
D.G. Rossetti / 1872
oil on canvas, 85.1 x 67.3 cm
Manchester City Galleries
figure 68

The outdoor setting is unusual in Rossetti's work; in fact this landscape was based on a much earlier canvas, painted in 1850 during Rossetti's only, uncompleted, foray into open-air painting. William Michael Rossetti thought that the subject of the earlier painting might have been *The Meeting of Dante and Beatrice in Paradise* – if so, it could have been a much larger oil version of cat. 43. The change in subject matter is telling: the new composition is very much up to date for the early 1870s, a scene of music-making and dancing in the spirit of 'art for art's sake', or what was beginning to be called 'Aestheticism'. The doves and roses suggest that this is also the ideal 'bower', or private garden, of Venus or love.

The musical instruments doubtless come from Rossetti's motley collections of aesthetic objects, again an important influence on Aesthetic Movement tastes, and the pearl hair ornament is one of Rossetti's favourite accessories (also seen in cats. 106, 109, 141). The models for the foreground figures were Marie Spartali Stillman (left) and Alexa Wilding (right), both regarded as classically beautiful (they were also the models for the handmaids in *Dante's Dream*, cat. 147).

149
Roman Widow (Dìs Manibus)
(s 236)
signed and dated lower left: D.G. Rossetti / 1874; inscribed on urn: DÎS MANIBUS / L. AELIO AQUINO / MARITO CARISSIMO / PAPIRIA GEMINA / FECIT / AVE DOMINE. VALE DOMINE
oil on canvas, 103.7 x 91.2 cm
Museo de Arte de Ponce, Puerto Rico
figure 70

A widow of ancient Rome sits beside the cinerary urn containing her husband's ashes; she plays two musical instruments in her husband's honour and in expression of her grief. Rossetti is usually seen as a medievalist, like his friends Burne-Jones and Morris, not a classicist like Frederic Leighton, George Frederic Watts or Lawrence Alma-Tadema (all of whom were also friends, although more distant ones). Yet a surprising number of his pictorial subjects derive from classical sources. More-over, he never lost the Latin he learned at school and was often able to make sophisti-

cated use of Latin titles and inscriptions (cats. 104, 108, 145). On this occasion, however, he borrowed the inscription from a Roman cinerary urn in his own collection (D & W, III, p. 1228): 'To the deities of the Underworld' – a standard invocation in Latin epitaphs – 'Papiria Gemina has made this for her dearest husband Lucius Aelius Aquinus: Hail, master, and farewell, master'. The magnificent array of shades of white is a *tour de force*; indeed one cannot help sus-pecting Rossetti of attempting to rival Alma-Tadema, who was becoming famous at just this date for his representation of white marble. Moreover, the care Rossetti takes with archaeological details also responds to the newly fashionable classicism of Alma-Tadema. The marble cinerary urn, the silver marriage-girdle that hangs on the urn, the figure's white mourning draperies and the musical instruments are all researched from archaeological sources. William Michael Rossetti suggested that the two instruments may correspond to the final two phrases of the inscription with which Papiria Gemina pays respect and bids farewell to her husband: 'Ave Domine' and 'Vale Domine' (W.M. Rossetti 1889, p. 92).

cat. 148

cat. 149

150

The Death of Lady Macbeth

(S 242 B)

c. 1875

ink and sepia wash on paper, 46.7 x 61.6 cm

Visitors of the Ashmolean Museum, Oxford

In the 1870s Rossetti showed a renewed
interest in subjects from Shakespeare; in
addition to *Mariana* (cat. 141), he was planning, in the final years of his life, a painting
of *Desdemona's Death Song* (from *Othello*, Act
IV, scene 3), never advanced, although Jane
Morris gave at least one sitting for it (B & T,
p. 185). This subject from *Macbeth* seems
never to have been started on canvas, but
it exists in three slightly different designs
(the others are at Tullie House Museum
and Art Gallery, Carlisle, and Birmingham
Museums & Art Gallery, S 242, 242 A).
Lady Macbeth's death occurs offstage in
Shakespeare's play. Rossetti therefore con-
structs the composition using elements
of her last appearance, when she is observed
obsessively rubbing her hands, imagining
that they are bloodstained, and crying:
'Out, damn'd spot! Out, I say!' (Act V,
scene 1). Rossetti regroups this scene and
adds further figures. A taper burns at the
rear, perhaps alluding to Macbeth's famous
speech, when he is told of his wife's death,
'Out, out brief candle!'(Act V, scene 5).
Perhaps this subject struck a chord with
Rossetti, still troubled by guilt about
Elizabeth Siddal's death.

151

Orpheus and Eurydice

(S 243)

1875

pencil on paper, 61 x 51.4 cm

The British Museum, London

This is a tale of a husband and wife separated
by the wife's death, briefly reunited in the
scene we see, but doomed to lose one another again. Orpheus, the husband, is the
great musician of ancient legend, able to
charm wild animals and even trees and stones;
in later art and literature he can represent
the archetypal creative artist. Here he plays
his lyre to Pluto and Proserpina, king and
queen of the Underworld; Pluto, swayed by
the beauty of the music, draws back the cur-
tain to allow Orpheus to lead his dead bride,
Eurydice, up the stairs to the land of the
living; a bird, faintly indicated in the pencil
drawing, flies before them. Proserpina,
though, leans her head on her hand, perhaps in dejection: she too longs to leave
the Underworld but can do so only for half
the year (see cat. 155). The drawing alludes
to previous and subsequent events in the
tale, as told in Ovid's *Metamorphoses*, Book X.
The snake that has killed Eurydice by biting
her ankle is sketched writhing on the floor,
and the tragic denouement is hinted in the
figures' poses: Orpheus, commanded not
to look back at Eurydice until they have gained
the upper air, is unable to resist, and Eurydice will slip back into death.

152

The Blessed Damozel

(S 244 R I)

c. 1875–81

signed on predella: DG Rossetti

oil on canvas, III x 82.7 cm; predella,
36.5 x 82.8 cm

National Museums Liverpool
(Lady Lever Art Gallery, Port Sunlight)

figure 103

This composition, which exists in two oil
versions (cat. 152 and fig. 69), represents
the sole occasion when Rossetti based
a pictorial work on a pre-existing poem
of his own – his most famous poem, written
before the formation of the Pre-Raphaelite
Brotherhood, published in the Pre-
Raphaelite literary magazine, *The Germ*,
in 1850 and reprinted as the first of the
Poems of 1870 (cat. 161). Most of the poem
describes the Damozel in Heaven and
records her speech; interspersed with these
passages are stanzas and phrases in parenth-
eses, representing the lover's utterances as
he strains to hear and see, or perhaps only
to remember, the Damozel. The picture
captures this alternation of voices, by presenting the Damozel in the large upper canvas
and the lover in the smaller predella below.
Only the lower space, on earth, obeys
normal post-Renaissance perspective; in
the upper canvas a heavenly realm beyond
space or time is envisaged, as in the poem.
The painting follows the text closely:

cat. 150

cat. 151

cat. 152

The blessed damozel leaned out
   From the gold bar of Heaven;
Her eyes were deeper than the depth
   Of waters stilled at even;
She had three lilies in her hand,
   And the stars in her hair were seven.

...

Herseemed she scarce had been a day
   One of God's choristers;
The wonder was not yet quite gone
   From that still look of hers;
Albeit, to them she left, her day
   Had counted as ten years.

On earth the lover responds:
   (To one, it is ten years of years.
      . . . Yet now, and in this place,
   Surely she leaned o'er me – her hair
      Fell all about my face. . .
   Nothing: the autumn-fall of leaves.
      The whole year sets apace.)

(D.G. Rossetti 1911, p. 3)

The model for the Damozel was Alexa Wilding (see cats. 104, 107–8, 119). For further discussion of this picture, see pp. 100-1.

153
Astarte Syriaca
(S 249)
signed and dated bottom left:
D.G. Rossetti. 1877
oil on canvas, 182.9 x 106.7 cm
Manchester City Galleries
exhibited at Liverpool only
figure 66

'I think that my brother was always wont to regard this as his most exalted performance,' wrote William Michael Rossetti (W.M. Rossetti 1889, p. 98). It is the largest of Rossetti's paintings of female figures (the only larger works are multiple-figure scenes, cats. 64, 147). Designed in 1875 and completed in 1877, it is the last major composition based on Jane Morris that came to fruition, and in many ways the culminating example of the series. The subject is the Syrian goddess of love, Astarte, more ancient even than the Greco-Roman Venus (cat. 104), and more elemental in this presentation with the luminous discs of the sun and moon above her head. As he often did, Rossetti wrote a sonnet when the picture was nearing completion:

Mystery: lo! Betwixt the sun and moon
   Astarte of the Syrians: Venus Queen
   Ere Aphrodite was. In silver sheen
Her twofold girdle clasps the infinite boon
Of bliss whereof the heaven and earth commune:
   And from her neck's inclining flower-stem lean
   Love-freighted lips and the absolute eyes that wean
The pulse of hearts to the spheres' dominant tune.

Torch-bearing, her sweet ministers compel
   All thrones of light beyond the sky and sea
   The witnesses of Beauty's face to be:
That face, of Love's all-penetrative spell
Amulet, talisman, and oracle,–
   Betwixt the sun and moon a mystery.

(D.G. Rossetti 1911, p. 226)

The face is instantly recognizable as that of Jane Morris, yet it also reaches an extreme of abstraction – 'amulet, talisman, and oracle', as the sonnet has it – uncanny in its perfect symmetry and absolutely frontal. At least one of the torchbearers was modelled on Jane's own daughter May, enhancing the effect of repetition in the faces, and the two flanking figures are also perfectly symmetrical; the flaming torch in antiquity could be a symbol of either love or death, since it was carried at both marriages and funerals.

   The commanding figure of Astarte, with its long, powerful limbs, recalls Michelangelo or the Mannerist painters; the hands take to an extreme the elongation of the fingers and the bending of the joints characteristic of Rossetti's representations of Jane Morris's

cat. 153

fig. 103
The Blessed Damozel
c. 1875–81
National Museums Liverpool,
(Lady Lever Art Gallery, Port Sunlight)
cat. 152

hands. They are arranged in a mannered version of the traditional *pudicitia* pose, used in ancient nude statues modestly to cover the breast and genital areas. Since this figure is not nude, the hands relate instead to the two girdles, evidently based on a silver belt that Jane eventually owned (cat. 178). Nonetheless, as the sonnet indicates, the two girdles encircle the areas of the female body associated with the *pudicitia* pose, with sexual 'bliss', or perhaps with the womb between them. Together, then, the picture and poem make the most sexually explicit subject in Rossetti's art. Yet this is balanced, in the sonnet, by the emphasis on 'mystery', and, in the picture, by the lofty stance of the figure and the rather dry, austere handling of the paint. According to William Michael Rossetti, this balance between the sensual and the spiritual was the guiding idea of the picture (W.M. Rossetti 1889, p. 99).

154
The Day Dream
(s 259)
signed and dated lower right:
D.G. Rossetti 1880
oil on canvas, 158.7 x 92.7 cm
Victoria & Albert Museum, London
exhibited at Liverpool only
figure 71

The subject matter of this work evolved through a number of vicissitudes. It began as a drawing of Jane Morris, certainly in existence by 1872, when Rossetti referred to it simply as 'the lady seated in a tree with a book in her lap' (D & W, III, pp. 1067–8). Thus the visual image, as often in Rossetti's work, seems to have predated any specific idea for a subject, although the resonances of the motif of the woman in a tree are intriguing. As Andrew Wilton has noted, this motif, important in the Symbolist art of the later 19th century, might recall any of the women in ancient myths who are metamorphosed into trees, or Eve and the Tree of Knowledge (Wilton and Upstone 1997, p. 11; perhaps the book alludes to the idea of knowledge).

In 1879 Rossetti was commissioned to execute the design as a full-scale painting, and he worked assiduously at it throughout the next year. At first he called it *Vanna Primavera*, with reference to a passage in the *Vita Nuova* in which Dante sees a woman called Giovanna ('Vanna') but nicknamed 'Primavera' (or 'Spring') walking before Beatrice (D.G. Rossetti 1911, p. 331). But the spring flowers Rossetti planned, a snowdrop and a primrose, proved too delicate for the extraordinary shape of Jane Morris's hand, as painted by Rossetti; meanwhile, the foliage of the sycamore tree grew too full for the season. Finally he abandoned the spring subject and renamed the picture *The Day Dream*. The new title preserves the emphasis on dreaming characteristic of many of Rossetti's Dante subjects; it also recalls the earlier drawing of Jane Morris, *Reverie* (cat. 139). Finally, Rossetti wrote a sonnet, which clearly relates not to the first conception of the picture, but to the way it had developed in the working process:

The thronged boughs of the shadowy sycamore
  Still bear young leaflets half the summer through;
  From when the robin 'gainst the unhidden blue
Perched dark, till now, deep in the leafy core,
The embowered throstle's urgent wood-notes soar
  Through summer silence. Still the leaves come new;
  Yet never rosy-sheathed as those which drew
Their spiral tongues from spring-buds heretofore.

Within the branching shade of Reverie
Dreams even may spring till autumn; yet none be
  Like woman's budding day-dream spirit-fann'd.
Lo! tow'rd deep skies, not deeper than her look,
She dreams; till now on her forgotten book
  Drops the forgotten blossom from her hand.

(D.G. Rossetti 1911, p. 231)

The picture is among Rossetti's finest designs, particularly in the subtle management of shades of green (the dress appears to be the same green silk as in *Astarte Syriaca*, cat. 153, and *Proserpine*, cat. 155) and in the complex intertwining curves of the limbs and branches. Most fascinating of all is the honeysuckle, slightly wilted, in the long, wan hand resting wearily on the book – 'forgotten', as the sonnet says, along with the spring subject, but at the same time a poignant reminder of the importance of flowers, as symbols of perfect beauty, throughout Rossetti's work.

cat. 154

155

Proserpine
(S 233 R 3)
signed and dated on scroll at lower left:
DANTE GABRIEL ROSSETTI 1882;
on scroll at top right: the sonnet
'Proserpine' (see below)
oil on canvas, 77.5 x 37.5 cm
Birmingham Museums & Art Gallery.
Purchased by the Public Picture Gallery
Fund
figure 62

Rossetti began eight canvases with this composition, three of which reached completion; the composition was also repeated several times in drawing media. Replication and translation into another medium were central practices of Rossetti's and crucial to his art (see pp. 90-1). There are also two versions of the accompanying sonnet, in Italian and English. The oil version catalogued here is smaller than the earlier versions (for example fig. 104). However, it is distinctive in other respects: it was the eighth and last, completed just a few days before the artist's death, and the only one to bear the English version of the sonnet. For this version only, he replaced Jane Morris's dark hair with red, the colour of Elizabeth Siddal's hair (he did this also when he retouched *Dante's Dream*, cat. 147, in 1881 for the Walker Art Gallery).

Proserpina was the unwilling wife of Pluto, who abducted her as she was picking flowers in the vale of Enna and carried her down to the Underworld to become his queen (see cat. 151). Her mother, Ceres, obtained permission from Jupiter for her return to earth, provided she had eaten nothing in the Underworld. But she had partaken of a pomegranate; thus she was doomed to spend half the year underground, and only half on earth. This tale of a woman trapped in an unhappy marriage has often been interpreted biographically, as a representation of Jane Morris. Yet the sonnet Rossetti wrote for the picture gives the subject a more universal significance; the repetitions of the word 'afar' dwell on the pain of separation — from daylight, from flowers, from the sky and from the days of the past, even from oneself:

Afar away the light that brings cold cheer
   Unto this wall, — one instant and no more
   Admitted at my distant palace-door.
Afar the flowers of Enna from this drear
Dire fruit, which, tasted once, must thrall me here.
   Afar those skies from this Tartarean gray
   That chills me: and afar, how far away
The nights shall be from the days that were.

Afar from mine own self I seem, and wing
   Strange ways in thought, and listen for a sign:
   And still some heart unto some soul doth pine,
(Whose sounds mine inner sense is fain to bring
Continually together murmuring,)—
   'Woe's me for thee, unhappy Proserpine!'

(D.G. Rossetti 1911, p. 253)

The square of light on the rear wall is, then, a ray from the world above, but the sonnet tells us that it will last only 'one instant'. The ivy clinging to the wall and the lamp on the foreground parapet are both symbols of memory, but like the light they only emphasize how far away is the remembered happiness of the past, or of the sunlit world of ordinary mortals. The lamp smokes, but provides no light. This is perhaps Rossetti's most famous composition, and certainly among his most powerful; it is also his most deeply mournful, the most vivid of his evocations of death and memory, the constant preoccupations of his late work. Yet the pomegranate, the cause of Proserpina's relegation for half the year to hell, is also used in Christian symbolism to stand for the hope of resurrection, since Proserpina returns each year to the upper earth. Thus it is an attribute of Dante, whose descent into hell is followed by his visions of Purgatory and Paradise (cats. 40–1). Perhaps we may, then, interpret the ray of light on the background wall not only as a memory of past bliss, but as a sign of hope.

cat. 155

fig. 104
Proserpine
1873–7
private collection

Rossetti as designer

Frames

Rossetti cared deeply about the way his art was presented. He conceived of his paintings not just as representations of his ideas but as beautiful objects in themselves. His use of line, composition and pattern emphasized the physical qualities of his pictures such as their flat surfaces; he denied the illusion of depth by arranging figures in shallow spaces parallel to the picture plane. Rossetti's frames were designed to bring about similar effects; they were integral to his conception of a work of art as a beautiful object.

Rossetti disliked the bulbous, neo-rococo gilt frames, the 'swept' outlines, the naturalistic designs or busy all-over patterns preferred by contemporary artists for their frames. He was a pioneer in the use of simpler, rectilinear frames with large areas devoid of decoration. He used ornaments sparingly against plain flat backgrounds; the ornamental motifs on his frames were personal and original, some abstract, some echoing the symbolism of his paintings. Rossetti was a pioneer of frame design, but it is difficult to be precise about dating, because of his habit of framing or reframing pictures long after they had been completed.

A number of frame types recur in his work, though often used with variations. He devised a broad, heavy type of frame for many of his small watercolours, to hold in the brilliance of their colour. These frames consist of a wide gilt 'flat' with narrower mouldings on the outer and inner edges. The flats were often incised with circular or

fig. 105
Fair Rosamund
1861
National Museums and Galleries of Wales,
Cardiff
cat. 96

star motifs and lines of poetry (cats. 43, 51). Whilst the earlier frames of this kind were covered in gesso and given a burnished gilt finish, Rossetti later preferred the wood of the flat to be painted in gold directly on to the wood, revealing its grain, and to have vertical joins instead of diagonal mitres at each corner (cats. 20, 116).

Rossetti also designed the so-called thumbnail pattern, a moulding with a triangular section projecting to a ridge, relieved by a snaking pattern of curved shapes gouged out in relief (cat. 97, fig. 105). Another favoured design was a narrow reeded frame, ebonized in black but relieved with crude gold painted squares, creating a striped effect (cat. 100). Later he used the same reeded moulding but entirely gilt and relieved by square motifs at each corner and circular wheel-like motifs on the verticals and horizontals (cat. 13). This type of moulding was usually seen on the outside of a broad gold-painted flat as already described. Sometimes the reeded outer edge was replaced by a more conventional plaster 'leaf and berry' pattern (cats. 42, 85).

For his late oils, Rossetti used a different style again, a big, heavy frame smoothly gilded, with a broad flat and narrower mouldings at outer and inner edges. In these frames, however, the flats were bevelled, sloping inwards towards the painting, and were relieved by much larger and more complex raised circular motifs, as well as lines of poetry (cat. 153, figs. 100, 104).

In addition to these types, Rossetti designed one-off frames for some of his most important works, for example the frame of *Beata Beatrix* (cat. 98) with its roundels of the sun, moon and stars relating to the complex symbolism of the picture; or the Italianate frame of *The Blessed Damozel* (cat. 152) with the main picture above a smaller panel, in the manner of a Renaissance altarpiece and its predella. Rossetti's frame-makers were Green; Foord and Dickinson; and Charles Rowley of Manchester (Grieve 1973a).

Bookbindings

Rossetti took as much care over the appearance of his books as he did over his paintings, and also designed bindings for books of poetry by his sister Christina and by his friend Swinburne. Rossetti thought that most commercial bindings were ugly: 'bad colours and most unpleasant texture' (D & W, II, p. 786). He took a great deal of trouble to choose the colour and feel of the cloths and to position the gold lines and motifs of his designs subtly, to emphasize the relationship between the fronts, backs and spines of his books. His designs were spare, simple and elegant, far more advanced in these respects than contemporary Victorian bindings; but Rossetti's bindings were inexpensive, using cheap, easily available materials. Most of the bindings were made for Rossetti by the bookbinding firm of James Burn (Grieve 1973c).

156
Dante and his Circle 1100–1200–1300 by D.G. Rossetti
published by Smith, Elder and Co., 1874
18.5 x 13.2 cm
Stephen Calloway

This originally appeared in 1861 as *The Early Italian Poets from Ciullo d'Alcamo to Dante Alighieri...translated by D.G. Rossetti* (see cat. 90). The 1861 edition was bound in black cloth; this copy is the revised and rearranged edition of 1874, when the book

cat. 156

cat. 157 b

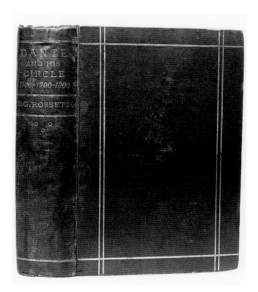

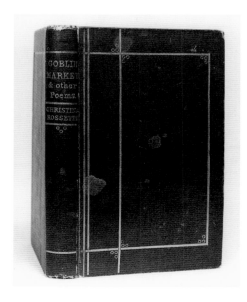

was reissued in a blue cloth binding, otherwise identical to the binding of the first edition. The design of the front cover is extremely simple, with two pairs of vertical gold lines and two single horizontal lines, which continue across the spine. Below the lettering on the spine is a design of three small gold circles.

157

Goblin Market and other poems
by Christina Rossetti (a)
published by Macmillan and Co., 1862
17.7 x 11.5 cm
The British Museum, London

Goblin Market and other poems
by Christina Rossetti (b)
published by Macmillan and Co., 1865
17.7 x 11.5 cm
Stephen Calloway

This was originally published in 1862 in a black cloth binding, with a design blocked in gold on the front and blind stamped on the back cover. In 1865 the book was reissued in a blue cloth, which Rossetti disliked. Both editions employ simple gold lines, but the design of the new edition was subtly altered. The placing of the vertical lines is asymmetrical, with a pair of lines close to the spine, and two single vertical lines creating a narrow outer margin and a wider inner one by the spine. The vertical lines weave over and under the horizontal ones, and the intersections are emphasized with the motif of three gold circles. In the

1862 edition the gold lines extend to the edges of the cover at top and bottom right, creating squares in the corners, whereas in the 1865 edition the extensions are omitted. The effect of this small alteration is to emphasize the central panel and to give more weight to the left side of the book and the spine.

158

The Comedy of Dante Allighieri [sic]: part I – the Hell.
Translated by William Michael Rossetti
published by Macmillan and Co., 1865
17.6 x 12 cm
The British Library, London

Bound in black cloth, the front cover has motifs blocked in gold, an alpha and omega set in a circle in each corner, and in the centre a square containing three circles for the three parts of the *Divine Comedy*. One is decorated with stars for Paradise, another with flames for Hell, and the third, for Purgatory, has a mixture of both. On the back cover is the circle with flames representing Hell, the subject of this volume. William Michael's blank verse translation of Dante's *Inferno* was intended to be the first of a set of volumes comprising the whole of the *Divine Comedy*, but only the first was published. The binding bears the label of the bookbinder James Burn. The flyleaf of this copy is inscribed: 'William Morris. With the affectionate regard of W.M. Rossetti'.

159

Atalanta in Calydon by A.C. Swinburne
published by Edward Moxon and Co., 1865
22.3 x 17.8 cm
Stephen Calloway

The book is bound in white buckram, which gives a more luxurious effect than the more utilitarian dark cloths of the previous bindings. Despite its impracticality, Rossetti insisted on the buckram being stretched over whitened boards to make it look as white as possible. The decorations are the result of close collaboration between Swinburne and Rossetti, for the gilt roundels contain stylized plant forms based on the patterns of Greek vases, to complement the classical spirit of Swinburne's poem.

160

The Prince's Progress and other poems
by Christina Rossetti
published by Macmillan and Co., 1866
17.7 x 11.5 cm
The British Museum, London

The sparse gold lines on Christina's first book of poems have been given elegant spiral terminations like those on the metal hinges of medieval doors. The design, on apple-green cloth, passes across the spine to link the front and back of the book. The binding of this copy bears the label of the bookbinder James Burn.

cat. 158

cat. 159

cat. 160

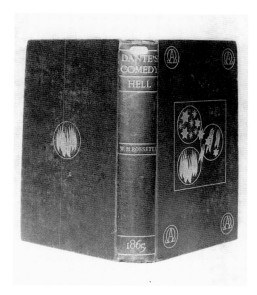

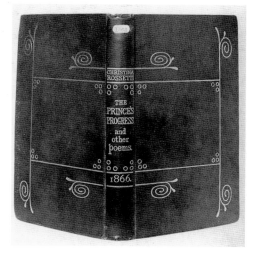

161
Poems by Dante Gabriel Rossetti (a)
published by F.S. Ellis, 1870

Poems by Dante Gabriel Rossetti (b)
published by F.S. Ellis, 4th edition 1870

Poems by Dante Gabriel Rossetti (c)
published by F.S. Ellis, new edition 1881

19.6 x 14 cm
Stephen Calloway

For his own collected poems, Rossetti
devised a less austere design than any of the
previous bindings, but it was equally carefully considered. The rectilinear division of
the cover into rectangular and square panels
is still present, but the dividing lines have
been omitted. Instead, the central and corner
panels have been filled in with a decorative
gold design of small flowers seen against a
network of curling lines. The cloth is a dull
green. The design passes across the spine,
linking front and back covers, and is repeated
on the endpapers, printed in indigo on
a blue-green paper. For the endpapers,
Rossetti seems to have used a paper brought
by his father from Malta or Naples (McGann
2000, p. 76). Rossetti's many letters to
his publisher show his meticulous concern
to obtain the precise effects he wanted
(D & W, II, pp. 785 ff.). The book was published in April, but the spine was too wide,
with the end of the book having to be filled
up with blank pages, so Rossetti had the
spine redesigned for the second printing.

162
Songs before Sunrise by A.C. Swinburne
published by F.S. Ellis, 1871
19.5 x 14 cm
Stephen Calloway

For his second design for Swinburne,
Rossetti went back to the one he had
made for Swinburne's *Atalanta in Calydon*
(cat. 159), using roundels on a plain colour.
The roundels now incorporate the rising
sun, the moon and the stars, and were
adapted from the roundels on the frame
for *Beata Beatrix* (cat. 98). The binding is
a blue-green cloth, but twenty-five large
paper copies were printed with a white buckram binding similar to *Atalanta in Calydon*.

Stained glass

In April 1861 Rossetti joined his friend
William Morris in his new design venture
Morris, Marshall, Faulkner & Co. and took
part in their work. Rossetti designed a small
amount of stained glass for domestic and
ecclesiastical commissions, usually as part
of a more comprehensive scheme involving
other designers. He produced far less glass
than Morris, Burne-Jones or Brown and
seems to have lost interest in the medium
around 1864 (Sewter 1975, I, pp. 66–8).

163
The Sermon on the Mount
(S 142)
c. 1861
signed bottom left corner: DGR (monogram)
ink on paper, 72.4 x 53.3 cm
William Morris Gallery
(London Borough of Waltham Forest)

Design for a window in the south aisle
at All Saints Church, Selsley. The saints
depicted are identifiable from the inscriptions on their haloes; the models are said
to have been members of the Rossetti circle.
Christ in the centre is George Meredith,
and the other figures are, left to right,
Swinburne as St John, Simeon Solomon
as St James, Christina Rossetti as the Virgin
Mary, the red-haired Fanny Cornforth as
Mary Magdalene, Ernest Gambart the art
dealer, whom Rossetti loved to hate, as Judas,
and William Morris himself as St Peter.
This is the finished design; Morris would

cat. 161 a

cat. 162

cat. 163

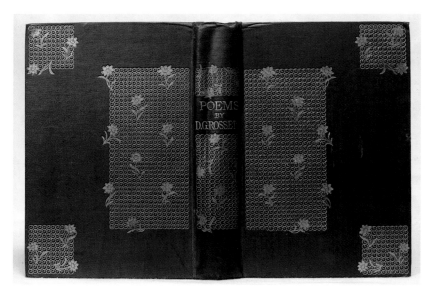

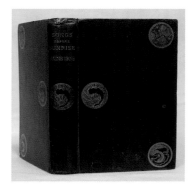

have made a tracing of it, to which he would have added the lead lines. Rossetti was fairly cavalier about his glass designs and did not adjust his drawing style or simplify his complex meandering outlines to make them easier to cut. This is the second version of the design; he carelessly drew the first (Leeds City Art Gallery, s 142 A) to the incorrect size, and it had to be redrawn. This bears out the opinion of Ford Madox Brown that Rossetti's maxim was 'Anything will do for stained glass' (Hueffer 1896, p. 343).

164
King René's Honeymoon (Music)
(S 175 A)
signed and dated bottom right:
DGR (monogram) / 1862
inscribed bottom left with title, probably in another hand
ink and wash on paper, 43.2 x 33.7 cm
Williamson Art Gallery & Museum, Birkenhead; Wirral Museums Service

The subject comes from Sir Walter Scott's novel *Anne of Geierstein*, which recounts imaginary incidents in the honeymoon of the art-loving King René of Anjou. Rossetti shows him kissing the future Queen Isabella as she plays the organ, on the end of which are written the names of the Kingdoms of which René was titular ruler, Jerusalem, Sicily, Cyprus and Navarre. It is one of four subjects from the same source, the others being *Architecture* by Ford Madox Brown, and *Sculpture* and *Painting* by Burne-Jones. They were originally commissioned

from Morris, Marshall, Faulkner & Co. as painted panels for a large piece of furniture, the King René's Honeymoon cabinet, designed by the architect J.P. Seddon and shown at the London International Exhibition of 1862. Rossetti also painted a smaller panel for the cabinet (see cat. 171).

This drawing is for the stained glass version of the designs, commissioned from Morris, Marshall, Faulkner and Co. by the artist Myles Birket Foster for his house, The Hill, at Witley, Surrey. Both the cabinet and the stained glass panels are now in the Victoria & Albert Museum (Parry 1996, pp. 170, 123).

165
The fight between Sir Tristram and Sir Marhaus
1862–3
stained glass panel, 68 x 61 cm
inscribed with title: How Sir Tristram fought with Sir Marhaus the King's son of Ireland for the tribute of Cornwall and how Sir Tristram wounded him sore, of which wound Sir Marhaus died.
Bradford Art Gallery
figure 106

166
Sir Tristram and la Belle Ysoude drinking the love potion
1862–3
stained glass panel, 68.5 x 63 cm
inscribed with title: How, as they sailed towards Cornwall, they saw on a day the flasket wherein was the love-filtre which the Queen of Ireland was sending by the hand of Dame Brangwaine for Isoude to drink with King Mark, and how Tristram drank it with her, both unwitting and how they loved each other ever after.
Bradford Art Gallery
figure 107

Two scenes from a set of thirteen stained glass panels of the story of Tristram and Ysoude as told in Malory's *Morte d'Arthur* (these two incidents are from Book VIII, chapters 6–8 and chapter 24). The glass was commissioned from Morris, Marshall, Faulkner & Co. by a Bradford merchant, Walter Dunlop, for his house, Harden Grange, near Bingley, Yorkshire, and was one of the firm's first domestic commissions. The subjects were shared amongst several artists: Arthur Hughes, Valentine Prinsep, Burne-Jones, Ford Madox Brown and William Morris designed the other panels in the series.

Malory recounts how Sir Tristram, having killed Sir Marhaus, son of the King of Ireland, sailed for Cornwall with Ysoude, daughter of the King of Ireland, whom he was bringing in marriage to his uncle King Mark of Cornwall. During the voyage they

cat. 164

cat. 165

cat. 166

How Sir Tristram fought with Sir Marhaus the King's son of Ireland for the tribute of Cornwal and how Sir Tristram wounded him sore, of which wound Sir Marhaus died

fig. 106
**The fight between Sir Tristram
and Sir Marhaus**
1862–3
Bradford Art Gallery
cat. 165

How, as they sailed towards Cornwall, they saw on a day the flasket wherein was the love-filtre which the Queen of Ireland was sending by the hand of Dame Brangwine for Isoude to drink with King Mark, and how Tristram drank it with her, both unwitting and how they loved each other ever after

fig. 107
Sir Tristram and la Belle Ysoude drinking the love potion
1862–3
Bradford Art Gallery
cat. 166

drank the love potion that was intended for Ysoude to drink with King Mark, and they fell deeply in love. The story was one of Morris's favourite episodes from Malory. It was also retold by Mathew Arnold in a poem of 1852, but the version that led to its wider currency was Wagner's opera *Tristan und Isolde*, first produced in 1865.

Furniture

Rossetti's first furniture work took the form of pictorial decoration. He painted scenes on some of the first pieces of furniture designed by William Morris for his rooms at Red Lion Square. Rossetti decorated the backs of two tall medieval-style chairs (1856–7, Delaware Art Museum), representing Gwendolen and Sir Galahad from Morris' poems, and he also painted doors for a massive settle destined for Red House; his panels were later removed from the settle and framed like easel paintings: *The Salutation of Beatrice* (1859, National Gallery of Canada, Ottawa, S 116) and *Dantis Amor* (fig. 93, see cat. 46). After 1861, when Morris launched the firm of Morris, Marshall, Faulkner and Co. as a collaborative venture, Rossetti also took part in early commissions, painting an *Annunciation* (S 131) on the pulpit at St Martin's Scarborough, for which he also designed stained glass, and painting two panels for the King René's Honeymoon cabinet (see cats. 164, 171).

Rossetti was not often involved with the actual design of furniture, but when he did put his mind to it, as in other fields of the decorative arts, his contribution was markedly original and refined. The sofa exhibited in 1862 (fig. 108) began as an imaginary prop in the background to a drawing of a Biblical subject (cat. 167); when realized in three dimensions, it was spare and light, in keeping with the most advanced contemporary designs of the Aesthetic Movement. The rush-seated armchair

named after Rossetti and manufactured by Morris's firm (cat. 170) is also light and informal, but the sofa he designed for his house in Cheyne Walk (see cat. 172), where he moved in 1862, is a more conventional upholstered piece. Its design, whilst not as radical as the 1862 sofa, is nevertheless original: it has painted panels, small ovals and roundels with stylized allegorical motifs (Fitzwilliam Museum, Cambridge). Rossetti is also known to have designed a sideboard 'which licks all creation' that was delivered to his house at Cheyne Walk in July 1863 (Marsh 1999a, p. 266; see Dunn 1984, p. 36).

167
Joseph accused before Potiphar
(S 122)
signed and dated bottom left:
DGR (monogram) / 1860
ink on paper, 15 x 14.5 cm
Birmingham Museums & Art Gallery.
Presented by subscribers

The story comes from Genesis 39. When Joseph came to Egypt, he became the trusted servant of Potiphar, one of Pharaoh's captains. Potiphar's wife attempted to seduce Joseph. When he refused, she unjustly accused him of rape and had him arrested and imprisoned. Rossetti shows the moment of arrest. Potiphar, in the centre, reproaches Joseph and takes back the keys with which he has been entrusted, whilst two men place a chain round his neck. Joseph denies any wrongdoing, whilst Potiphar's wife looks on from the left,

cat. 167

fig. 108

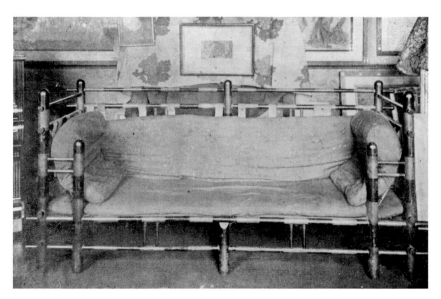

twisting her arms, with an evil expression on her face. The figures are placed in a shallow frieze, and Rossetti fills the drawing with quaint detail. Potiphar's wife has a winged headdress and an elaborate necklace, and there are numerous different patterned surfaces, fish-scales for Potiphar's tunic, lozenges for his sash, stripes for Joseph's sash and a herringbone design for the straw matting and the sofa (see cat. 168).

The drawing may be connected with Dalziel's *Bible Gallery*, an ambitious series of wood-engraved Bible illustrations commissioned from a number of different artists. Though there is no evidence that Rossetti was asked to contribute, the Dalziel brothers were approaching artists, including the leading Pre-Raphaelites, from 1859 and throughout the 1860s. (The illustrations were not published until 1881.)

168
Two designs for a sofa
(S 122 A)
inscribed with dimensions and notes, some by William Morris
pencil and ink on paper, 25.2 x 35.2 cm
Birmingham Museums & Art Gallery.
Presented by subscribers

The drawing shows two variants of the same design, one symmetrical and, below it, another in the style of a chaise longue with one end lower than the other. The symmetrical one is remarkably similar to that shown in the ink drawing of *Joseph accused before Potiphar* (cat. 167) of 1860 and is a rare

instance of an imaginative invention from a drawing being realized: a sofa to this design was manufactured by Morris, Marshall, Faulkner & Co. (fig. 108) and shown in the firm's display at the London International Exhibition of 1862.

In the *Potiphar* drawing the sofa is upholstered in Japanese straw matting, with a roll of straw matting at the left, and the uprights were decorated with palmette-shaped fans. This was before such straw matting and fans became fashionable in aesthetic circles. When the sofa was made up for exhibition, the fans were omitted and the matting was replaced by cushions and bolsters of red serge decorated with bars of music. The wooden poles were made of ebonized and white wood.

Charles Dickens ridiculed the sofa as uncomfortable, 'straight and angular, and stuffed, possibly with discarded horse-hair shirts' (*All the Year Round*, 30 August 1862, pp. 584–5), but the *Athenaeum* thought it was excellent, showing 'considerable ingenuity in applying straps to support the cushions, and admirable taste for colour in the covers as a whole' (27 September 1862, p. 407). The piece was priced at £30. Its present whereabouts, if it survives at all, are unknown, but a photograph of it was published in 1900, when it belonged to Harold Rathbone, the ceramicist and former pupil of Ford Madox Brown (fig. 108, *The Furnisher* III, 13, Nov. 1900; Parry 1996, pp. 170–1).

169
Jewel casket
before 1862
painted wood, with iron frame, hinges and clasp, 17.7 x 29.2 x 17.7 cm
The Society of Antiquaries of London (Kelmscott Manor)
exhibited at Liverpool only

The casket is in a medieval style with a gabled top, hinged along both sides. It has fourteen panels, seven of which retain their original painted decoration. The painting is by Rossetti and Elizabeth Siddal; she died in 1862, hence the dating. The casket subsequently belonged to Jane Morris and was presumably given to her by Rossetti. Several of the painted panels show scenes of elegantly dressed medieval courtiers. One of the scenes, showing two lovers by a rose trellis, derives from a medieval manuscript in the British Museum, the early 15th-century *Poems of Christine de Pisan* (Banham and Harris 1984, pp. 120–1).

The form of the casket recalls the larger and much more elaborately decorated St Ursula reliquary in the St John's Hospital at Bruges, with painted panels by Hans Memling (before 1489). Rossetti visited the Hospital on his trip to Bruges in 1849 and particularly admired Memling's pictures there (F, I, p. 129). On the gabled roof of the St Ursula shrine are painted panels of angels playing musical instruments, including many of the medieval instruments seen in Rossetti's paintings. He visited

cat. 168

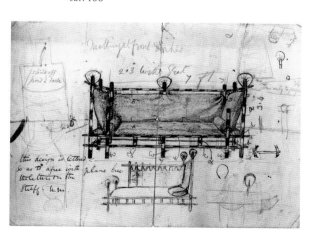

cat. 169

Bruges and saw the shrine again in 1863 in company with his brother.

170

'Rossetti' armchair

Made by Morris, Marshall, Faulkner & Co., possibly to a design by Rossetti
in production from c. 1863
ebonized beech with rush seat,
(a) 89 x 50 x 46 cm, private collection
(b) 89 x 41 x 46 cm, Robert Wilson

The chair is traditionally known as the Rossetti armchair and was marketed under this name by Morris & Co., but there is no documentary evidence proving that Rossetti was responsible for the design. It is based on French country chairs of the early 19th century. Examples of this chair differ slightly from each other in detail and proportion; the differences are accounted for because they were all made by individual craftsmen. The earlier examples of the Rossetti armchair are trimmed with red painted lines (cat. 170a); some chairs have a thin banding nailed around the edge to protect the rushing (cat. 170b).

An example of the chair is seen in a photograph of 1863 showing Rossetti in the garden at Cheyne Walk with John Ruskin and William Bell Scott (fig. 88). The more famous (and much cheaper) rush-seated armchairs from the Sussex range were first made c. 1860 and were in production c. 1865 (Parry 1996, pp. 169, 176).

171

Gardening (Spring)

(s 132)
signed and dated bottom right:
DGR (monogram)/ 1864; inscribed bottom
left: Spring
watercolour on paper, 22.5 x 20 cm
private collection

This is a watercolour version of a design originally made for one of the smaller painted panels on the King René's Honeymoon cabinet (see cat. 164), each panel illustrating the artistic interests of the King. Fanny Cornforth was the model for the girl, who is shown cutting flowering branches from a tree with a pair of scissors.

cat. 170 a

cat. 171

Rossetti as a collector

Rossetti's studios

Rossetti decorated the interiors of his homes and studios in typically unconventional style, in advance of fashion. His first studio was at his rooms at 14 Chatham Place, Blackfriars, overlooking the Thames, where he moved in 1852. In November 1860, following his marriage in May, he and his wife, Elizabeth Siddal, took the second floor of the next-door house, no. 13, to live in. They hung it with pictures 'in profusion' (F, II, p. 328) and in the drawing room put up a wallpaper designed by Rossetti, depicting stylized trees as if growing from floor to ceiling. 'I shall have it printed on common brown packing paper and on blue grocer's paper, to try which is best'(F, II, p. 342).

After his wife's death he moved to a new home and studio at Chelsea, also overlooking the river. Tudor House, 16 Cheyne Walk (fig. 89), was an early 18th-century house with a large garden. (The name Tudor House came from the site, originally part of Chelsea Manor, built by Henry VIII.) Rossetti painted the wooden panelled rooms in rich colours and furnished the rooms in an idiosyncratic style, filling them with bric-à-brac found in curiosity shops in Leicester Square and Hammersmith. This was a deliberately uncoordinated look very much in advance of its time, juxtaposing junk with high quality, an eclectic mixture of Chinese and Japanese objects with Delft tiles, Old English china, brass, pewter, Spanish cabinets, Sheraton furniture, oriental rugs, velvets and chintzes. A particular feature was

cat. 172

fig. 109
Henry Treffry Dunn
**D.G. Rossetti and Theodore Watts-Dunton
in the sitting room at Cheyne Walk**
1882
National Portrait Gallery, London
cat. 172

the abundance of mirrors. The contents were dispersed in a sale on 5–7 July 1882, but several pieces of furniture from Cheyne Walk are preserved at Kelmscott Manor.

172

Henry Treffry Dunn (1838–1899)
D.G. Rossetti and Theodore Watts-Dunton in the sitting room at Cheyne Walk
signed and dated bottom right:
H. TREFFRY DUNN 1882
watercolour on paper, 54 x 82.6 cm
National Portrait Gallery, London
figure 109

'I was ushered into one of the prettiest and most curiously furnished old-fashioned parlours that I had ever seen. Mirrors and looking-glasses of all shapes, sizes and design lined the walls. Whichever way I looked I saw myself gazing at myself.

What space there was left was filled up with pictures, chiefly old and of an interesting character. The mantelpiece was a most original make-up of Chinese black-lacquered panels bearing designs of birds, animals, flowers and fruit in gold relief. The effect was very good. On either side of the grate were inlaid a series of old blue Dutch tiles, mostly of Biblical subjects done in the serious comic manner that existed at the period. The firegrate was a beautifully wrought specimen of 18th Century design and workmanship of brass with fire-irons and fender to match. In one corner of the room stood an old English china cupboard; inside was

displayed a quantity of Spode ware. I sat myself down on a dear little cosy sofa with landscapes and figures painted on the panels of the Cipriani period' (Dunn 1984, p. 14). Rossetti is seen reading the proofs of *Ballads and Sonnets* to Watts-Dunton. Above the latter hangs the double portrait of Frances Lavinia and Christina Rossetti (cat. 121) and at the right is a portrait of Christina.

173

Henry Treffry Dunn (1838–1899)
Rossetti's Drawing Room at Cheyne Walk
signed and dated bottom right:
H. TREFFRY DUNN 1882
watercolour on paper, 68.6 x 94 cm
private collection

'When the party was an exceptional one, I mean for the number of friends invited, the table was laid in the so-called drawing room – an apartment comprising the whole width of the house, boasting of five windows giving an extensive and interesting view of Chelsea Reach.... A beautiful room by day when the sun streamed in and lit up all the curious collection of Indian cabinets, couches, old Nankin and miscellaneous odds and ends with which it was crowded ... but at night when the heavy Utrecht velvet curtains were drawn and the dining-table extended to its utmost limits, when the huge Flemish brass wrought candelabra with its two dozen wax lights that hung suspended from the ceiling midway over the table was lit up and the central old-fashioned silver

epergne filled with flowers, then the room was filled with a pleasant glow and warmth anticipatory of the company expected' (Dunn 1984, p. 43).

The wicker chair on the left, similar to that seen in the photographs of Jane Morris, is now at Wightwick Manor, on loan from the Ashmolean Museum.

174

Henry Treffry Dunn (1838–1899)
Rossetti's bedroom at Cheyne Walk
c. 1882
inscribed bottom left: Cheyne Walk;
bottom right: Gabriels' Bedroom
watercolour on paper, diameter 33 cm
Wightwick Manor (The National Trust,
by kind gift of Mrs H. Guglielmini)

The bedroom was on the first floor at the back of the house. Dunn painted the view of the room as reflected in a convex mirror that hung there: 'I thought it a most unhealthy place to sleep in. Thick curtains heavy with crewel work in designs of print and foliage hung closely drawn round an antiquated four-post bedstead. This he had bought out of an old furniture shop somewhere in the slums of Lambeth.... A massive panelled oak mantelpiece reached from the floor to the ceiling, fitted up with numerous shelves and cupboard-like recesses, all filled with a medley assortment of brass repoussé dishes, blue china vases filled with peacocks' feathers, oddly-fashioned early English and foreign candlesticks, Chinese monstrosities in bronze and various other curiosities, the

cat. 173

cat. 174

whole surmounted by an ebony and ivory crucifix. The only modern thing I could see anywhere was a Bryant and May's box of safety matches' (Dunn 1984, p. 24).

cat. 175

cat. 176

Jewellery

The jewels worn by Rossetti's models were carefully selected to contribute to the particular aesthetic effect of each picture, complementing the textiles, dresses, flowers and other accessories. They were not invented but painted from real pieces, mostly copied literally, though sometimes Rossetti would simplify details or alter the appearance to fit in with his colour scheme. Both *The Blue Bower* and *The Beloved* (cats. 105, 106) include Chinese hair ornaments made of kingfisher feathers: in *The Beloved* Rossetti has changed the colour of the feathers from turquoise blue to red.

Rossetti kept a cabinet at Cheyne Walk full of necklaces, featherwork, Japanese crystals and knick-knacks of all kinds (Dunn 1984, p. 18). Many of the ornaments were cheap items of costume jewellery and not especially rare or precious. Some were bought from curiosity shops and others were borrowed from friends: Boyce lent him the necklace seen on the black boy's head in *The Beloved*, as well as the Japanese robe worn by the bride. The spiral pearl pin featuring in *The Beloved*, *Monna Vanna* (1866, Tate, S 191), *A Christmas Carol* (cat. 109), *Mariana* (cat. 141) and *The Bower Meadow* (cat. 148) was a particular favourite: Rossetti was angry when it was taken away by Charles Augustus Howell and not returned promptly.

Most of Rossetti's collection of jewellery was sold after his death and cannot now be traced, but the four items in this section are part of a group of jewellery bequeathed to

cat. 177

the Victoria & Albert Museum by Jane Morris's daughter May. Apart from Jane Morris's own wedding ring, the three other pieces may originally have belonged to Rossetti and been given to Jane as tokens of love (Bury 1976).

175
Jane Morris's wedding ring on a gold chain
ring, 22 carat gold, with London hallmark for 1858, maker's mark JO
chain, stamped gold links, English 1830–40
diameter of ring 1.89 cm, length of chain 121.9 cm
Victoria & Albert Museum, London

In *The Blue Silk Dress* (cat. 125) of 1868 and *Mariana* (cat. 141) of 1870 Rossetti painted her wearing a similar gold chain looped around her neck, though in *Mariana* the chain appears to be longer.

176
Bracelet
South Indian or Burmese, perhaps mid-19th century
gold set with rubies, diameter 17.6 cm, width 0.63 cm
Victoria & Albert Museum, London

The central motif of the bracelet is a pair of water monsters on each side of a water pot with lion masks grasping the plaited chain in their jaws. Rossetti first used this exotic piece in 1864 in *Monna Pomona* (Tate, S 171), and it can be clearly seen worn by the bride

cat. 178

on her left wrist in *The Beloved* (cat. 106) of 1865–6.

177

Heart-shaped brooch

probably European, mid-19th century
silver with applied rosettes, set with three
large pieces of coloured glass, 3.5 x 2.84 cm
Victoria & Albert Museum, London

The brooch consists of two red pieces of
coloured glass and one green one below,
within a heart-shaped mount with small
rosettes and leaves filling the gaps. Though
it was made with a vertical pin to be worn as
a brooch, in *The Blue Bower* (cat. 105) Fanny
Cornforth wears it as a pendant, hanging
provocatively at her throat on a chain.
A colourful and obviously cheap piece
of costume jewellery, it expresses Fanny's
personality and echoes her red lips and
the green silk of her robe. A similar brooch,
though not heart-shaped, fastens the headdress of the bridesmaid on the left of *The
Beloved* (cat. 106).

178

Belt and hanger

probably German or Tyrolean, 17th century
silver with links of cast floral ornament,
length 104 cm, width 2.52 cm
Victoria & Albert Museum, London

The belt is worn by the central figure in
Astarte Syriaca (cat. 153). Rossetti has not
painted this piece literally but changed it
from silver to silver-gilt, added two long
pendant drops, and simplified the design
of each of the main links from a stylized
spray of eight flowers to a single sprig.

cat. 179

Chinese and Japanese art

Rossetti was an early participant in the
craze for collecting Chinese blue-and-
white china, part of a vogue for Oriental
art that included Japanese as well as Chinese
artefacts. The fashion was started by artists:
in 1856 a workman in Paris found a volume
of prints by Hokusai used for packing china,
and the prints were eventually purchased
by the artist Félix Bracquemond. In 1862
Mme Desoye opened a shop in the Rue de
Rivoli selling Oriental wares, which num-
bered among its customers Manet, Fantin-
Latour, Tissot and Whistler. It was from
Whistler that Rossetti caught the bug.
In September 1863 Rossetti and his brother
were in Antwerp, where they bought a jar
with blue-and-white birds, and in April
the following year Rossetti enthusiastically
invited Ford Madox Brown to see his collection: 'My pots now baffle description
altogether…COME AND SEE THEM' (D & W,
II, p. 501).

Rossetti obtained many of his best examples
of 'Nankin ware', as it was known, from the
dealer Murray Marks, who was to advise all
the great late Victorian collectors of Chinese
porcelain. Marks first met Rossetti as early
as 1861, but their acquaintance became closer
in 1864; calling to see Rossetti's pots, he
reported that 'it was a poor collection, and
consisted chiefly of the common stuff which
was to be picked up in London at that time'
(Williamson 1919, p. 52). Marks agreed to
obtain top-quality pieces for Rossetti and to
give him first refusal on them, and in return

cat. 180

cat. 181

cat. 182

Rossetti would introduce buyers to Marks from his own circle of clients. Rossetti also obtained porcelain from the notoriously dishonest Charles Augustus Howell. Both Marks and Howell became unofficial dealers to Rossetti, selling his paintings as well as buying and selling porcelain for him.

Marks was one of the first to create the taste for the large ginger jars decorated with prunus blossom over a brilliant blue 'cracked ice' ground, for which Rossetti coined the name 'hawthorn pots'. In the 1860s these could be bought for about twelve shillings and sixpence, but their stock rose rapidly and by 1905 a price of £ 6,000 was not unusual for a good one. Rossetti painted a design based on the hawthorn pattern, but applied to octagonal tiles, an invented form, as the background to *The Blue Bower* (cat. 105), and he portrayed Mrs F.R. Leyland with a fine example of a hawthorn pot in *Monna Rosa* (1867, private collection, s 198). Rossetti's enthusiasm for collecting Nankin wares was the subject of many practical jokes and anecdotes: at a dinner party Rossetti was so keen to see the marks on a prized porcelain dish that he turned it over, forgetting that there was food in it, and upset a salmon all over his hostess's tablecloth (Holiday 1914, p. 76).

All the pieces in this section were formerly owned by Rossetti.

179
Pair of beaker shaped vases
Chinese, Kangxi period (1662–1722)
painted in underglaze blue with ladies on the upper part, sprays of flowers round the middle and children at play below, height 26.4 cm
paper labels on both bases with DGR monogram and inscription: A101 and A102
Victoria & Albert Museum, London

180
Pair of lidded baluster vases with dog-shaped knobs
Chinese, Kangxi period (1662–1722)
painted in underglaze blue with blue strokes forming spirals, separated by cross-hatched borders, height 34 cm
Wightwick Manor, The Mander Collection (The National Trust)

181
Narrow-necked bottle
Chinese, Yung Cheng period (1722–36)
mottled with robin's egg blue glaze, height 17 cm
Wightwick Manor, The Mander Collection (The National Trust)

182
Pair of ewers
Chinese, Kangxi period (1662–1722)
painted in underglaze blue with a design of rocks and flowering plants, height 28 cm
National Museums Liverpool (Lady Lever Art Gallery, Port Sunlight)

183
Jar and cover
Chinese, Kangxi period (1662–1722)
painted in underglaze blue with an imperial couple in a garden, height 20.3 cm
National Museums Liverpool (Lady Lever Art Gallery, Port Sunlight)

184
Pair of jars
Chinese, Kangxi period (1662–1722)
with handles in the form of elephant heads and loops; painted in underglaze blue with ladies and plants, height 28.5 cm
Said to have been a present from Rossetti to his mother.
Syndics of the Fitzwilliam Museum, Cambridge

185
Tsunenobu (1636–1713)
Blossoming cherry in the mist
fragment of a painting mounted as a hanging scroll
ink, colour and gold on silk, 17.9 x 50.5 cm (painting)
The British Museum, London

Given by Rossetti to the painter G.F. Britten. The subsequent owner, Arthur Morrison, had it mounted as a hanging scroll: it may have been framed when owned by Rossetti.

cat. 183

cat. 184

cat. 185

Chronology

1828

born 12 May; baptized Gabriel Charles Dante Rossetti

second of four children of Gabriele Rossetti (exiled Italian patriot, Dante scholar, and from 1830 Professor of Italian, King's College London) and Frances Polidori Rossetti (governess and teacher); his elder sister, Maria Francesca, born the previous year

1829

William Michael Rossetti born

1830

Christina Georgina Rossetti born

1837

Queen Victoria accedes to the throne

Gabriel enters King's College School, London, joined shortly by William Michael

1842

enrols at Sass's, a private drawing school which prepared students for the Royal Academy Schools

1845

admitted to Royal Academy Schools

1848

year of European revolutions; both Rossetti brothers write political sonnets

participates in Cyclographic Society (an art-students' club which circulated drawings for criticism by members; see cat. 8)

writes to Leigh Hunt about prospects for a career as poet

writes to Ford Madox Brown requesting tuition; this initiates a lifelong friendship; at Brown's suggestion, enrols in Dickinson's Life Class, Maddox Street

admires William Holman Hunt's *The Eve of St Agnes* at the Royal Academy exhibition, and initiates friendship; shares Hunt's studio in Cleveland Street

translates Dante's *Vita Nuova*, and lists thirteen subjects for pictorial treatment

copies his original poems, as 'Songs of an Art-Catholic', and sends them to William Bell Scott, initiating another lifelong friendship

formation of the Pre-Raphaelite Brotherhood (PRB), probably by the end of December, with seven members: James Collinson, William Holman Hunt, John Everett Millais, Dante Gabriel Rossetti, William Michael Rossetti, Frederic George Stephens, Thomas Woolner

1849

begins to sign himself Dante Gabriel Rossetti

first exhibition season of the PRB.: Rossetti exhibits *The Girlhood of Mary Virgin* (cat. 12) at the Free Exhibition; Hunt, Millais and Collinson exhibit at the Royal Academy

William Michael Rossetti begins the *P.R.B. Journal* on 15 May, as the first exhibited pictures begin to make their impact

with Hunt, travels to Paris and Belgium in the autumn; admires paintings of Hippolyte Flandrin, Jan Van Eyck and Hans Memling

1850

The Germ, Pre-Raphaelite literary magazine, published January – May (4 issues); Rossetti's contributions include 'The Blessed Damozel' (see cat. 152) and the short story 'Hand and Soul'

second exhibition season of the PRB: Rossetti exhibits *Ecce Ancilla Domini!* (cat. 13) at the National Institution (successor to the Free Exhibition); after the existence of the PRB is revealed in the press, many critics respond with hostility

in the autumn, paints out of doors at Knole Park, Sevenoaks, Kent, where Hunt and Stephens are also working; Rossetti fails to finish his picture but later uses the landscape background for *The Bower Meadow* of 1872 (cat. 148)

shares rooms in Red Lion Square with Walter Deverell

by the end of 1850, William Michael Rossetti records in the *P.R.B. Journal* that PRB group meetings have fallen into abeyance

1851

moves to Ford Madox Brown's studio in Newman Street

begins to draw and paint from Elizabeth Siddal; according to William Michael Rossetti, his brother and Siddal are informally engaged by the end of the year or soon afterwards

John Ruskin writes to *The Times* and publishes a pamphlet, *Pre-Raphaelitism*, in defence of the PRB

1852

in July, Woolner emigrates to Australia, with two other artists, to seek his fortune in the goldfields (see cat. 15)

in November, Rossetti moves to 14 Chatham Place, Blackfriars Bridge, where he will live until 1862

1853

on 12 April the remaining members of the PRB make portraits of one another to send to Woolner in Australia (cats. 16–17)

in the summer, Rossetti visits William Bell Scott in Newcastle; they visit Carlisle (see cat. 71); Rossetti tours Warwickshire on his return journey

Siddal uses Rossetti's studio at Blackfriars while he is away, and works on a self-portrait; from about this date she stops sitting as model to other artists and develops her own practice as an artist

by autumn, designs made for *Found* (cats. 56–7)

in November, Millais is elected Associate of the Royal Academy; Rossetti writes to his sister, 'So now the whole Round Table is dissolved' (F, I, p. 294)

1854

William Holman Hunt leaves in January for Egypt and Palestine

Walter Deverell dies in February; Gabriele Rossetti (Rossetti's father) dies in April

Ruskin writes to Rossetti, visits his studio and begins to take special interest in his art

Siddal's ill health begins to cause serious concern; she convalesces in Hastings, where Rossetti visits her (see cats. 25, 27)

begins to take interest in book design and illustration; executes *The Maids of Elfen-Mere* (cats. 74–5) for a volume by his friend, the poet William Allingham

1855

begins teaching at Working Men's College, at Ruskin's urging

introduces Siddal to Ruskin, who gives her an allowance to allow her to pursue her artistic career and seeks medical advice for her; she is sent to the South of France for the winter

visits Paris to meet Siddal and to see the Exposition Universelle of 1855

1856

meets Edward Burne-Jones and William Morris, undergraduates at the University of Oxford, and encourages them to begin artistic careers

receives his first major commission, for an altarpiece in Llandaff Cathedral

1857

Pre-Raphaelite Exhibition held privately in Russell Place, Fitzroy Square; Rossetti and Siddal exhibit watercolours and drawings

organizes mural decorations for the new Debating Hall of the Oxford Union Society, assembling a group of artists including Burne-Jones and Morris; they meet Jane Burden (cats. 122–123) and Algernon Charles Swinburne (cat. 116)

Moxon Tennyson published (see cats. 76–83)

1858

formation of Hogarth Club, a private exhibiting society

1859

paints *Bocca Baciata* (cat. 94, exhibited at the Hogarth Club in 1860)

William Morris and Jane Burden marry

1860

Rossetti and Siddal, who is seriously ill, marry on 23 May and honeymoon in Paris; after a brief stay in Hampstead they settle in Chatham Place

Burne-Jones and Georgiana Macdonald (cat. 115) marry

Morrises move to Red House, Bexleyheath, Kent, designed for them by Philip Webb; they collaborate with friends on furniture and interior decorations

1861

Morris, Marshall, Faulkner & Co. begin trading in April, with seven partners including Rossetti, Burne-Jones, Webb, Brown and Morris (reorganized 1875 as Morris & Co. under Morris's sole proprietorship); in the early years of the firm Rossetti is an active participant especially as a designer of stained glass

Dante Gabriel and Elizabeth Rossetti's daughter is stillborn on 2 May

Rossetti's translations, *The Early Italian Poets from Ciullo d'Alcamo to Dante Alighieri*, published in December

1862

Elizabeth Siddal Rossetti dies of an overdose on 11 February; Rossetti places the manuscript of his poems in her coffin

Rossetti moves to Tudor House, 16 Cheyne Walk, Chelsea, in the autumn; at first he shares the house with Swinburne, the poet George Meredith and William Michael Rossetti; begins to amass diverse collections of fine and applied art, including Japanese and Chinese ceramics; employs Walter John Knewstub as pupil-assistant

Meets James McNeill Whistler

1863

travels to Belgium with William Michael Rossetti

1864

finishes last section of Llandaff altarpiece and retouches the whole in position (cat. 64)

travels to Paris in the autumn; escorted by Henri Fantin-Latour, visits studios of Gustave Courbet and Edouard Manet and cafés frequented by artists

1865

commissions series of photographs of Jane Morris, posed in the garden at Tudor House, just before the Morrises leave Red House to settle in Queen Square, London; begins to make drawings of Jane Morris

1867

employs Henry Treffry Dunn as studio assistant

1868

executes portrait of Jane Morris (cat. 125); begins series of formal drawings of her, which form the basis for later subject pictures

stays at Penkill Castle, Perthshire, with Alice Boyd and William Bell Scott; has trouble with his eyes and fears blindness

resumes writing poetry

1869

Henry James visits Rossetti's studio and the Morrises' house, and is impressed by Rossetti's paintings and drawings of Jane Morris

Jane Morris's health declines; in the autumn the Morrises visit the spa at Bad Ems in Germany; Rossetti returns to Penkill Castle

Disinterment of Siddal's coffin to recover the manuscript volume of Rossetti's poems

1870

Poems published in April; the volume attracts favourable reviews and sells briskly, reaching a sixth printing

1871

Rossetti and William Morris take joint tenancy of Kelmscott Manor, Oxfordshire; in the summer Morris travels to Iceland, leaving Rossetti, Jane Morris and the Morris children at Kelmscott

'The Fleshly School of Poetry', attacking Rossetti (and other poets and artists in his circle) for immorality and aestheticism, published by Robert Buchanan (writing under the pseudonym 'Thomas Maitland') in the *Contemporary Review* for October; Rossetti replies in 'The Stealthy School of Criticism', published in the *Athenaeum* in December

1872

mental and physical breakdown in June; convalesces in Scotland, then at Kelmscott, designs *Proserpine*, and starts it on four canvases by early 1873 (see cat. 155)

1873

plans to translate Michelangelo sonnets translations of early Italian poetry reissued as *Dante and his Circle*

1874

William Morris takes sole tenancy of Kelmscott Manor; Rossetti returns to Tudor House

William Michael Rossetti and Lucy Madox Brown marry

1875

stays at Aldwick Lodge, Bognor Regis, over the winter, with visits from Jane Morris; works on *Astarte Syriaca* (cat. 153)

1877

declines invitation to exhibit at the Grosvenor Gallery, a new exhibiting venue where members of his circle, particularly Burne-Jones, achieve great success

undergoes an operation in June; convalesces at Herne Bay, on the Kent coast, in autumn, joined by his mother and sister (cats. 120-1)

1881

publishes a new edition of *Poems* and a volume of *Ballads and Sonnets*

Liverpool Corporation buys *Dante's Dream* (cat. 147) for the Walker Art Gallery

Jane Morris sits to Rossetti for the last time in September, for the hands in a projected picture of *Desdemona's Death-Song*

1882

seriously ill, taken to Birchington-on-Sea, on the North Kent coast, where he composes his last poems and finishes the eighth and last version of *Proserpine* (cat. 155)

William Michael Rossetti writes in his diary: 'My dear Gabriel, the pride & glory of our family, died on 9 April, Easter Sunday, about 9:31 p.m.' (Fredeman 1982, p. 239)

winter 1882–83

memorial exhibitions of Rossetti's work at the Royal Academy and the Burlington Fine Arts Club

Bibliography

Abbreviations

B & T
John Bryson and Janet Camp Troxell (eds.), *Dante Gabriel Rossetti and Jane Morris: Their Correspondence*, Oxford 1976.

D & W
Oswald Doughty and John Robert Wahl (eds.), *Letters of Dante Gabriel Rossetti*, Oxford 1965–7, 4 vols.

F
William E. Fredeman (ed.), *The Correspondence of Dante Gabriel Rossetti: The Formative Years 1835–1862*, Cambridge 2002, 2 vols.

S
Virginia Surtees, *The Paintings and Drawings of Dante Gabriel Rossetti (1828–1882): A Catalogue Raisonné*, Oxford 1971, 2 vols. (references are to vol. 1).

Ainsworth 1976
Maryan Wynn Ainsworth (ed.), *Dante Gabriel Rossetti and the Double Work of Art*, exh. cat., New Haven (Yale University Art Gallery) 1976.

Allen 1984
Virginia M. Allen, ' "One Strangling Golden Hair": Dante Gabriel Rossetti's *Lady Lilith*', *Art Bulletin* 66, June 1984, pp. 285–94.

Banham and Harris 1984
Joanna Banham and Jennifer Harris (eds.), *William Morris and the Middle Ages*, exh. cat., Manchester (Whitworth Art Gallery) 1984.

Tim Barringer, *The Pre-Raphaelites: Reading the Image*, London 1998.

Mary Bennett, *Artists of the Pre-Raphaelite Circle: The First Generation: Catalogue of Works in the Walker Art Gallery, Lady Lever Art Gallery and Sudley Art Gallery*, London 1988.

Bentley 1976
D.R.M. Bentley, 'Rossetti and the Hypnerotomachia Poliphili,' *English Language Notes* 14, 1976–7, pp. 279–83.

Boyce 1980
George Price Boyce, *The Diaries of George Price Boyce*, ed. Virginia Surtees, Norwich 1980.

Brown 1981
Ford Madox Brown, *The Diary of Ford Madox Brown*, ed. Virginia Surtees, New Haven & London 1981.

Browne 1994
Max Browne, *The Romantic Art of Theodor von Holst*, London 1994.

Burne-Jones 1904
Georgiana Burne-Jones, *Memorials of Edward Burne-Jones*, London 1904, 2 vols.

Bury 1976
Shirley Bury, 'Rossetti and his Jewellery', *Burlington Magazine* 118, February 1976, pp. 94–102.

Casteras 1984
Susan P. Casteras, *English Pre-Raphaelitism and its Reception in America in the Nineteenth Century*, Cranbury, London & Mississauga (Ontario) 1984.

Casteras 1995
Susan P. Casteras, 'The Pre-Raphaelite Legacy to Symbolism: Continental Response and Impact on Artists in the Rosicrucian Circle', in Susan P. Casteras and Alicia Craig Faxon (eds.), *Pre-Raphaelite Art in its European Context*, London & Toronto 1995, pp. 33-49.

Christian 1973
John Christian, 'Early German Sources for Pre-Raphaelite Designs', *Art Quarterly* 36, nos. 1 & 2, 1973, pp. 56–83.

Cruise 1996
Colin Cruise, ' "Lovely devils": Simeon Solomon and Pre-Raphaelite masculinity', in Ellen Harding (ed.), *Re-framing the Pre-Raphaelites: historical and theoretical essays*, Aldershot (Hants) 1996, pp. 195–210.

Dietrich 2000
Flavia Dietrich, 'Art history painted. The Pre-Raphaelite view of Italian art: some works by Rossetti,' *The British Art Journal* 2, no. 1, Autumn 2000, pp. 61–9.

Oswald Doughty, *A Victorian Romantic: Dante Gabriel Rossetti*, London 1963, 2nd ed. (first published 1949).

Drewery, Moore and Whittick 2001
Anne Drewery, Julian Moore and Christopher Whittick, 'Re-presenting Fanny Cornforth: The makings of an historical identity', *The British Art Journal* 2, no. 3, Spring / Summer 2001, pp. 3–15.

Dubernard-Laurent 1996
Annie Dubernard-Laurent, *Le Pré-Raphaélisme en Angleterre. Les Arts et les Lettres en France : essai d'étude comparative*, diss. Paris (Sorbonne – Paris IV) 1996, 2 vols.

Dunn 1984
Henry Treffry Dunn, *Recollections of Dante Gabriel Rossetti and his Circle: or Cheyne Walk Life*, ed. Rosalie Mander, Westerham (Kent) 1984.

Duret 1883
Théodore Duret, 'Les Expositions de Londres: Dante Gabriel Rossetti', *Gazette des Beaux-Arts* 18, 2nd series, 1 July 1883, pp. 49–58.

Rowland Elzea, *The Samuel and Mary R. Bancroft, Jr. and Related Pre-Raphaelite Collections*, Wilmington (Delaware Art Museum) 1984, rev. ed.

Erdman 1973
David V. Erdman (ed.), *The Notebook of William Blake*, Oxford 1973.

Faxon 1989
Alicia Craig Faxon, *Dante Gabriel Rossetti*, New York, London & Paris 1989.

Fredeman 1975
William E. Fredeman (ed.), *The PRB Journal*, Oxford 1975.

Fredeman 1982
William E. Fredeman (ed.), 'A Shadow of Dante: Rossetti in the Final Years (Extracts from W.M. Rossetti's Unpublished Diaries, 1876–1882)', *Victorian Poetry* 20, Autumn / Winter 1982, pp. 217–45.

Fry 1916
Roger Fry, 'Rossetti's Water Colours of 1857', *Burlington Magazine* 29, June 1916, pp. 100–9.

J.A. Gere, *Pre-Raphaelite Drawings in the British Museum*, London 1994.

Gilchrist 1863
Alexander Gilchrist, *Life of William Blake*, London 1863 (supplementary chapter by DGR).

Grieve 1973a
Alastair Grieve, 'The Applied Art of D.G. Rossetti – 1. His Picture-Frames', *Burlington Magazine* 115, January 1973, pp. 16–24.

Grieve 1973b
Alastair Grieve, *The Art of Dante Gabriel Rossetti: The Pre-Raphaelite Period*, Hingham (Norfolk) 1973.

Grieve 1973c
Alastair Grieve, 'Rossetti's Applied Art Designs: 2. Book Bindings', *Burlington Magazine* 115, February 1973, pp. 79–83.

Grieve 1973d
Alastair Grieve, 'Rossetti's Illustrations to Poe', *Apollo* 97, February 1973, pp. 142–5.

Grieve 1976
Alastair Grieve, *The Art of Dante Gabriel Rossetti: 1. Found; 2. The Pre-Raphaelite Modern-Life Subject*, Norwich 1976.

Grieve 1978
Alastair Grieve, *The Art of Dante Gabriel Rossetti: The Watercolours and Drawings of 1850–1855*, Norwich 1978.

Grieve 1999
Alastair Grieve, 'Rossetti and the scandal of art for art's sake in the early 1860s', in Elizabeth Prettejohn (ed.), *After the Pre-Raphaelites: Art and Aestheticism in Victorian England*, Manchester 1999, pp. 17–35.

Heffner 1985
D.T. Heffner, 'Additional Typological Symbolism in D.G. Rossetti's The Girlhood of Mary Virgin,' *Journal of Pre-Raphaelite Studies* 5, no. 2, May 1985, pp. 68–77.

Holiday 1914
Henry Holiday, *Reminiscences of my Life*, London, 1914.

Hueffer 1896
Ford Madox Hueffer (later called Ford Madox Ford), *Ford Madox Brown: A Record of his Life and Work*, London, New York & Bombay 1896.

Hueffer 1902
Ford Madox Hueffer (later called Ford Madox Ford), *Rossetti: A Critical Essay on his Art*, London 1902 (repr. 1914).

James 1974
Henry James, *Henry James Letters*, ed. Leon Edel, London 1974, vol. I.

Kassner 1900
Rudolf Kassner, *Die Mystik, die Künstler und das Leben. Über englische Dichter und Maler im 19. Jahrhundert*, Leipzig 1900.

Lang 1959
Cecil Y. Lang (ed.), *The Swinburne Letters*, New Haven & London 1959–62, vol. I.

Lasner 1990
Mark Samuels Lasner, 'William Allingham', *Book Collector* 39, 1990, pp. 175–95.

McGann 2000
Jerome McGann, *Dante Gabriel Rossetti and the Game That Must Be Lost*, New Haven & London 2000.

Dianne Sachko Macleod, 'Dante Gabriel Rossetti and Titian', *Apollo* 121, January 1985, pp. 36–9.

Macleod 1987
Dianne Sachko Macleod, 'Art Collecting and Victorian Middle-Class Taste', *Art History* 10, September 1987, pp. 328–50.

Mancoff 2000
Debra N. Mancoff, *Jane Morris: The Pre-Raphaelite Model of Beauty*, San Francisco 2000.

Henry Currie Marillier, *Dante Gabriel Rossetti: An Illustrated Memorial of his Art and Life*, London 1899.

Marsh 1996
Jan Marsh, '"For the wolf or the babe he is seeking to devour?" The hidden impact of the American Civil War on British art', in Ellen Harding (ed.), *Re-framing the Pre-Raphaelites: historical and theoretical essays*, Aldershot (Hants) 1996, pp. 115–26.

Marsh 1999a
Jan Marsh, *Dante Gabriel Rossetti: Painter and Poet*, London 1999.

Marsh 1999b
Jan Marsh, 'Rossetti's "Nativity" and "The Seed of David"', *Burlington Magazine* 141, October 1999, pp. 606–12.

Milbank 1998
Alison Milbank, *Dante and the Victorians*, Manchester & New York 1998.

Muther 1896
Richard Muther, *The History of Modern Painting*, London 1896, vol. III.

Myers 1883
F.W.H. Myers, 'Rossetti and the Religion of Beauty', *Essays Modern* (vol. II of *Essays Classical and Modern*), London 1883, pp. 312–34.

Linda Nochlin, 'Lost and *Found*: Once More the Fallen Woman', *Art Bulletin* 60, March 1978, pp. 140–53.

Ormond 1967
Richard Ormond, 'Portraits to Australia: a group of Pre-Raphaelite drawings', *Apollo* 85, 1967, pp. 25–7.

Leonée Ormond, 'Dress in the Painting of Dante Gabriel Rossetti', *Costume* 8, 1974, pp. 26–9.

Østermark-Johansen 1998
Lene Østermark-Johansen, *Sweetness and Strength: The Reception of Michelangelo in Late Victorian England*, Aldershot (Hants) & Brookfield (Vermont) 1998.

Parris 1984
Parris, Leslie (ed.), *The Pre-Raphaelites*, exh. cat., London (Tate) 1984.

Parry 1996
Linda Parry (ed.), *William Morris*, exh. cat., London (Victoria & Albert Museum) 1996.

Pater 1889
Walter Pater, 'Dante Gabriel Rossetti' (1883), *Appreciations*, London 1889, pp. 228–42.

Pater 1895
Walter Pater, *Greek Studies: A Series of Essays*, London 1895 (repr. 1901).

Pater 1980
Walter Pater, *The Renaissance: Studies in Art and Poetry: The 1893 Text*, ed. Donald L. Hill, Berkeley, Los Angeles & London 1980.

Patmore 1857
Coventry Patmore, 'Walls and wall painting at Oxford,' *Saturday Review*, 26 December 1857, pp. 583–4.

Pearce 1991
Lynne Pearce, *Woman / Image / Text: Readings in Pre-Raphaelite Art and Literature*, Toronto & Buffalo 1991.

Phelps Smith 1978
Sarah Phelps Smith, 'Dante Gabriel Rossetti's Flower Imagery and the Meaning of his Painting', Ph.D. diss., University of Pittsburgh, 1978 (facsimile, Ann Arbor, Michigan, 1993).

Sarah Phelps Smith, 'Dante Gabriel Rossetti's "Lady Lilith" and the "Language of Flowers" ', *Arts Magazine* 53, February 1979, pp. 142–5.

Pollock 1988
Griselda Pollock, 'Woman as sign: psycho-analytic readings', in *Vision and Difference: Femininity, feminism and histories of art*, London & New York 1988, pp. 120–54.

Powell 1993
Kirsten H. Powell, 'Object, Symbol, and Metaphor: Rossetti's Musical Imagery', *Journal of Pre-Raphaelite Studies*, n.s. vol. 2, Spring 1993, pp. 16–29.

Elizabeth Prettejohn, *Rossetti and his Circle*, London 1997.

Prettejohn 1999
Elizabeth Prettejohn (ed.), *After the Pre-Raphaelites: Art and Aestheticism in Victorian England*, Manchester 1999.

Elizabeth Prettejohn, *The Art of the Pre-Raphaelites*, London 2000.

Psomiades 1997
Kathy Alexis Psomiades, *Beauty's Body: Femininity and Representation in British Aestheticism*, Stanford (California) 1997.

Reid 1928
Forrest Reid, *Illustrators of the 1860s*, London 1928.

Roberts 1974
Helene E. Roberts, 'The Dream World of Dante Gabriel Rossetti', *Victorian Studies* 17, June 1974, pp. 371–93.

Robertson 1933
W. Graham Robertson, *Time Was*, London 1933.

D.G. Rossetti 1911
Dante Gabriel Rossetti, *The Works of Dante Gabriel Rossetti*, ed. William Michael Rossetti, London 1911, rev. ed.

D.G. Rossetti 1999
Dante Gabriel Rossetti, *Collected Writings*, ed. Jan Marsh, London 1999.

W.M. Rossetti 1884
William Michael Rossetti, 'Some Notes on Rossetti and his Works', *Art Journal*, 1884, p. 16.

W.M. Rossetti 1889
William Michael Rossetti, *Dante Gabriel Rossetti as Designer and Writer*, London 1889.

W.M. Rossetti 1895
William Michael Rossetti (ed.), *Dante Gabriel Rossetti: His Family-Letters: With a Memoir*, London 1895, 2 vols.

W.M. Rossetti 1903
William Michael Rossetti (ed.), *Rossetti Papers: 1862 to 1870*, London 1903.

W.M. Rossetti 1906
William Michael Rossetti, *Some Reminiscences*, London 1906, 2 vols.

Ruskin 1903–12
John Ruskin, *The Works of John Ruskin*, Library Edition, ed. E.T. Cook and Alexander Wedderburn, London 1903–12, 39 vols.

Sewter 1975
A.C. Sewter, *The Stained Glass of William Morris and his Circle*, London 1975, 2 vols.

Sharp 1882
William Sharp, *Dante Gabriel Rossetti: a Record and Study*, London 1882.

Shields 1890
Frederic Shields, 'A Note upon Rossetti's Method of Drawing in Crayons', *Century Guild Hobby Horse* 5, 1890, pp. 70–3.

Sinclair 1971
John D. Sinclair, *The Divine Comedy of Dante Alighieri*, Italian text with translation and comment, London, Oxford & New York 1971 (vol. I: Inferno, vol. II: Purgatorio, vol. III: Paradiso).

Smit 1998
Mathijs Smit, ' "Schoonheid als een absolute macht..." Dante Gabriel Rossetti in Nederland', *Literatuur* 15, March / April 1998, 2nd series, pp. 75-83.

Smith 1996
Alison Smith, *The Victorian Nude: Sexuality, morality and art*, Manchester & New York 1996.

Spencer-Longhurst 2000
Paul Spencer-Longhurst, *The Blue Bower: Rossetti in the 1860s*, exh. cat., Birmingham (The Barber Institute of Fine Arts) 2000.

Richard L. Stein, *The Ritual of Interpretation: The Fine Arts as Literature in Ruskin, Rossetti, and Pater*, Cambridge (Mass.) 1975.

Stephens 1865
Frederic George Stephens, 'Mr. Rossetti's Pictures', *Athenaeum*, no. 1982, 21 October 1865, pp. 545-6 (published anonymously).

Stephens 1894
Frederic George Stephens, *Dante Gabriel Rossetti*, *Portfolio* monograph, London 1894.

Surtees 1972
Virginia Surtees, 'The Early Italian Poets by D.G. Rossetti with his Illustrations', in R.S. Fraser (ed.), *Essays on the Rossettis*, Princeton 1972.

Surtees 1973
Virginia Surtees, 'A Conversation Piece at Blackfriars', *Apollo* 97, February 1973, pp. 146-7.

Virginia Surtees, *Dante Gabriel Rossetti: Painter and Poet*, exh. cat., London (Royal Academy of Arts) & Birmingham (City Museums & Art Gallery) 1973.

Surtees 1979
Virginia Surtees (ed.), *Reflections of a Friendship: John Ruskin's Letters to Pauline Trevelyan 1848–1866*, London 1979.

Surtees 1991
Virginia Surtees, *Rossetti's Portraits of Elizabeth Siddal*, Oxford (Ashmolean Museum) 1991.

Swinburne 1868
Algernon Charles Swinburne in William Michael Rossetti and Algernon Charles Swinburne, *Notes on the Royal Academy Exhibition, 1868*, London 1868, pp. 31–51.

Taylor 1863
Tom Taylor, 'English Painting in 1862', *Fine Arts Quarterly Review* 1, May 1863, pp. 1–26.

The Times 1883
The Times, 'The Royal Academy: IV' (review of Rossetti's memorial exhibition), 13 January 1883, p. 4.

Treuherz 1984
Julian Treuherz, 'The Pre-Raphaelites and Mediaeval Manuscripts', in Leslie Parris (ed.), *Pre-Raphaelite Papers*, London (Tate) 1984, pp. 153–69.

Watts 1883
Theodore Watts (later called Watts-Dunton), 'The Truth about Rossetti', *The Nineteenth Century* 13, March 1883, pp. 404–23.

Wildman 1995
Wildman, Stephen, *Visions of Love and Life, Pre-Raphaelite Art from Birmingham Museums and Art Gallery*, Alexandria (Virginia) 1995.

Williamson 1919
G.C. Williamson, *Murray Marks and his Friends*, London 1919.

Wilton and Upstone 1997
Andrew Wilton and Robert Upstone (eds.), *The Age of Rossetti, Burne-Jones & Watts: Symbolism in Britain 1860–1910*, exh. cat., London (Tate) 1997–8, Munich (Haus der Kunst) 1998 & Hamburg (Hamburger Kunsthalle) 1998.

Woolner 1917
Amy Woolner, *Thomas Woolner, R.A., Sculptor and Poet: His Life in Letters*, London 1917.

Website (still in progress)
The Complete Writings and Pictures of Dante Gabriel Rossetti: A Hypermedia Research Archive, ed. Jerome McGann, 2000 and forthcoming, http://jefferson.village.virginia.edu/rossetti/rossetti.ht

Index

Numbers in bold type refer to pages with illustrations

246